STUDIES IN CONTEMPORARY ENGLISH LITERATURE

STUDIES IN CONTEMPORARY ENGLISH LITERATURE

L. D' Souza

CYBER TECH PUBLICATIONS
4264/3, Ansari Road, Daryaganj, New Delhi-110002 (India)
Ph.: 011-23244078, 011-43559448 Fax: 011-23280028
E-Mail: cyberpublicationsdelhi@yahoo.com
Website: www.cybertechpublications.com

STUDIES IN CONTEMPORARY ENGLISH LITERATURE

L. D' Souza

First Edition 2011

Published by :

G.S. Rawat for **Cyber Tech Publications**
4264/3, Ansari Road, Daryaganj, New Delhi-110002 (India)
Ph.: 011-23244078, 011-43559448 Fax: 011-23280028
E-Mail: cyberpublicationsdelhi@yahoo.com
Website: www.cybertechpublications.com

CONTENTS

Preface

The organisation of material in this book conforms with that of the other books in this series. After a brief consideration of the historical background and time-spirit of the different phases of the contemporary period, the method of procedure is topical. Within the topical divisions of poetry, novel, drama, and miscellaneous prose, the arrangement is generally chronological. In the treatment of particular movements and groups, however, it has seemed more practicable at times to proceed from a discussion of major figures to those of lesser importance. In the many instances in which an author's works extend to several literary forms, the works, regardless of type, are considered in the principal entry of the particular author. Thus Hardy's novels and poetry, Galsworthy's novels and dramas are considered under the entries of Hardy and Galsworthy respectively.

The general bibliographies are arranged according to literary type, with subdivisions indicated in so far as they prove helpful. The reference works on poetry, for example, are subdivided into anthologies, biographical and critical studies, and discussions of poetic theory and principle. In

the bibliographies of individual authors, the order of arrangement is generally from comprehensive treatment to the treatment of particular facets of the author's life and works. The chronologies of authors' works and the lists of bibliographical items are often selective rather than exhaustive; and in the reference works, reviews and newspaper notices are not included. Only places of publication other than New York and London are listed in the bibliographies.

—*Author*

1

Introduction

Different historical periods have emphasized various characteristics of literature. Early works often had an overt or covert religious or didactic purpose. Moralizing or prescriptive literature stems from such sources. The exotic nature of romance flourished from the Middle Ages onwards, whereas the Age of Reason manufactured nationalistic epics and philosophical tracts. Romanticism emphasized the popular folk literature and emotive involvement, but gave way in the 19th-century West to a phase of so-called realism and naturalism, investigations into what is real. The 20th century brought demands for symbolism or psychological insight in the delineation and development of character.

The Muslim Scientist and Philosopher Imam Ja'far al-Sadiq defined Literature as follows: "Literature is the garment which one puts on what he says or writes so that it may appear more attractive."

FORMS OF LITERATURE

Poetry

A poem is commonly defined as a composition written in verse (although verse has been equally used for epic and dramatic fiction). Poems rely heavily on imagery, precise word choice, and metaphor; they may take the form of measures consisting of patterns of stresses (metric feet) or of patterns of different-length syllables (as in classical prosody); and they may or may not utilize rhyme. One cannot readily characterize poetry precisely. Typically though, poetry as a form of literature makes some significant use of the formal properties of the words it uses-the properties attached to the written or spoken form of the words, rather than to their meaning. Metre depends on syllables and on rhythms of speech; rhyme and alliteration depend on words that have similar pronunciation. Some recent poets, such as E. E. Cummings, made extensive use of words' visual form. Poetry perhaps pre-dates other forms of literature: early known examples include the Sumerian Epic of Gilgamesh (dated from around 2700 B.C.), parts of the Bible, the surviving works of Homer (the Iliad and the Odyssey), and the Indian epics Ramayana and Mahabharata. In cultures based primarily on oral traditions the formal characteristics of poetry often have a mnemonic function, and important texts: legal, genealogical or moral, for example, may appear first in verse form. Much poetry uses specific forms: the haiku, the limerick, or the sonnet, for example. A haiku must have seventeen syllables, distributed over three lines in groups of five, seven, and five, and should have an image of a season and something to do with nature. A limerick has five lines, with a rhyme scheme of AABBA, and line lengths of 3,3,2,2,3 stressed syllables. It traditionally has a less reverent attitude towards nature.

Language and tradition dictate some poetic norms: Persian poetry always rhymes, Greek poetry rarely rhymes, Italian or French poetry often does, English and German can go either way (although modern non-rhyming poetry often, perhaps unfairly, has a more "serious" aura). Perhaps the most paradigmatic style of English poetry, blank verse, as exemplified in works by Shakespeare and by Milton, consists of unrhymed iambic pentameters. Some languages prefer longer lines; some shorter ones. Some of these conventions result from the ease of fitting a specific language's vocabulary and grammar into certain structures, rather than into others; for example, some languages contain more rhyming words than others, or typically have longer words. Other structural conventions come about as the result of historical accidents, where many speakers of a language associate good poetry with a verse form preferred by a particular skilled or popular poet.

Works for theatre traditionally took verse form. This has now become rare outside opera and musicals, although many would argue that the language of drama remains intrinsically poetic.

In recent years, digital poetry has arisen that takes advantage of the artistic, publishing, and synthetic qualities of digital media.

Drama

A play or drama offers another classical literary form that has continued to evolve over the years. It generally comprises chiefly dialogue between characters, and usually aims at dramatic / theatrical performance rather than at reading. During the eighteenth and nineteenth centuries, opera developed as a combination of poetry, drama, and music. Nearly all drama took verse form until comparatively recently.

Greek drama exemplifies the earliest form of drama of which we have substantial knowledge. Tragedy, as a dramatic genre, developed as a performance associated with religious and civic festivals, typically enacting or developing upon well-known historical or mythological themes. Tragedies generally presented very serious Theme.

With the advent of newer technologies, scripts written for non-stage media have been added to this form. War of the Worlds (radio) in 1938 saw the advent of literature written for radio broadcast, and many works of Drama have been adapted for film or television. Conversely, television, film, and radio literature have been adapted to printed or electronic media.

Essays

An essay consists of a discussion of a topic from an author's personal point of view, exemplified by works by Francis Bacon or by Charles Lamb.

'Essay' in English derives from the French 'essai', meaning 'attempt'. Thus one can find open-ended, provocative and/or inconclusive essays. The term "essays" first applied to the self-reflective musings of Michel de Montaigne, and even today he has a reputation as the father of this literary form.

Genres related to the essay may include:

- the memoir, telling the story of an author's life from the author's personal point of view
- the epistle: usually a formal, didactic, or elegant letter.
- the blog, an informal short rant about a particular topic or topics, usually opinion

Prose Fiction

Prose consists of writing that does not adhere to any particular formal structures (other than simple grammar); "non-poetic writing," writing, perhaps. The term sometimes appears pejoratively, but prosaic writing simply says something without necessarily trying to say it in a beautiful way, or using beautiful words. Prose writing can of course take beautiful form; but less by virtue of the formal features of words (rhymes, alliteration, metre) but rather by style, placement, or inclusion of graphics. But one need not mark the distinction precisely, and perhaps cannot do so. Note the classifications:

- "prose poetry", which attempts to convey the aesthetic richness typical of poetry using only prose
- "free verse", or poetry not adhering to any of the structures of one or another formal poetic style

Narrative fiction (narrative prose) generally favours prose for the writing of novels, short stories, graphic novels, and the like. Singular examples of these exist throughout history, but they did not develop into systematic and discrete literary forms until relatively recent centuries. Length often serves to categorize works of prose fiction. Although limits remain somewhat arbitrary, modern publishing conventions dictate the following:

- A Mini Saga is a short story of exactly 50 words
- A Flash fiction is generally defined as a piece of prose under a thousand words.
- A short story comprises prose writing of less than 10,000 to 20,000 words, but typically more than 500 words, which may or may not have a narrative arc.
- A story containing between 20,000 and 50,000 words falls into the novella category.
- A work of fiction containing more than 50,000 words falls squarely into the realm of the novel.

A novel consists simply of a long story written in prose, yet the form developed comparatively recently. Icelandic prose sagas dating from about the 11th century bridge the gap between traditional national verse epics and the modern psychological novel. In mainland Europe, the Spaniard Cervantes wrote perhaps the first influential novel: Don Quixote, the first part of which was published in 1605 and the second in 1615. Earlier collections of tales, such as Boccaccio's Decameron and Chaucer's The Canterbury Tales, have comparable forms and would classify as novels if written today. Earlier works written in Asia resemble even more strongly the novel as we now think of it-for example, works such as the Chinese Romance of the Three Kingdoms and the Japanese

Tale of Genji by Lady Murasaki. Compare to The Book of One Thousand and One Nights.

Early novels in Europe did not, at the time, count as significant literature, perhaps because "mere" prose writing seemed easy and unimportant. It has become clear, however, that prose writing can provide aesthetic pleasure without adhering to poetic forms. Additionally, the freedom authors gain in not having to concern themselves with verse structure translates often into a more complex plot or into one richer in precise detail than one typically finds even in narrative poetry. This freedom also allows an author to experiment with many different literary and presentation styles-including poetry-in the scope of a single novel.

Other Prose Literature

Philosophy, history, journalism, and legal and scientific writings traditionally ranked as literature. They offer some of the oldest prose writings in existence; novels and prose stories earned the names "fiction" to distinguish them from factual writing or nonfiction, which writers historically have crafted in prose.

The "literary" nature of science writing has become less pronounced over the last two centuries, as advances and specialization have made new scientific research inaccessible to most audiences; science now appears mostly in journals. Scientific works of Euclid, Aristotle, Copernicus, and Newton still possess great value; but since the science in them has largely become outdated, they no longer serve for scientific instruction, yet they remain too technical to sit well in most programmes of literary study. Outside of "history of science" programmes students rarely read such works. Many books "popularizing" science might still deserve the title "literature"; history will tell.

Philosophy, too, has become an increasingly academic discipline. More of its practitioners lament this situation than occurs with the sciences; nonetheless most new philosophical work appears in academic journals. Major philosophers through history--Plato, Aristotle, Augustine, Descartes, Nietzsche--have become as canonical as any writers. Some recent philosophy works are argued to merit the title "literature", such as some of the works by Simon Blackburn; but much of it does not, and some areas, such as logic, have become extremely technical to a degree similar to that of mathematics.

A great deal of historical writing can still rank as literature, particularly the genre known as creative nonfiction. So can a great deal of journalism, such as literary journalism. However these areas have become extremely large, and often have a primarily utilitarian purpose: to record data or convey immediate information. As a result the writing in these fields often lacks a literary quality, although it often and in its better moments has that quality.

Major "literary" historians include Herodotus, Thucydides and Procopius, all of whom count as canonical literary figures. Law offers a less clear case. Some writings of Plato and Aristotle, or even the early parts of the Bible, might count as legal literature.

The law tables of Hammurabi of Babylon might count. Roman civil law as codified in the Corpus Juris Civilis during the reign of Justinian I of the Byzantine Empire has a reputation as significant literature. The founding documents of many countries, including the United States Constitution, can count as literature; however legal writing now rarely exhibits literary merit.

Game Design Scripts-In essence never seen by the player of a game and only by the developers and/or publishers, the audience for these pieces is usually very small. Still, many game scripts contain immersive stories and detailed worlds making them hidden literary gems.

Most of these fields, then, through specialization or proliferation, no longer generally constitute "literature" in the sense under discussion. They may sometimes count as "literary literature"; more often they produce what one might call "technical literature" or "professional literature".

Related Narrative Forms

- Graphic novels and comic books present stories told in a combination of sequential artwork, dialogue and text.
- Films, videos and broadcast soap operas have carved out a niche which often parallels the functionality of prose fiction.
- Interactive fiction, a term for a prose-based genre of computer games, occupies a small literary niche.
- Electronic literature is a developing literary genre meant to be read on a computer screen, often making use of hypertext.

Genres of Literature

A literary genre refers to the traditional divisions of literature of various kinds according to a particular criterion of writing.

Literary Techniques

A Literary technique or literary device may be used by works of literature in order to produce a specific effect on the reader. Literary technique is distinguished from literary genre as military tactics are from military strategy. Thus, though David Copperfield employs satire at certain moments, it belongs to the genre of comic novel, not that of satire. By contrast, Bleak House employs satire so consistently as to belong to the genre of satirical novel. In this way, use of a technique can lead to the development of a new genre, as was the case with one of the first modern novels, Pamela by Samuel Richardson, which by using the epistolary technique strengthened the tradition of the epistolary novel, a genre which had been practiced for some time already but without the same acclaim.

Literature by Country, Language, or Cultural Group

Literary Criticism

Literary criticism implies a critique and evaluation of a piece of literature and in some cases is used to improve a work in progress or classical piece. There are many types of literary criticism and each can be used to critique a piece in a different way or critique a different aspect of a piece. The major types of literary criticism are Marxism, Human studies, which umbrellas homosexual studies and feminism, historical, and Traditional, also known as New Criticism.

Themes in Literature

Theme is a broad idea in a story, or a message conveyed by a work. This message is usually about life, society or human nature. Themes are usually implied rather than explicitly stated. Deep thematic content is not required in literature; however, some readers would say that all stories inherently project some kind of outlook on life that can be taken as a theme, regardless of whether or not this is the intent of the author. Analysis of changes in dynamic characters can provide insight into a particular theme.

WESTERN CANON

The Western canon is a term used to denote a canon of books, and, more widely, music and art, that has been the most influential in shaping Western culture. It asserts a compendium of the greatest works of artistic merit. Such a canon is important to the theory of educational perennialism and the development of high culture. Although previously held in high regard, it has been the subject of increasing contention through the latter half of the 20th century. In practice, debates, and attempts to actually define the Canon in lists, are essentially restricted to books of various sorts: Literature, including Poetry, Fiction and Drama, autobiographical writings and Letters, Philosophy and History. A few accessible books on the Sciences are usually included.

Examples

Examples of shorter canonical lists include (in which the selectors have attempted to list only the most important ones):

- The Harvard Classics
- Great Books
- Great Books of the Western World
- Harold Bloom's Western Canon link

University reading lists are also good indicators of what is considered to be in the Western canon:

- St. John's College reading list
- Columbia College Core Curriculum

Longer lists (in which the selectors have attempted to be more comprehensive):

- Loeb Classical Library (Greek and Latin authors)
- I Tatti Renaissance Library (Renaissance authors)
- Everyman's Library (Modern works)

Origins

The process of listmaking-defining the boundaries of the canon-is endless. One of the notable attempts in the English-speaking world was the Great Books of the Western World program. This program, developed in the middle third of the 20th century, grew out of the curriculum at the University of Chicago. University president Robert

Hutchins and his collaborator Mortimer Adler developed a program that offered reading lists, books, and organizational strategies for reading clubs to the general public. An earlier attempt, the Harvard Classics (1909) was promulgated by Harvard University president Charles W. Eliot, whose thesis was the same as Carlyle's:... The greatest university of all is a collection of books.-Thomas Carlyle

Debate

There has been an ongoing, intensely political debate over the nature and status of the canon since at least the 1960s. In the USA, in particular, it has been attacked as a compendium of books written mainly by "dead white European males", that thus do not represent the viewpoints of many others in contemporary societies around the world. Others, notably Allan Bloom in his 1987 book The Closing of the American Mind, have disagreed strongly. Authors such as Yale Professor of Humanities Harold Bloom (no relation) have also spoken strongly in favor of the canon, and in general the canon remains as a represented idea in most institutions, though its implications continue to be debated heavily.

Defenders maintain that those who undermine the canon do so out of primarily political interests, and that the measure of quality represented by the works of the canon is of an aesthetic rather than political nature. Thus, any political objections aimed at the canon are ultimately irrelevant. One of the main objections to a canon of literature is the question of authority-who should have the power to determine what works are worth reading and teaching?

Works

Works which are commonly included in the canon include works of fiction such as some epic poems, poetry, music, drama, novels, and other assorted forms of literature from the many diverse Western (and more recently non-Western) cultures. Many non-fiction works are also listed, primarily from the areas of religion, mythology, science, philosophy, economics, politics, and history. Works which directly address the canon (both for and against):

- The Western Canon: The Books and School of the Ages by Harold Bloom

- Shakespeare: The Invention of the Human by Harold Bloom
- The Dead Father by Donald Barthelme
- The History of Western Literature by Otto Maria Carpeaux (eight volumes, only available in Portuguese)

ENGLISH LITERATURE

The term English literature refers to literature written in the English language, including literature composed in English by writers not necessarily from England; Joseph Conrad was Polish, Robert Burns was Scottish, James Joyce was Irish, Dylan Thomas was Welsh, Edgar Allan Poe was American, Salman Rushdie is Indian, V.S. Naipaul is Trinidadian. In other words English literature is as diverse as the varieties and dialects of English spoken around the world. In academia, the term often labels departments and programmes practising English studies in secondary and tertiary educational systems.

MIDDLE AGES

The first works in English, written in the Anglo-Saxon dialect now called Old English, appear in the early Middle Ages (the oldest surviving text is Cædmon's Hymn). The oral tradition was very strong in early British culture and most literary works were written to be performed. Epic poems were thus very popular and many, including Beowulf, have survived to the present day in the rich corpus of Anglo-Saxon literature.

These are languages that closely resemble today's Norwegian or, better yet, Icelandic, though much Anglo-Saxon verse in the extant manuscripts is probably a "milder" adaptation of the earlier Viking and German war poems from the continent.

When such poetry was brought to England it was still being handed down orally from one generation to another, and the constant presence of alliterative verse, or consonant rhyme (today's newspaper headlines and marketing abundantly uses this technique such as in Big is Better) helped the Anglo-Saxon peoples remember it. Such rhyme is a feature of Germanic languages and is opposed to vocalic or end-rhyme of Romance languages. But the first written literature dates to the early Christian monasteries founded by St. Augustine of Canterbury and his disciples and it is reasonable to believe that it was somehow adapted to suit to needs of Christian readers.

Even without their crudest lines, Viking war poems still smell of blood feuds and their consonant rhymes sound like the smashing of swords under the gloomy northern sky: there is always a sense of imminent danger in the narratives. Sooner or later, all things must come to an end, as Beowulf eventually dies at the hands of the huge monster he spends his life fighting.

The feelings of Beowulf that nothing lasts, that youth and joy will turn to death and sorrow entered Christianism and were to dominate the future landscape of English fiction. The "ubi sunt" theme is, for example, recurrent in Hamlet ("Alas, poor Yorick"), not to mention much Jacobean poetry. With the exception of the relatively light-hearted and optimistic Restoration and the Augustan Age, melancholia and angst remain a favorite theme with English-speaking writers, through the Gothic novel and Pre-romanticism to the birth of modern romantic sensibility.

When William the Conqueror makes England a part of the Anglo-Norman realm in 1066 bringing Norman, there is a period of Anglo-Norman literature, though Old English poetry continues to be read and its language widely spoken. It was not until the early 13th century when Albion becomes independent and severs its relations to France that the language really changes. As the Normans are assimilated into mainstream culture, their French penetrates the lower orders of society changing much of the grammar and lexicon of Old English. Though it does not become a Romance language, Chaucer's English is much closer to present-day English than the language that people spoke a century before. The average English-speaker cannot read Chaucer (Middle English) without difficulty but can nonetheless grasp the gist of the story, while he needs to read Beowulf in modern English--in translation.

In the late medieval period (1200-1500), the ideals of courtly love entered England and authors began to write romances, either in verse or prose. Especially popular were tales of King Arthur and his court. The poem Sir Gawain and the Green Knight shows many of the key features of literature at this time: a setting in the legendary time of King Arthur, an emphasis on chivalry and knightly behavior, and religious overtones.

English drama at this time was overtly religious. Mystery plays were enacted in cities and towns to celebrate major holidays, and the less formal mummers plays also conveyed Christian themes. England's first great author, Geoffrey Chaucer (1340-1400), wrote in Middle English. His most famous work is The Canterbury Tales, a collection of stories in a variety of genres, ostensibly told by a group of pilgrims on their way to Canterbury. Remarkably, they are from all walks of life, which is reflected as much in the language they use as in the content of their stories. But, though Chaucer is most certainly an English author, he was inspired by literary developments taking place elsewhere in Europe, especially in Italy. Chaucer's The Canterbury Tales are quite indebted to Giovanni Boccaccio's Decameron. The Renaissance was making its way to Britain.

EARLY MODERN RENAISSANCE

Following the introduction of a printing press into England by William Caxton in 1476, vernacular literature flourished. The Reformation inspired the production of vernacular liturgy which led to the Book of Common Prayer, a lasting influence on literary English language. The poetry, drama, and prose produced under both Queen Elizabeth I and King James I constitute what is today labelled as Early modern (or Renaissance). This literature is noted for its interest in the human being as a worthy subject (due in large part to the importation of humanism from Italy). Unlike the literature of Medieval England, which was almost entirely religious in nature, Early modern literature offered readers a more secular literature; though it should be noted, Early modern literature does appear overtly religious in many ways when compared with modern secularism.

Elizabethan Literature

The Elizabethan era saw a great flourishing of literature, especially in the field of drama. The Italian Renaissance had rediscovered the ancient Greek and Roman theatre, which was then beginning to evolve apart from the old mystery and miracle plays of the Middle Ages. The Italians were particularly inspired by Seneca (a major tragic playwright and philosopher, the tutor of Nero) and Plautus (its comic clichés, especially that of the boasting soldier had a powerful influence on the Renaissance and after). However, the Italian tragedies embraced a principle contrary to Seneca's ethics: showing blood and violence on the stage. In Seneca's plays such scenes were only acted by the characters. But the English playwrights were intrigued by Italian model: a conspicuous community of Italian actors had settled in London and Giovanni Florio had brought much of the Italian language and culture to England.

It is also true that the Elizabethan Era was a very violent age and that the high incidence of political assassinations in Renaissance Italy (embodied by Niccolò Machiavelli's The Prince) did little to calm fears of popish plots. As a result, representing that kind of violence on the stage was probably more cathartic for the Elizabethan spectator. Following earlier Elizabethan plays such as Gorboduc by Sackville & Norton and The Spanish Tragedy by Kyd that was to provide much material for Hamlet, William Shakespeare stands out in this period as a poet and playwright as yet unsurpassed. Shakespeare was not a man of letters by profession, and probably had only some grammar school education. He was neither a lawyer, nor an aristocrat as the "university wits" that had monopolised the English stage when he started writing. But he was very gifted and incredibly versatile, and he surpassed "professionals" as Greene who mocked this "shake-scene" of low origins. Though most dramas met with great success, it is in his later years (marked by the early reign of James I) that he wrote what have been considered his greatest plays: Hamlet, Othello, King Lear, Macbeth, Antony and Cleopatra, and The Tempest, a tragicomedy that inscribes within the main drama a brilliant pageant to the new king. This 'play within a play' takes the form of a masque, an interlude with music and dance colored by the novel special effects of the new indoor theaters.

Critics have shown that this masterpiece, which can be considered a dramatic work in its own right, was written for James's court, if not for the monarch himself. The magic arts of Prospero, on which depend the outcome of the plot, hint at the fine relationship between art and nature in poetry. Significantly for those times (the arrival of the first colonists in America), The Tempest is (though not apparently) set on a Bermudan island, as research on the Bermuda Pamphlets (1609) has shown, linking Shakespeare to the Virginia Company itself. The "News from the New World", as Frank Kermode points out, were already out and Shakespeare's interest in this respect is remarkable. Shakespeare also popularized the English sonnet which made significant changes to Petrarch's model.

The sonnet was introduced into English by Thomas Wyatt in the early 16th century. Poems intended for to be set to music as songs, such as by Thomas Campion, became popular as printed literature was disseminated more widely in households. Other important figures in Elizabethan theatre include Christopher Marlowe, Thomas Dekker, John Fletcher and Francis Beaumont. Had Marlowe (1564-1593) not been stabbed at twenty-nine in a tavern brawl, says Anthony Burgess, he might have rivalled, if not equalled Shakespeare himself for his poetic gifts. Remarkably, he was born only a few weeks before Shakespeare and must have known him well. Marlowe's subject matter, though, is different: it focuses more on the moral drama of the renaissance man than any other thing. Marlowe was fascinated and terrified by the new frontiers opened by modern science. Drawing on German lore, he introduced Dr. Faustus to England, a scientist and magician who is obsessed by the thirst of knowledge and the desire to push man's technological power to its limits.

He acquires supernatural gifts that even allow him to go back in time and wed Helen of Troy, but at the end of his twenty-four years' covenant with the devil he has to surrender his soul to him. His dark heroes may have something of Marlowe himself, whose untimely death remains a mystery. He was known for being an atheist, leading a lawless life, keeping many mistresses, consorting with ruffians: living the 'high life' of London's underworld. But many suspect that this might have been a cover-up for his activities as a secret agent for Elizabeth I, hinting that the 'accidental stabbing' might have been a premeditated assassination by the enemies of The Crown. Beaumont and Fletcher are less-known, but it is almost sure that they helped Shakespeare write some of his best dramas, and were quite popular at the time. It is also at this time that the city comedy genre develops. In the later 16th century English poetry was characterised by elaboration of language and extensive allusion to classical myths. The most important poets of this era include Edmund Spenser and Sir Philip Sidney.

Jacobean Literature

After Shakespeare's death, the poet and dramatist Ben Jonson was the leading literary figure of the Jacobean era (The reign of James I). However, Jonson's aesthetics harks back to the Middle Ages rather than to the Tudor Era: his characters embody the theory of humors. According to this contemporary medical theory, behavioral differences result from a prevalence of one of the body's four "humors" (blood, phlegm, black bile, and yellow bile) over the other three; these humors correspond with the four elements of the universe, air, water, fire, and earth. This leads Jonson to exemplify such differences to the point of creating types, or clichés.

Jonson is a master of style, and a brilliant satirist. His Volpone shows how a group of scammers are fooled by a top con-artist, vice being punished by vice, virtue meeting its reward.

Others who followed Jonson's style include Beaumont and Fletcher, who wrote the brilliant comedy, The Knight of the Burning Pestle, a mockery of the rising middle class and especially of those nouveau riches who pretend to dictate literary taste without knowing much literature at all. In the story, a couple of grocers wrangle with professional actors to have their illiterate son play a leading role in a drama. He becomes a knight-errant wearing, appropriately, a burning pestle on his shield. Seeking to win a princess's heart, the young man is ridiculed much in the way Don Quixote was, although Don Quixote had not yet been written. One of Beaumont and Fletcher's chief merits was that of realising how feudalism and chivalry had turned into snobbery and make-believe and that new social classes were on the rise.

Another popular style of theatre during Jacobean times was the revenge play, popularized by John Webster and Thomas Kyd. George Chapman wrote a couple of subtle revenge tragedies, but must be remembered chiefly on account of his famous translation of Homer, one that had a profound influence on all future English literature, even inspiring John Keats to write one of his best sonnets.

The King James Bible, one of the most massive translation projects in the history of English up to this time, was started in 1604 and completed in 1611. It represents the culmination of a tradition of Bible translation into English that began with the work of William Tyndale.

It became the standard Bible of the Church of England, and some consider it one of the greatest literary works of all time. This project was headed by James I himself, who supervised the work of forty-seven scholars. Although many other translations into English have been made, some of which are widely considered more accurate, many aesthetically prefer the King James Bible, whose meter is made to mimic the original Hebrew verse.

Besides Shakespeare, whose figure towers the early 1600s, the major poets of the early 17th century included John Donne and the other Metaphysical poets. Influenced by continental Baroque, and taking as his subject matter both Christian mysticism and eroticism, metaphysical poetry uses unconventional or "unpoetic" figures, such as a compass or a mosquito, to reach surprise effects. For example, in one of Donne's Songs and Sonnets, the points of a compass represent two lovers, the woman who is home, waiting, being the center, the farther point being her lover sailing away from her. But the larger the distance, the more the hands of the compass lean to each other: separation makes love grow fonder. The paradox or the oxymoron is a constant in this poetry whose fears and anxieties also speak of a world of spiritual certainties shaken by the modern discoveries of geography and science, one that is no longer the center of the universe.

Apart from the metaphysical poetry of Donne, the 17th century is also celebrated for its Baroque poetry. Baroque poetry served the same ends as the art of the period; the Baroque style is lofty, sweeping, epic, and religious. Many of these poets have an overtly Catholic sensibility (namely Richard Crashaw) and wrote poetry for the Catholic counter-Reformation in order to establish a feeling of supremacy and mysticism that would ideally persuade newly emerging Protestant groups back toward Catholicism.

Caroline and Cromwellian Literature

The turbulent years of the mid-17th century, during the reign of Charles I and the subsequent Commonwealth and Protectorate, saw a flourishing of political literature in English. Pamphlets written by sympathisers of every faction in the English civil war ran from vicious personal attacks and polemics, through many forms of propaganda, to high-minded schemes aiming to reform the nation. Of the latter type Leviathan by Thomas Hobbes would prove to be one of the most important works of British political philosophy. Hobbes' writings are some of the only political works from the era which are still regularly published whilst John Bramhall, who was Hobbes' chief critic, is mostly forgotten. The period also saw a flourishing of news books, the precursors to the British newspaper, with journalists such as Henry Muddiman, Marchamont Needham, John Birkenhead representing the views and activities of the contending parties. The frequent arrests of authors and the suppression of their works, with the consequence of foreign or underground printing, led to the idea of licensing being proposed. The Areopagitica, a political pamphlet by John Milton, was written in opposition to licensing and is regarded as one of the most eloquent defences of press freedom ever written.

Other forms of literature written during this period are usually ascribed political subtexts or their authors' are grouped along political lines. The cavalier poets, active mainly before the civil war, owed much to the earlier school of metaphysical poets. The forced retirement of royalist officials after the execution of Charles I was a good thing in the case of Izaak Walton as it gave him time to work on his book The Compleat Angler. Published in 1653 the book, ostensibly a guide to fishing, is much more; being a meditation on life, leisure and contentment. The two most important poets of Oliver Cromwell's England were Andrew Marvell and John Milton with both producing works praising the new government; such as Marvell's An Horatian Ode upon Cromwell's Return from Ireland. Despite their republican beliefs they escaped punishment upon the Restoration of Charles II after which Milton wrote some of his greatest poetical works with any possible political message hidden under allegory. Thomas Browne was another writer of the period; a learned man with an extensive library, he wrote prolifically on science, religion, medicine and the esoteric.

Restoration Literature

Restoration literature includes both Paradise Lost and the Earl of Rochester's Sodom, the high spirited sexual comedy of The Country Wife and the moral wisdom of Pilgrim's Progress. It saw Locke's Treatises on Government, the founding of the Royal Society, the experiments of Robert Boyle and the holy meditations of Boyle, the hysterical attacks on theaters from Jeremy Collier, the pioneering of literary criticism from Dryden, and the first newspapers. The official break in literary culture caused by censorship and radically moralist standards under Cromwell's Puritan regime created a gap in literary tradition, allowing a seemingly fresh start for all forms of literature after the Restoration. During the Interregnum, the royalist forces attached to the court of Charles I went into exile with the twenty-year old Charles II. The nobility who travelled with Charles II were therefore lodged for over a decade in the midst of the continent's literary scene. Charles spent his time attending plays in France, and he developed a taste for Spanish plays. Those nobles living in Holland began to learn about mercantile exchange as well as the tolerant, rationalist prose debates that circulated in that officially tolerant nation.

The largest and most important poetic form of the era was satire. In general, publication of satire was done anonymously. There were great dangers in being associated with a satire. On the one hand, defamation law was a wide net, and it was difficult for a satirist to avoid prosecution if he were proven to have written a piece that seemed to criticize a noble. On the other hand, wealthy individuals would respond to satire as often as not by having the suspected poet physically attacked by ruffians. John Dryden was set upon for being merely suspected of having written the Satire on Mankind. A consequence of this anonymity is that a great many poems, some of them of merit, are unpublished and largely unknown.

Prose in the Restoration period is dominated by Christian religious writing, but the Restoration also saw the beginnings of two genres that would dominate later periods: fiction and journalism. Religious writing often strayed into political and economic writing, just as political and economic writing implied or directly addressed religion. Thomas Sprat wrote his The Dead Poet's Society in 1667 and set forth, in a single document, the goals of empirical science ever after. The Restoration was also the time when John Locke wrote many of his philosophical works. Locke's empiricism was an attempt at understanding the basis of human understanding itself and thereby devising a proper manner for making sound decisions.

These same scientific methods led Locke to his three Treatises on Government, which later inspired the thinkers in the American Revolution. As with his work on understanding, Locke moves from the most basic units of society toward the more elaborate, and, like Thomas Hobbes, he emphasizes the plastic nature of the social contract. For an age that had seen absolute monarchy overthrown, democracy attempted, democracy corrupted, and limited monarchy restored, only a flexible basis for government could be satisfying. The Restoration moderated most of the more strident sectarian writing, but radicalism persisted after the Restoration. Puritan authors such as John Milton were forced to retire from public life or adapt, and those Digger, Fifth Monarchist, Leveller, Quaker, and Anabaptist authors who had preached against monarchy and who had participated directly in the regicide of Charles I were partially suppressed. Consequently, violent writings were forced underground, and many of those who had served in the Interregnum attenuated their positions in the Restoration. John Bunyan stands out beyond other religious authors of the period. Bunyan's The Pilgrim's Progress is an allegory of personal salvation and a guide to the Christian life. Instead of any focus on eschatology or divine retribution, Bunyan instead writes about how the individual saint can prevail against the temptations of mind and body that threaten damnation.

The book is written in a straightforward narrative and shows influence from both drama and biography, and yet it also shows an awareness of the grand allegorical tradition found in Edmund Spenser. During the Restoration period, the most common manner of getting news would have been a broadsheet publication. A single, large sheet of paper might have a written, usually partisan, account of an event. However, the period saw the beginnings of the first professional and periodical (meaning that the publication was regular) journalism in England. Journalism develops late, generally around the time of William of Orange's claiming the throne in 1689. Coincidentally or by design, England began to have newspapers just when William came to court from Amsterdam, where there were already newspapers being published.

It is impossible to satisfactorily date the beginning of the novel in English. However, long fiction and fictional biographies began to distinguish themselves from other forms in England during the Restoration period. An existing tradition of Romance fiction in France and Spain was popular in England The "Romance" was considered a feminine form, and women were taxed with reading "novels" as a vice. One of the most significant figures in the rise of the novel in the Restoration period is Aphra Behn. She was not only the first professional female novelist, but she may be among the first professional novelists of either sex in England. Behn's most famous novel was Oroonoko in 1688. This was a biography of an entirely fictional African king who had been enslaved in Suriname. Behn's novels show the influence of tragedy and her experiences as a dramatist.

As soon as the previous Puritan regime's ban on public stage representations was lifted, the drama recreated itself quickly and abundantly. The most famous plays of the early Restoration period are the unsentimental or "hard" comedies of John Dryden, William Wycherley, and George Etherege, which reflect the atmosphere at Court, and celebrate an aristocratic macho lifestyle of unremitting sexual intrigue and conquest. After a sharp drop in both quality and quantity in the 1680s, the mid-90s saw a brief second flowering of the drama, especially comedy. Comedies like William Congreve's Love For Love (1695) and The Way of the World (1700), and John Vanbrugh's The Relapse (1696) and The Provoked Wife (1697) were "softer" and more middle-class in ethos, very different from the aristocratic extravaganza twenty years earlier, and aimed at a wider audience. The playwrights of the 1690s set out to appeal to more socially mixed audiences with a strong middle-class element, and to female spectators, for instance by moving the war between the sexes from the arena of intrigue into that of marriage. The focus in comedy is less on young lovers outwitting the older generation, more on marital relations after the wedding bells.

Diarists John Evelyn and Samuel Pepys depicted everyday London life and the cultural scene of the times.

Augustan Literature

The term Augustan literature derives from authors of the 1720's and 1730's themselves, who responded to a term that George I of England preferred for himself. While George I meant the title to reflect his might, they instead saw in it a reflection of Ancient Rome's transition from rough and ready literature to highly political and highly polished literature. Because of the aptness of the metaphor, the period from 1689-1750 was called "the Augustan Age" by critics throughout the 18th century (including Voltaire and Oliver Goldsmith). The literature of the period is overtly political and thoroughly aware of critical dictates for literature. It is an age of exuberance and scandal, of enormous energy and inventiveness and outrage, that reflected an era when English, Scottish, and Irish people found themselves in the midst of an expanding economy, lowering barriers to education, and the stirrings of the Industrial Revolution. The most outstanding poet of. the age is Alexander Pope, but Pope's excellence is partially in his constant battle with other poets, and his serene, seemingly neo-Classical approach to poetry is in competition with highly idiosyncratic verse and strong competition from such poets as Ambrose Philips. It was during this time that James Thomson produced his melancholy The Seasons and Edward Young wrote Night Thoughts. It is also the era that saw a serious competition over the proper model for the pastoral. In criticism, poets struggled with a doctrine of decorum, of matching proper words with proper sense and of achieving a diction that matched the gravity of a subject. At the same time, the mock-heroic was at its zenith. Pope's Rape of the Lock and The Dunciad are still the greatest mock-heroic poems ever written.

In prose, the earlier part of the period was overshadowed by the development of the English essay. Joseph Addison and Richard Steele's The Spectator established the form of the British periodical essay, inventing the pose of the detached observer of human life who can meditate upon the world without advocating any specific changes in it. However, this was also the time when the English novel, first emerging in the Restoration, developed into a major artform. Daniel Defoe turned from journalism and writing criminal lives for the press to writing fictional criminal lives with Roxana and Moll Flanders. He also wrote a fictional treatment of the travels of Alexander Selkirk called Robinson Crusoe (1719). The novel would benefit indirectly from a tragedy of the stage, and in mid-century many more authors would begin to write novels.

If Addison and Steele overawed one type of prose, then Jonathan Swift did another. Swift's prose style is unmannered and direct, with a clarity that few contemporaries matched. He was a profound skeptic about the modern world, but he was similarly profoundly distrustful of nostalgia. He saw in history a record of lies and vanity, and he saw in the present a madness of vanity and lies. Core Christian values were essential, but these values had to be muscular and assertive and developed by constant rejection of the games of confidence men and their gullies. Swift's A Tale of a Tub announced his skeptical analysis of the claims of the modern world, and his later prose works, such as his war with Patridge the astrologer, and most of all his derision of pride in Gulliver's Travels left only the individual in constant fear and humility safe. After his "exile" to Ireland, Swift reluctantly began defending the Irish people from the predations of colonialism. His A Modest Proposal and the Drapier Letters provoked riots and arrests, but Swift, who had no love of Irish Roman Catholics, was outraged by the abuses and barbarity he saw around him.

Drama in the early part of the period featured the last plays of John Vanbrugh and William Congreve, both of whom carried on the Restoration comedy with some alterations. However, the majority of stagings were of lower farces and much more serious and domestic tragedies. George Lillo and Richard Steele both produced highly moral forms of tragedy, where the characters and the concerns of the characters were wholly middle class or working class. This reflected a marked change in the audience for plays, as royal patronage was no longer the important part of theatrical success. Additionally, Colley Cibber and John Rich began to battle each other for greater and greater spectacles to present on stage.

The figure of Harlequin was introduced, and pantomime theater began to be staged. This "low" comedy was quite popular, and the plays became tertiary to the staging. Opera also began to be popular in London, and there was significant literary resistance to this Italian incursion. This trend was broken only by a few attempts at a new type of comedy. Pope and John Arbuthnot and John Gay attempted a play entitled Three Hours After Marriage that failed. In 1728, however, John Gay returned to the playhouse with The Beggar's Opera. Gay's opera was in English and retold the story of Jack Sheppard and Jonathan Wild. However, it seemed to be an allegory for Robert Walpole and the directors of the South Sea Company, and so Gay's follow up opera was banned without performance. In 1737, 18th century drama almost ends, for that was the year of the Licensing Act. At that point, there was official state censorship of all plays.

An effect of the Licensing Act was to cause more than one aspiring playwright to switch over to writing novels. Henry Fielding began to write prose satire and novels after his plays could not pass the censors. Henry Brooke also turned to novels. In the interim, Samuel Richardson had produced a novel intended to counter the deleterious effects of novels in Pamela, or Virtue Rewarded (1749). Henry Fielding attacked the absurdity of this novel with two of his own works, Joseph Andrews and Shamela, and then countered Richardson's Clarissa with Tom Jones. Brooke wrote The Man of Feeling and indirectly began the sentimental novel.

Laurence Sterne attempted a Swiftian novel with a unique perspective on the impossibility of biography (the model for most novels up to that point) and understanding with Tristram Shandy, even as his detractor

Tobias Smollett elevated the picaresque novel with his works. Each of these novels represents a formal and thematic divergence from the others. Each novelist was in dialog and competition with the others, and, in a sense, the novel established itself as a diverse and open-formed genre in this explosion of creativity. The most lasting effects of the experimentation would be the psychological realism of Richardson, the bemused narrative voice of Fielding, and the sentimentality of Brooke.

18th Century During the Age of Sensibility, literature reflected the worldview of the Age of Enlightenment (or Age of Reason)-a rational and scientific approach to religious, social, political, and economic issues that promoted a secular view of the world and a general sense of progress and perfectibility. Led by the philosophers who were inspired by the discoveries of the previous century (Newton) and the writings of Descartes, Locke and Bacon. They sought to discover and to act upon universally valid principles governing humanity, nature, and society. They variously attacked spiritual and scientific authority, dogmatism, intolerance, censorship, and economic and social restraints. They considered the state the proper and rational instrument of progress. The extreme rationalism and skepticism of the age led naturally to deism; the same qualities played a part in bringing the later reaction of romanticism. The Encyclopédie of Denis Diderot epitomized the spirit of the age. Increased emphasis on instinct and feeling, rather than judgment and restraint. A growing sympathy for the Middle Ages during the Age of Sensibility sparked an interest in medieval ballads and folk literature.

The Romanticism

The changing landscape of Britain brought about by the steam engine has two major outcomes: the boom of industrialism with the expansion of the city, and the consequent depopulation of the countryside as a result of the enclosures, or privatisation of pastures. Most peasants poured into the city to work in the new factories.

This abrupt change is revealed by the change of meaning in five key words: industry (once meaning "creativity"), democracy (once disparagingly used as "mob-rule"), class (from now also used with a social connotation), art (once just meaning "craft"), culture (once only belonging to farming).

But the poor condition of workers, the new class-conflicts and the pollution of the environment causes a reaction to urbanism and industrialisation prompting poets to rediscover the beauty and value of nature. Mother earth is seen as the only source of wisdom, the only solution to the ugliness caused by machines.

The superiority of nature and instinct over civilisation had been preached by Jean Jacques Rousseau and his message was picked by almost all European poets. The first in England were the Lake Poets, a small group of friends including William Wordsworth and Samuel Taylor Coleridge.

These early Romantic Poets brought a new emotionalism and introspection, and their emergence is marked by the first romantic Manifesto in English literature, the "Preface to the Lyrical Ballads". This collection was mostly contributed by Wordsworth, although Coleridge must be credited for his long and impressive Rime of the Ancient Mariner, a tragic ballad about the survival of one sailor through a series of supernatural events on his voyage through the south seas which involves the slaying of an albatross, the death of the rest of the crew, a visit from Death and his mate, Life-in-Death, and the eventual redemption of the Mariner.

Coleridge and Wordsworth, however, understood romanticism in two entirely different ways: while Coleridge sought to make the supernatural "real" (much like sci-fi movies use special effects to make unlikely plots believable), Wordsworth sought to stir the imagination of readers through his down-to-earth characters taken from real life (for eg. in "The Idiot Boy"), or the beauty of the Lake District that largely inspired his production (as in "Lines Composed a Few Miles Above Tintern Abbey").

The "Second generation" of Romantic Poets includes Lord Byron, Percy Bysshe Shelley, Mary Shelley and John Keats. Byron, however, was still influenced by 18th-century satirists and was, perhaps the least 'romantic' of the three. His amours with a number of prominent but married ladies was also a way to voice his dissent on the hypocrisy of a high society that was only apparently religious but in fact largely libertine, the same that had derided him for being physically impaired. His first trip to Europe resulted in the first two cantos of Childe

Harold's Pilgrimage, a mock-heroic epic of a young man's adventures in Europe but also a sharp satire against London society.

Despite Childe Harold's success on his return to England, accompanied by the publication of The Giaour and The Corsair his alleged incestuous affair with his half-sister Augusta Leigh in 1816 actually forced him to leave England for good and seek asylum on the continent. Here he joined Percy Bysshe Shelley, his wife Mary, with his secretary Dr. John Polidori on the shores of Lake Geneva during the 'year without a summer' of 1816.

Although his is just a short story, Polidori must be credited for introducing The Vampyre, conceived from the same competition which spawned Mary Shelley's Frankenstein, to English literature. Percy, like Mary, had much in common with Byron: he was an aristocrat from a famous and ancient family, had embraced atheism and free-thinking and, like him, was fleeing from scandal in England.

Shelley had been expelled from college for openly declaring his atheism. He had married a 16-year-old girl, Harriet Westbrook whom he had abandoned soon after for Mary (Harriet took her own life after that). Harriet did not embrace his ideals of free love and anarchism, and was not as educated as to contribute to literary debate. Mary was different: the daughter of philosopher and revolutionary William Godwin, she was intellectually more of an equal, shared some of his ideals and was a feminist like her late mother, Mary Wollstonecraft, author of Vindication of the Rights of Women.

One of Shelley's best works is the Ode to the West Wind. Despite his apparent refusal to believe in God, this poem is considered a homage to pantheism, the recognition of a spiritual presence in nature.

Mary Shelley did not go down in history for her poetry, but for giving birth to science fiction: the plot for the novel is said to have come from a nightmare during stormy nights on Lake Geneva in the company of Percy Shelley, Lord Byron, and John Polidori. Her idea of making a body with human parts stolen from different corpses and then animating it with electricity was perhaps influenced by Alessandro Volta's invention and Luigi Galvani's experiments with dead frogs. Frankenstein's chilling tale also suggests modern organ transplants, tissue regeneration, reminding us of the moral issues raised by today's medicine.

But the creature of Frankenstein is incredibly romantic as well. Although "the monster" is intelligent, good and loving, he is shunned by everyone because of his ugliness and deformity, and the desperation and envy that result from social exclusion turn him against the very man who created him.

John Keats did not share Byron's and Shelley's extremely revolutionary ideals, but his cult of pantheism is as important as Shelley's. Keats was in love with the ancient stones of the Parthenon that Lord Elgin had brought to England from Greece, also known as the Elgin Marbles). He celebrates ancient Greece: the beauty of free, youthful love couples here with that of classical art. Keats's great attention to art, especially in his Ode on a Grecian Urn is quite new in romanticism, and it will inspire Walter Pater's and then Oscar Wilde's belief in the absolute value of art as independent from aesthetics.

The most popular novelist of the era was Sir Walter Scott, whose grand historical romances inspired a generation of painters, composers, and writers throughout Europe. By contrast, Jane Austen wrote novels about the life of the landed gentry, seen from a woman's point of view, and wryly focused on practical social issues, especially marriage and money.

Victorian Literature

It was in the Victorian era (1837-1901) that the novel became the leading form of literature in English. Most writers were now more concerned to meet the tastes of a large middle class reading public than to please aristocratic patrons. The best known works of the era include the emotionally powerful works of the Brontë sisters; the satire Vanity Fair by William Makepeace Thackeray; the realist novels of George Eliot; and Anthony Trollope's insightful portrayals of the lives of the landowning and professional classes.

Charles Dickens emerged on the literary scene in the 1830s, confirming the trend for serial publication. Dickens wrote vividly about London life and the struggles of the poor, but in a good-humoured fashion which was acceptable to readers of all classes. His early works such as the Pickwick Papers are masterpieces of comedy. Later his works became darker, without losing his genius for caricature.

An interest in rural matters and the changing social and economic situation of the countryside may be seen in the novels of Thomas Hardy, Elizabeth Cleghorn Gaskell, and others.

Leading poetic figures of the Victorian era included Alfred Tennyson, Robert Browning and his wife, Elizabeth Barrett Browning, Matthew Arnold and Dante Gabriel Rossetti and his sister, Christina Rossetti.

Literature for children was published during the Victorian period, some of which has become globally well-known, such as the work of Lewis Carroll who was a proponent of nonsense verse, as was Edward Lear.

MODERNISM

The movement known as English literary modernism grew out of a general sense of disillusionment with Victorian era attitudes of certainty, conservatism, and objective truth. The movement was greatly influenced by the ideas of Romanticism, Karl Marx's political writings, and the psychoanalytic theories of Sigmund Freud. The continental art movements of Impressionism, and later Cubism, were also important inspirations for modernist writers.

Although literary modernism reached its peak between the First and Second World Wars, the earliest examples of the movement's attitudes appeared in the mid to late nineteenth century. Gerard Manley Hopkins, A. E. Housman, and the poet and novelist Thomas Hardy represented a few of the major early modernists writing in England during the Victorian period.

The first decades of the twentieth century saw several major works of modernism published, including the seminal short story collection Dubliners by James Joyce, Joseph Conrad's Heart of Darkness, and the poetry and drama of William Butler Yeats.

Important novelists between the World Wars included Virginia Woolf, E. M. Forster, Evelyn Waugh, P.G. Wodehouse, D. H. Lawrence and T. S. Eliot, the preeminent English poet of the period. Across the Atlantic writers like William Faulkner, Ernest Hemingway, and the poets Wallace Stevens and Robert Frost developed a more American take on the modernist aesthetic in their work. Perhaps the most contentiously important figure in the development of the modernist movement was the American poet Ezra Pound. Credited with "discovering" both T. S. Eliot and James Joyce, whose stream of consciousness novel Ulysses is considered to be one of the century's greatest literary achievements, Pound also advanced the cause of imagism and free verse, forms which would dominate English poetry into the twenty-first century.

Other notable writers of the period included W. H. Auden, Vladimir Nabokov, William Carlos Williams, Ralph Ellison, Dylan Thomas, R.S. Thomas and Graham Greene. However, some of these writers are more closely associated with what has become known as post-modernism, a term often used to encompass the diverse range of writers who succeeded the modernists.

POSTMODERNISM

Postmodernism is an idea that has been extremely controversial and difficult to define among scholars, intellectuals, and historians, because the term implies to many that the modern historical period has passed. Nevertheless, most agree that postmodern ideas have influenced philosophy, art, critical theory, literature, architecture, design, marketing/ business, interpretation of history, and culture since the late 20th century. Postmodernity, a separate term, describes social and cultural conditions connected to the era in which postmodernism arose.

An Overview

Scholars and historians most commonly hold postmodernism to be a movement of ideas contrary to modernism. Modernism places a great deal of importance on ideals such as rationality, objectivity, and progress--as well as other ideas rooted in the Enlightenment, and as positivist and realist movements from the late 19th century. Postmodernism questions whether these ideals can actually exist at all.

In a nutshell, the pro-postmodernism argument runs that economic and technological conditions of our age have given rise to a decentralized, media-dominated society in which ideas are simulacra and only inter-referential representations and copies of each other, with no real original, stable or objective source for communication and meaning. Globalization, brought on by innovations in communication, manufacturing and transportation, is often cited as one force which has driven the decentralized modern life, creating a culturally pluralistic and interconnected global society lacking any single dominant center of political power, communication, or intellectual production.

Postmodernism's adherents often argue that their ideals have arisen as the result of particular economic and social conditions, including what is described as "late capitalism" and the growth of broadcast media, and that such conditions have pushed society into a new historical period. However, a large number of thinkers and writers hold that postmodernism is at best simply a period, variety, or extension of modernism and not actually a separate period or idea.

Postmodern scholars argue that such a decentralized society inevitably creates responses/perceptions that are described as post-modern, such as the rejection of what are seen as the false, imposed unities of meta-narrative and hegemony; the breaking of traditional frames of genre, structure and stylistic unity; and the overthrowing of categories that are the result of logocentrism and other forms of artificially imposed order.

Scholars who accept the division of post-modernity as a distinct period believe that society has collectively eschewed modern ideals and instead adopted ideas that are rooted in the reaction to the restrictions and limitations of those ideas, and that the present is therefore a new historical period. While the characteristics of postmodern life are sometimes difficult to grasp, most postmodern scholars point to concrete and visible technological and economic changes that they claim have brought about the new types of thinking.

Critics of the idea claim that it does not represent liberation, but rather a failure of creativity, and the supplanting of organization with syncreticism and bricolage. They argue that post-modernity is obscurist, overly dense, and makes assertions about the sciences that are demonstrably false.

There are often strong political overtones to this debate, with conservative commentators often being the harshest critics of post-modernism. There is a great deal of disagreement over whether or not recent technological and cultural changes represent a new historical period, or merely an extension of the modern one. Complicating matters further, others have argued that even the postmodern era has already ended, with some commentators asserting culture has entered a post-postmodern period. Alan Kirby has argued, in his essay "The Death of Postmoderrism, and Beyond", that we now inhabit an entirely new cultural landscape, which he calls "pseudo-modernism".

Meaning and Definitions

As with many other divisions, the use of the term is subject to the lumpers and splitters problem. There are those who use very small and exact definitions of postmodernism, often for theories perceived as relativist, nihilist, counter-Enlightenment or antimodern. Others believe the world has changed so profoundly that the term applies to nearly everything, and use postmodernism in a broad cultural sense. People who believe postmodernism is really just an aspect of the modern period may instead use terms such as "late modernism".

"Postmodernism is incredulity towards metanarratives."

Jean-Francois Lyotard: "The theory of rejecting theories."

Tony Cliff: "A generation raised on channel-surfing has lost the capacity for linear thinking and analytical reasoning."

Chuck Colson: "Postmodernist fiction is defined by its temporal disorder, its disregard of linear narrative, its mingling of fictional forms and its experiments with language."

Barry Lewis, Kazuo Ishiguro: "Weird for the sake of being weird."

Moe Szyslak, of The Simpsons: "It's the combination of narcissism and nihilism that really defines postmodernism,"

Al Gore: "Post-modernism swims, even wallows, in the fragmentary and the chaotic currents of change as if that is all there is."

David Harvey, The Condition of Postmodernity, Oxford: Basil Blackwell, 1989.: "We could say that every age has its own post-modern, just as every age has its own form of mannerism (in fact, I wonder if postmodern is not simply the modern name for *Manierismus*...). I believe that every age reaches moments of crisis like those described by Nietzsche in the second of the Untimely Considerations, on the harmfulness of the study of history (Historiography). The sense that the past is restricting, smothering, blackmailing us."

Development of Postmodernism

From Modernism

Modernity is defined as a period or condition loosely identified with the Industrial Revolution, or the Enlightenment. One "project" of modernity is said to have been the fostering of progress, which was thought to be achievable by incorporating principles of rationality and hierarchy into aspects of public and artistic life.

Although useful distinctions can be drawn between the modernist and postmodernist eras, this does not erase the many continuities present between them. (These continuities are the reason that some refer to post-modernism as both the continuation as well as the cessation of modernism.) One of the most significant differences between modernism and postmodernism is its interest in universality or totality. While modernist artists aimed to capture universality or totality in some sense, postmodernists have rejected these ambitions as "metanarratives." This usage is ascribed to the philosophers Jean-François Lyotard and Jean Baudrillard.

Lyotard understood modernity as a cultural condition characterized by constant change in the pursuit of progress, and postmodernity as the culmination of this process, where constant change has become a status quo and the notion of progress, obsolete. Following Ludwig Wittgenstein's critique of the possibility of absolute and total knowledge, Lyotard also further argued that the various "master-narratives" of progress, such as positivist science, Marxism, and Structuralism, were defunct as a method of achieving progress.

Writers such as John Ralston Saul among others have argued that postmodernism represents an accumulated disillusionment with the promises of the Enlightenment project and its progress of science, so central to modern thinking.

Notable Philosophical Contributors

Thinkers in the mid and late 19th century and early 20th century, like Søren Kierkegaard and Friedrich Nietzsche, through their arguments against objectivity, and emphasis on skepticism (especially concerning social morals and norms), laid the groundwork for the existentialist movement of the 20th century. Writers such as Jean-Paul Sartre, Albert Camus, and Samuel Beckett, drew heavily from Kierkegaard and Nietzsche, and other previous thinkers, and brought about a new sense of subjectivity, and forlornness, which greatly influenced contemporary thinkers, writers, and artists. Karl Barth's fideist approach to theology and lifestyle, brought an irreverence for reason, and the rise of subjectivity. Post-colonialism after World War II contributed to the idea that one cannot have an objectively superior lifestyle or belief. This idea was taken further by the anti-foundationalist philosophers: Heidegger, then Ludwig Wittgenstein, then Derrida, who examined the fundamentals of knowledge; they argued that rationality was neither as sure nor as clear as modernists or rationalists assert. Features of postmodern culture begin to arise in the 1920s with the emergence of the Dada art movement. Both World Wars contributed to postmodernism; it is with the end of the Second World War that recognizably post-modernist attitudes begin to emerge. Some identify the burgeoning anti-establishment movements of the 1960s as an early trend toward postmodernism. The theory gained some of its strongest ground early on in French academia. In 1979 Jean-François Lyotard wrote a short but influential work The Postmodern Condition: A report on knowledge. Also, Richard Rorty wrote Philosophy and the Mirror of Nature (1979). Jean Baudrillard, Michel Foucault, and Roland Barthes are also influential in 1970s postmodern theory.

Marxist critics argue that postmodernism is symptomatic of "late capitalism" and the decline of institutions, particularly the nation-state. The literary critic Fredric Jameson and the geographer David Harvey have also identified post-modernity with "late capitalism" or "flexible accumulation". This situation, called finance capitalism, is characterized by a high degree of mobility of labor and capital, and what Harvey called "time and space compression." They suggest that this coincides with the breakdown of the Bretton Woods system which they believe defined the economic order following the Second World War. Other thinkers assert that post-modernity is the natural reaction to mass broadcasting and a society conditioned to mass production and mass politics. Related to this critical perspective on the economic, political and ideological realities of capitalist modernity is the work of Alasdair MacIntyre, who informs the versions of postmodernism elaborated by such authors as Murphy and Bielskis. On their account, MacIntyre's postmodern revision of Aristotelianism poses a challenge to the kind of consumerist ideology that now promotes capital accumulation.

The movement has had diverse political ramifications: its anti-ideological ideas appear to have been conducive to, and strongly associated with, the feminist movement, racial equality movements, gay rights movements, most forms of late 20th century anarchism, and even the peace movement, as well as various hybrids of these in the current anti-globalization movement. Unsurprisingly, none of these institutions entirely embraces all aspects of the postmodern movement in its most concentrated definition, but they reflect, or borrow from, some of its core ideas.

DECONSTRUCTION

Deconstruction is a term which is used to denote the application of post-modern ideas of criticism, or theory, to a "text" or "artifact". A deconstruction is meant to undermine the frame of reference and assumptions that underpin the text or the artifact.

In its original use, a "deconstruction" is an important textual "occurrence" described and analyzed by many postmodern authors and philosophers. They argue that aspects in the text itself would undermine its own authority or assumptions and that internal contradictions would erase boundaries or categories which the work relied on or asserted. Post-structuralists beginning with Jacques Derrida, who coined the term, argued that the existence of deconstructions implied that there was no intrinsic essence to a text, merely the contrast of difference. This is analogous to the scientific idea that only the variations are real, that there is no established norm to a genetic population, or the idea that the difference in perception between black and white is the context. A deconstruction is created when the "deeper" substance of text opposes the text's more "superficial" form.

This idea too is not isolated to post-structuralists, but is related to the idea of hermeneutics in literature, intellectuals as early as Plato asserted it, and so did modern thinkers such as Leo Strauss. Derrida's argument is that deconstruction proves that texts have multiple meanings, and the "violence" between the different meanings of text may be elucidated by close textual analysis. Popularly, close textual analyses describing deconstruction within a text are often themselves called deconstructions. Derrida argued, however, that deconstruction is not a method or a tool, but an occurrence within the text itself. Writings about deconstruction are therefore referred to in academic circles as deconstructive readings.

Deconstruction is far more important to postmodernism than its seemingly narrow focus on text might imply. According to Derrida, one consequence of deconstruction is that the text may be defined so broadly as to encompass not just written words, but the entire spectrum of symbols and phenomena within Western thought. To Derrida, a result of deconstruction is that no Western philosopher has been able to escape successfully from this large web of text and reach that which is "signified", which they imagined to exist "just beyond" the text. The more common use of the term is the more general process of pointing to contradictions between the intent and surface of a work, and the assumptions about it. A work then "deconstructs" assumptions when it places them in context. For example, someone who can pass as the opposite sex is said to "deconstruct" gender identity, because there is a conflict between the superficial appearance, and the reality of the person's gender.

Social Construction, Structuralism, Post-structuralism

Often opposed to deconstruction are social constructionists, labelled as such within the analytic tradition, but not usually in the case of the continental tradition. The term was first used in Peter Berger and Thomas Luckmann's book The Social Construction of Reality. Usually in the continental tradition, the terms structuralism or post-structuralism are used. Maurice Merleau-Ponty is seen as the biggest contributor to structuralism, which is epitomized in the philosophy of Claude Levi-Strauss. Michel Foucault was also a structuralist, but then turned to what would be termed post-structuralism, although he himself disputed that his views had been post-structuralist.

Structuralism historically gave way to post-structuralism, often the role of postmodernism within the analytic tradition is played down, although works by major figures of the analytic tradition in the 20th century, including those of Thomas Kuhn, and Willard Van Orman Quine, show a similarity with works in the continental tradition for their lack of belief in absolute truth as well as in the pliability of language. In the continental tradition, most works argue that power dissimulates, and that society constructs reality, while its individuals remain powerless or almost powerless. Often, both continental and analytic sources argue for a renewed subjectivity, borrowing heavily from Immanuel Kant, while they largely reject his a priori/a posteriori distinction. They both minimize discussions of practical ethics, instead borrowing heavily from post-Holocaust accounts of the need for an ethics of responsibility, which is very rarely practically defined.

One of the large differences between analytic postmodern sources and continental postmodern sources is that the analytic tradition by and large guards at least some of the tenets of liberalism, while many continental sources flirt with, or completely immerse themselves in, Marxism.

Criticism

The term post-modernism is often used pejoratively to describe tendencies perceived as Relativist, Counter-enlightenment or antimodern, particularly in relation to critiques of Rationalism, Universalism or Science. It is also sometimes used to describe tendencies in a society that are held to be antithetical to traditional systems of morality. The criticisms of postmodernism are often complicated by the still fluid nature of the term, and in many cases the criticisms are clearly directed at poststructuralism and the philosophical and academic movements that it has spawned rather than the broader term postmodernism.

As Intellectually and Artistically Disingenuous

Charles Murray, a critic of postmodernism, defines the term: By contemporary intellectual fashion, I am referring to the constellation of views that come to mind when one hears the words multicultural, gender, deconstruct, politically correct, and Dead White Males. In a broader sense, contemporary intellectual fashion encompasses as well the widespread disdain in certain circles for technology and the scientific method. Embedded in this mind-set is hostility to the idea that discriminating judgments are appropriate in assessing art and literature, to the idea that hierarchies of value exist, hostility to the idea that an objective truth exists. Postmodernism is the overarching label that is attached to this perspective.

Charles Murray: Central to the debate is the concept of "objectivity" and what it means. Denial of the practical possibility of objectivity is held to be the postmodern position, and a hostility towards claims advanced on the basis of objectivity its defining feature. It is this underlying hostility towards the concept of objectivity, evident among many contemporary critical theorists, that is the common point of attack for critics of postmodernism. Many critics characterise postmodernism as an ephemeral phenomenon that cannot be adequately defined simply because, as a philosophy at least, it represents nothing more substantial than a series of disparate conjectures allied only in their distrust of modernism.

The most prominent recent criticism of postmodern art is that of John Gardner. Gardner wrote that the classification "post-modern" / "modern" applied to the art of his time was an evasion, a stab at nothing-i.e., a move to elude the basic function of criticism, which, according to Gardner, is to judge art's moral value.

The Stuckist art movement has issued a series of manifestos denouncing postmodernism for what they see as its "scientific materialism, nihilism and spiritual bankruptcy".

As a False Distinction

The antipathy of postmodernists towards modernism, and their consequent tendency to define themselves against it, has also attracted criticism. It has been argued that modernity was not actually a lumbering, totalizing monolith at all, but in fact was itself dynamic and ever-changing; the evolution, therefore, between "modern" and "postmodern" should be seen as one of degree, rather than of kind-a continuation rather than a "break." One theorist who takes this view is Marshall Berman, whose book All That is Solid Melts into Air (1982) (a quote from Marx) reflects in its title the fluid nature of "the experience of modernity." Some theorists such as Habermas argue that the supposed distinction between the "modern" and the "postmodern" does not exist, but that the latter is no more than a development within a larger, still-current, "modern" framework.

Many who make this argument are academics with Marxist leanings, such as Seyla Benhabib, Terry Eagleton, Fredric Jameson, and David Harvey (social geographer), who are concerned that postmodernism's undermining of Enlightenment values makes a progressive cultural politics difficult, if not impossible. That is, "How can 'we' effect any change in people's poor living conditions, in inequality and injustice, if 'we' don't accept the validity of underlying universals such as the 'real world' and 'justice' in the first place?" How is any progress to be made through a philosophy so profoundly skeptical of the very notion of progress, and of unified perspectives?

These critics argue that the postmodern vision of a tolerant, pluralist society in which every political ideology is perceived to be as valid, or as redundant, as the other, may encourage individuals to lead lives of a rather disastrous apathetic quietism. This reasoning leads Habermas to compare postmodernism with conservatism and the preservation of the status quo. Such critics often argue that, in fact, such postmodern premises are rarely, if ever, actually embraced-that if they were, we would be left with nothing more than a crippling radical subjectivism. They point to the continuity of the projects of the Enlightenment and modernity as alive and well, as can be seen in science, in political rights movements and in the very idea of universities. To some critics, there seems to be a glaring contradiction between maintaining the death of objectivity and privileged position on one hand, while the scientific community continues a project of unprecedented scope to unify various scientific disciplines into a theory of everything, on the other. Hostility toward hierarchies of value and objectivity becomes problematic to them when postmodernity itself attempts to analyse such hierarchies with, apparently, some measure of objectivity and make categorical statements concerning them.

As Empty Rhetoric

The criticism of Postmodernism as ultimately meaningless rhetorical gymnastics was demonstrated in the Sokal Affair, where Alan Sokal, a physicist, wrote a deliberately nonsensical article purportedly about interpreting physics and mathematics in terms of postmodern theory, which was nevertheless published by the Social Text, a journal which he and most of the scientific community considered postmodernist. Interestingly, Social Text never acknowledged that the article's publication was a mistake, but supported a counter-argument defending the "interpretative validity" of Sokal's false article, despite the author's rebuttal of his own article.

2

Early History of Literature

The history of literature is the historical development of writings in prose or poetry which attempt to provide entertainment, enlightenment, or instruction to the reader/hearer/observer, as well as the development of the literary techniques used in the communication of these pieces. Not all writings constitute literature. Some recorded materials, such as compilations of data (e.g., a check register) are not considered literature, and this article relates only to the evolution of the works defined in the first sentence above.

THE BEGINNING OF LITERATURE

Literature and writing, though obviously connected, are not synonymous. The very first writings from ancient Sumer by any reasonable definition do not constitute literature-the same is true of some of the early Egyptian hieroglyphics or the thousands of logs from ancient Chinese regimes. Scholars always have and always will disagree concerning when the earliest records-keeping in writing becomes more like "literature" than anything else: the definition is largely subjective.

Moreover, it must be borne in mind that, given the significance of distance as a cultural isolator in earlier centuries, the historical development of literature did not occur at an even pace across the world. The problems of creating a uniform global history of literature are compounded by the fact that many texts have been lost over the millennia, either deliberately, by accident, or by the total disappearance of the originating culture. Much has been written, for example, about the destruction of the Library of Alexandria in the 3rd century BCE, and the innumerable key texts which are believed to have been lost forever to the flames. The deliberate suppression of texts (and often their authors) by organisations of either a spiritual or a temporal nature further shrouds the subject.

Certain primary texts, however, may be isolated which have a qualifying role as literature's first stirrings. Very early examples are Epic of Gilgamesh, in its Sumerian version predating 2000 BCE, and the Egyptian Book of the Dead written down in the Papyrus of Ani in approximately 250 BCE but probably dates from about the 18th century BCE. Ancient Egyptian literature was not included in early studies of the history of literature because the writings of Ancient Egypt were not translated into European languages until the 19th century when the Rosetta stone was deciphered.

Many texts handed down by oral tradition over several centuries before they were fixed in written form are difficult or impossible to date. The core of the Rigveda may date to the mid 2nd millennium BCE. The Pentateuch is traditionally dated to the 15th century, although modern scholarship estimates its oldest part to date to the 10th century BCE at the earliest.

Homer's The Iliad and The Odyssey date to the 8th century BCE and mark the beginning of Classical Antiquity. They also stand in an oral tradition that stretches back to the late Bronze Age. Indian sruti texts post-dating the Rigveda (such as the Yajurveda, the Atharvaveda and the Brahmanas), as well as the Hebrew Tanakh and the a mystical collection of poems attributed to Lao Tze, the Tao te Ching, date to the Iron Age, but their dating is difficult and controversial. The great Hindu epics were also transmitted orally, likely predating the Maurya period. Other oral traditions were fixed in writing much later, such as the Elder Edda, written down in the 12th or 13th century.

There are various different possible answers to the question "Which was the first novel ever written?"

EARLY INDIAN LITERATURE

Indian epics such as Ramayana and Mahabharata, have influenced countless other works, including Balinese Kecak and other performances such as shadow puppetry (wayang), and many European influenced works. Pali literature has an important position in the rise of Buddhism.

EARLY CHINESE LITERATURE

The first great author on military tactics and strategy was Sun Tzu, whose The Art of War remains on the shelves of many modern military officers (and its advice has been applied to the corporate world as well). Philosophy developed far differently in China than in Greece-rather than presenting extended dialogues, the Analects of Confucius and Lao Zi's Tao Te Ching presented sayings and proverbs more directly and didactically.

THE GREEKS AND THE ROMANS

The Greeks

Ancient Greek society placed considerable emphasis upon literature. Many authors consider the western literary tradition to have begun with the epic poems The Iliad and The Odyssey, which remain giants in the literary canon for their skillful and vivid depictions of war and peace, honor and disgrace, love and hatred. Notable among later Greek poets was Sappho, who defined, in many ways, lyric poetry as a genre.

A playwright named Aeschylus changed Western literature forever when he introduced the ideas of dialogue and interacting characters to playwriting. In doing so, he essentially invented "drama": his Oresteia trilogy of plays is seen as his crowning achievement. Other refiners of playwriting were Sophocles and Euripides.

Sophocles is credited with skillfully developing irony as a literary technique, most famously in his play Oedipus the King. Euripedes, conversely, used plays to challenge societal norms and mores-a hallmark of much of Western literature for the next 2,300 years and beyond-and his works such as Medea, The Bacchae and The Trojan Women are still notable for their ability to challenge our perceptions of propriety, gender, and war. Aristophanes, a comic playwright, defines and shapes the idea of comedy almost as Aeschylus had shaped tragedy as an art form-Aristophanes' most famous plays include the Lysistrata and The Frogs.

Philosophy entered literature in the dialogues of Plato, who converted the give and take of Socratic questioning into written form. Aristotle, Plato's student, wrote dozens of works on many scientific disciplines, but his greatest contribution to literature was likely his Poetics, which lays out his understanding of drama, and thereby establishes the first criteria for literary criticism.

The Romans

In many respects, the writers of the Roman Republic and the Roman Empire chose to avoid innovation in favor of imitating the great Greek authors. Virgil's Aeneid, in many respects, emulated Homer's Iliad; Plautus, a comic playwright, followed in the footsteps of Aristophanes; Tacitus' Annals and Germania follow essentially the same historical approaches that Thucydides devised (the Christian historian Eusebius does also, although far more influenced by his religion than either Tacitus or Thucydides had been by Greek and Roman polytheism); Ovid and his Metamorphoses explore the same Greek myths again in new ways. It can be argued, and has been, that the Roman authors, far from being mindless copycats, improved on the genres already established by their Greek predecessors. For example Ovid's Metamorphoses creates a form which is a clear predecessor of the stream of consciousness genre. What is undeniable is that the Romans, in comparison with the Greeks, innovate relatively few literary styles of their own.

Satire is one of the few Roman additions to literature-Horace was the first to use satire extensively as a tool for argument, and Juvenal made it into a weapon. The New Testament is an unusual collection of texts--Paul's epistles are the first collection of personal letters to be treated as literature, the Gospels arguably present the first realistic biographies in Western literature, and John's Book of Revelation, though not the first of its kind, essentially defines apocalypse as a literary genre. Augustine of Hippo and his The City of God do for religious literature essentially what Plato had done for philosophy, but Augustine's approach was far less conversational and more didactive. His Confessions is perhaps the first true autobiography, and certainly it gives rise to the genre of confessional literature which is now more popular than ever.

TURKISH LITERATURE

The history of Turkish literature spans a period of nearly 1,500 years. The oldest extant records of written Turkish are the Orhon inscriptions, found in the Orhon River valley in central Mongolia and dating to the 8th century. Subsequent to this period, between the 9th and 11th centuries, there arose among the nomadic Turkic peoples of Central Asia/Turkistan a tradition of oral epics, such as the Book of Dede Korkut of the Oghuz Turks-ancestors of the modern Turkish people-and the Manas epic of the Kyrgyz Turks.

Among the early written prose Yusuf Has Hajib's "Kutat-Ku Bilik" (Blessings and Wisdom) a book on Turkic philosophy, the "Divan-i Lugat-it Turk" an encyclopedic dictionary written by Mahmut Kasgari and Mir Ali Shir Nava'i the Chaucer of the Turks are early epic masterpieces.

PERSIAN LITERATURE

The Medieval Period

After the fall of Rome (in roughly 476), many of the literary approaches and styles invented by the Greeks and Romans fell out of favor in Europe. In the millennium or so that intervened between Rome's fall and the Florentine Renaissance, medieval literature focused more and more on faith and faith-related matters, in part because the works written by the Greeks had not been preserved in Europe, and therefore there were few models of classical literature to learn from and move beyond. What little there was became changed and distorted, with new forms beginning to develop from the distortions. Some of these distorted beginnings of new styles can be seen in the literature generally described as Matter of Rome, Matter of France and Matter of Britain. Following Rome's fall, Islam's spread across Asia and Africa brought with it a desire to preserve and build upon the work of the Greeks, especially in literature. Although much had been lost to the ravages of time (and to catastrophe, as in the burning of the Library of Alexandria), many Greek works remained extant: they were preserved and copied carefully by Muslim scribes.

Among the innovations of Arabic literature was Ibn Khaldun's perspective on chronicling past events-by fully rejecting supernatural explanations, Khaldun essentially invented the scientific or sociological approach to history.

In Europe Hagiographies, or "lives of the saints", are frequent among early medieval texts. The writings of Bede-Historia ecclesiastica gentis Anglorum-and others continue the faith-based historical tradition begun by Eusebius in the early 300s. Playwriting essentially ceased, except for the mystery plays and the passion plays that focused heavily on conveying Christian belief to the common people. Around 400 AD the Prudenti Psychomachia began the tradition of allegorical tales. Poetry flourished, however, in the hands of the troubadours, whose courtly romances and chanson de geste amused and entertained the upper classes who were their patrons. Geoffrey of Monmouth wrote works which he claimed were histories of Britain. These were highly fanciful and included stories of Merlin the magician and King Arthur. Epic poetry continued to develop with the addition of the mythologies of Northern Europe: Beowulf and the Norse sagas have much in common with Homer and Virgil's approaches to war and honor, while poems such as Dante's Divine Comedy and Geoffrey Chaucer's The Canterbury Tales take much different stylistic directions.

From Persian culture the book which would, eventually, become the most famous in the west is the Rubaiyat of Omar Khayyam. The Rubáiyát is a collection of poems by the Persian mathematician and astronomer Omar Khayyám (1048-1122). "Rubaiyat" means "quatrains": verses of four lines.

In November 1095-Pope Urban II preached the First Crusade at the Council of Clermont. The crusades would affect everything in Europe and the Middle East for many years to come and literature would, along with everything else, be transformed by the wars between these two cultures. For instance the image of the knight would take on a different significance. Also the Islamic emphasis on scientific investigation and the presevation of the Greek philosophical writings would eventually affect European literature.

Between Augustine and The Bible, religious authors had numerous aspects of Christianity that needed further explication and interpretation. Thomas Aquinas, more than any other single person, was able to turn theology into a kind of science, in part because he was heavily influenced by Aristotle, whose works were returning to Europe in the 1200s.

LATER CHINESE LITERATURE

Lyric poetry advanced far more in China than in Europe prior to 1000, as multiple new forms developed in the Han, Tang, and Song dynasties: perhaps the greatest poets of this era in Chinese literature were Li Bai and Du Fu. Printing began in China. A copy of the Diamond Sutra, a key Buddhist text, found sealed in a cave in China in the early 20th century, is the oldest known dated printed book, with a printed date of 868. The method used was block printing.

Some authors feel that China originated the novel form with the Romance of the Three Kingdoms by Luo Guanzhong (in the 14th century), although others feel that this epic is distinct from the novel in key ways.

EUROPEAN RENAISSANCE LITERATURE

Had nothing occurred to change literature in the 1400s but the Renaissance, the break with medieval approaches would have been clear enough. The 1400s, however, also brought Johann Gutenberg and his invention of the printing press, an innovation (for Europe, at least) that would change literature forever.

Texts were no longer precious and expensive to produce-they could be cheaply and rapidly put into the marketplace. Literacy went from the prized possession of the select few to a much broader section of the population (though by no means universal). As a result, much about literature in Europe was radically altered in the two centuries following Gutenberg's unveiling of the printing press in 1455.

William Caxton was the first English printer and published English language texts including Le Morte d'Arthur (a collection of oral tales of the Arthurian Knights which is a forerunner of the novel) and Geoffrey Chaucer's Canterbury Tales. These are an indication of future directions in literature. With the arrival of the printing press a process begins in which folk yarns and legends are collected within a frame story and then mass published.

In the Renaissance, the focus on learning for learning's sake causes an outpouring of literature. Petrarch popularized the sonnet as a poetic form; Giovanni Boccaccio's Decameron made romance acceptable in prose as well as poetry; François Rabelais rejuvenates satire with Gargantua and Pantagruel; Michel de Montaigne single-handedly invented the essay and used it to catalog his life and ideas. Perhaps the most controversial and important work of the time period was a treatise printed in Nuremberg, entitled De Revolutionibus Orbium Coelestium: in it, the astronomer Nicolaus Copernicus removed the Earth from its privileged position in the universe, which had far-reaching effects, not only in science, but in literature and its approach to humanity, hierarchy, and truth.

THE EARLY MODERN PERIOD IN WESTERN EUROPE

A new spirit of science and investigation in Europe was part of a general upheaval in human understanding which began with the discovery of the New world in 1492 and continues through the subsequent centuries, even up to the present day.

The form of writing now commonplace acros the world-the novel-originated from the early modern period and grew in popularity in the next century. Before the modern novel became established as a form there first had to be a transitional stage when "novelty" began to appear in the style of the epic poem.

Plays for entertainment (as opposed to religious enlightenment) returned to Europe's stages in the early modern period. William Shakespeare is the most notable of the early modern playwrights, but numerous others made important contributions, including Christopher Marlowe, Molière, and Ben Jonson. From the 16th to the 18th century Commedia dell'arte performers improvised in the streets of Italy and France. Some Commedia dell'arte plays were written down.

Both the written plays and the improvisation were influential upon literature of the time, particularly upon the work of Molière. Shakespeare, and his associate Robert Armin, drew upon the arts of jesters and strolling players in creating new style comedies. All the parts, even the female ones, were played by men (en travesti) but that would change, first in France and then in England too, by the end of the 17th century. The epic Elizabethan poem The Faerie Queene by Edmund Spenser was published, in its first part, in 1590 and then in completed form in 1597. The Fairie Queen marks the transitional period in which "novelty" begins to enter in to the narative in the sense of overturning and playing with the flow of events. Theatrical forms known in Spenser's time such as The Masque and the Mummers' Play are incorporated into the poem in ways which twist tradition and turn it to political propaganda in the service of Queen Elizabeth I.

The earliest work considered an opera in the sense the work is usually understood dates from around 1597. It is Dafne, (now lost) written by Jacopo Peri for an elite circle of literate Florentine humanists who gathered as the "Camerata".

Miguel de Cervantes's Don Quixote de la Mancha has been called "the first novel" by many literary scholars (or the first of the modern

European novels). It was published in two parts. The first part was published in 1605 and the second in 1615. It might be viewed as a parody of Le Morte d'Arthur (and other examples of the chivalric romance), in which case the novel form would be the direct result of poking fun at a collection of heroic folk legends. This is fully in keeping with the spirit of the age of enlightenment which began from about this time and delighted in giving a satirical twist to the stories and ideas of the past. It's worth noting that this trend toward satirising previous writings was only made possible by the printing press. Without the invention of mass produced copies of a book it would not be possible to assume the reader will have seen the earlier work and will thus understand the references within the text.

The new style in English poetry during the 17th century was that of the metaphysical movement. The metaphysical poets were John Donne, George Herbert, Andrew Marvell, Thomas Traherne, Henry Vaughan and others. Metaphysical poetry is characterised by a spirit of intellectual investigation of the spiritual, rather than the mystical reverence of many earlier English poems. The metaphysical poets were clearly trying to understand the world around them and the spirit behind it, instead of accepting dogma on the basis of faith.

In the middle of the century the king of England was overthrown and a republic declared. In the new regime (which lasted from 1649 to 1653) the arts suffered. In England and the rest of the British Isles Oliver Cromwell's rule temporarily banned all theatre, festivals, jesters, mummers plays and frivolities. The ban was lifted when the monarchy was restored with Charles II. Thomas Killigrew and the Drury Lane theatre were favorites of King Charles.

In contrast to the metaphysical poets was John Milton's Paradise Lost, an epic religious poem in blank verse. Milton had been Oliver Cromwell's chief propagandist and suffered when the Restoration came. Paradise Lost is one of the highest developments of the epic form in poetry immediately preceding the era of the modern prose novel.

An allegorical novel, The Pilgrim's Progress from This World to That Which Is to Come was published by John Bunyan in 1678.

Other early novelists include Daniel Defoe (born 1660) and Jonathan Swift (born 1667).

RHETORIC

Rhetoric (from Greek word, rhêtôr, orator, teacher) is the art or technique of persuasion through the use of oral or written language. Rhetoric is one of the three original liberal arts or trivium (the other members are dialectic and grammar) in Western culture. In ancient and medieval times, grammar concerned itself with correct, accurate, pleasing, and effective language use through the study and criticism of literary models, dialectic concerned itself with the testing and invention of new knowledge through a process of question and answer, and rhetoric concerned itself with persuasion in public and political settings such as assemblies and courts of law. As such, rhetoric is said to flourish in open and democratic societies with rights of free speech, free assembly, and political enfranchisement for some portion of the population.

The concept of rhetoric has shifted widely during its 2500-year history. Today rhetoric is described more broadly as the art or practice of persuasion through any symbolic system, but especially language. Or, rhetoric can be described as the persuasive or "suasory" function of all human action, including symbolic action like language use. So while rhetoric clearly has a place in such arenas as politics, law, public relations, lobbying, marketing and advertising, many scholars also find elements of rhetoric in such apparently non-rhetorical fields as science, journalism, history, literature and even cartography or architecture.

The terms "rhetoric" and "sophistry" are also used today in a pejorative or dismissive sense, when someone wants to refer to demagogic politicians, distinguish between "empty" words and action, or between true or accurate information and misinformation, propaganda, or "spin." Another current use of the word rhetoric is to denigrate specific forms of verbal reasoning as irrelevant, fallacious, inflammatory, or spurious. Nonetheless, rhetoric, as the art of persuasion, continues to play an important function in contemporary public life.

The scholarly literature on the 2500-year history and theory of rhetoric in Western culture is far too voluminous to be listed at the end of this entry. Useful reference works include George Kennedy's Classical Rhetoric and its Christian and Secular Tradition from Ancient to Modern Times, Thomas O. Sloane, ed., Encyclopedia of Rhetoric (Oxford University Press, 2001); Heinrich Lausberg, Handbook of Literary Rhetoric: A Foundation for Literary Study (1960; 2nd ed. 1973; English trans, Brill, 1998); Richard A. Lanham, A Handlist of Rhetorical Terms

(University of California Press, 1968; 2nd ed. 1991). For overview surveys of the scholarly literature, see Winifred Bryan Horner, ed., The Present State of Scholarship in Historical and Contemporary Rhetoric (University of Missouri Press, 1983; rev. ed. 1990); and Theresa Enos and Stuart C. Brown, eds., Defining the New Rhetorics (Sage, 1993).

Ancient Greece

Western thinking about rhetoric grew out of the public and political life of Ancient Greece, much of which revolved around the use of oratory as the medium through which political and judicial decisions were made, and through which philosophical ideas were developed and disseminated. For modern students today, it can be difficult to remember that the wide use and availability of written texts is a phenomenon that was just coming into vogue in Classical Greece. In Classical times, many of the great thinkers and political leaders performed their works before an audience, usually in the context of a competition or contest for fame, political influence, and cultural capital; in fact, many of them are known only through the texts that their students, followers, or detractors wrote down. As has already been noted, rhetor was the Greek term for orator: A rhetor was a citizen who regularly addressed juries and political assemblies and who was thus understood to have gained some knowledge about public speaking in the process, though in general facility with language was often referred to as logôn techne, "skill with arguments" or "verbal artistry." See, Mogens Herman Hansen The Athenian Democracy in the Age of Demosthenes (Blackwell, 1991); Josiah Ober Mass and Elite in Democratic Athens (Princeton UP, 1989); Jeffrey Walker, Rhetoric and Poetic in Antiquity (Oxford UP, 2000).

Rhetoric thus evolved as an important art, one that provided the orator with the forms, means, and strategies of persuading an audience of the correctness of the orator's arguments. Today the term rhetoric can be used at times to refer only to the form of argumentation, often with the pejorative connotation that rhetoric is a means of obscuring the truth. Classical philosophers believed quite the contrary: the skilled use of rhetoric was essential to the discovery of truths, because it provided the means of ordering and clarifying arguments.

THE SOPHISTS

Organized thought about rhetoric began in ancient Greece. Possibly, the first study about the power of language may be attributed to the philosopher Empedocles (d. ca. 444 BC), whose theories on human knowledge would provide a basis for many future rhetoricians. The first written manual is attributed to Corax and his pupil Tisias. Their work, as well as that of many of the early rhetoricians, grew out of the courts of law; Tisias, for example, is believed to have written judicial speeches that others delivered in the courts. Rhetoric was popularized in the 5th century BC by itinerant teachers known as sophists, the best known of whom were Protagoras (c.481-420 BC), Gorgias (c.483-376 BC), and Isocrates (436-338 BC). The Sophists were a disparate group who travelled from city to city making public displays to attract students who were then charged a fee for their education. Their central focus was on logos or what we might broadly refer to as discourse. They defined parts of speech, analyzed poetry, parsed close synonyms, invented argumentation strategies, and debated the nature of reality. They claimed to make their students "better," or, in other words, to teach virtue.

They thus claimed that human "excellence" was not an accident of fate or a prerogative of noble birth, but an art or "techne" that could be taught and learned. Several sophists also questioned received wisdom about the gods and about the inherent supremacy of Greek culture, taken for granted by Greeks of their time. They argued, for example, that cultural practices were a function of convention or nomos rather than blood or birth or phusis, and further that the morality or immorality of any action could not be judged outside of the cultural context within which it occurred. The well-known phrase, "Man is the measure of all things" arises from this belief. One of their most famous, and infamous, doctrines has to do with probability and counter arguments. They taught that every argument could be countered with an opposing argument, that an argument's effectiveness derived from how "likely" it appeared to the audience (its probability of seeming true), and that any probability argument could be countered with an inverted probability argument. Thus, if it seemed likely that a strong, poor man were guilty of robbing a rich, weak man, the strong poor man could argue, on the contrary, that this very likelihood (that he would be a suspect) makes it unlikely that he committed the crime. Aristophanes famously parodies the clever inversions that sophists were known for in his play The Clouds.

The word "sophistry" has negative connotations today, but in ancient Greece sophists were popular and well-paid professionals, widely respected for their abilities but also widely criticized for their excesses.

ISOCRATES

Isocrates (436-338 BC), like the sophists, taught public speaking as a means of human improvement, but he worked to distinguish himself from the Sophists, whom he saw as claiming far more than they could deliver. He suggested that while an art of virtue or excellence did exist, it was only one piece, and the least, in a process of self-improvement that relied much more heavily on native talent and desire, constant practice, and the imitation of good models. Isocrates believed that practice in speaking publicly about noble themes and important questions would function to improve the character of both speaker and audience while also offering the best service to a state.

He thus wrote his speeches as "models" for his students to imitate in the same way that poets might imitate Homer or Hesiod. His was the first permanent school in Athens and it is likely that Plato's Academy and Aristotle's Lyceum were founded in part as a response to Isocrates. Though he left no handbooks, his speeches ("Antidosis" and "Against the Sophists" are most relevant to students of rhetoric) became models of oratory (he was one of the canonical "Ten Attic Orators") and he had a marked influence on Cicero and Quintilian, and through them, on the entire educational system of the west.

PLATO

Plato (427-347 BC) has famously outlined the differences between true and false rhetoric in a number of dialogues, but especially the Gorgias and the Phaedrus. Both dialogues are complex and difficult, but in both Plato disputes the Sophistic notion that an art of persuasion, the art of the Sophists which he calls "rhetoric" (after the public speaker or rhêtôr) can exist independent of the art of dialectic. Plato claims that since Sophists appeal only to what seems likely or probable, rather than to what is true, they are not at all making their students and audiences "better," but simply flattering them with what they want to hear. While Plato's condemnation of rhetoric is clear in the Gorgias, in the Phaedrus he seems to suggest the possibility of a true art of rhetoric based upon the knowledge produced by dialectic, and he relies on such a dialectically informed rhetoric to appeal to the main character, Phaedrus, to take up philosophy.

Plato's animosity against the Sophists derives not only from their inflated claims to teach virtue and their reliance on appearances, but from the fact that his teacher, Socrates, was accused of being a sophist and ultimately sentenced to death for his teaching. In his dialogues, Plato attempts to distinguish the rhetoric common to Socratic questioning from Sophistry.

ARISTOTLE

Plato's student Aristotle (384-322 BC) famously set forth an extended treatise on rhetoric that still repays careful study today.

In the first sentence of The Art of Rhetoric, Aristotle says that "rhetoric is the counterpart [literally, the antistrophe] of dialectic." As the "antistrophe" of a Greek ode responds to and is patterned after the structure of the "strophe" (they form two sections of the whole and are sung by two parts of the chorus), so the art of rhetoric follows and is structurally patterned after the art of dialectic because both are arts of discourse production. Thus, while dialectical methods are necessary to find truth in theoretical matters, rhetorical methods are required in practical matters such as adjudicating somebody's guilt or innocence when charged in a court of law, or adjudicating a prudent course of action to be taken in a deliberative assembly.

For Plato and Aristotle, dialectic involves persuasion, so when Aristotle says that rhetoric is the antistrophe of dialectic, he means that rhetoric as he uses the term has a domain or scope of application that is parallel to but different from the domain or scope of application of dialectic.

In Nietzsche Humanist (1998: 129), Claude Pavur explains that "the Greek prefix 'anti' does not merely designate opposition, but it can also mean 'in place of.'" When Aristotle characterizes rhetoric as the antistrophe of dialectic, he no doubt means that rhetoric is used in place of dialectic when we are discussing civic issues in a court of law or in a legislative assembly. The domain of rhetoric is civic affairs and practical decision making in civic affairs, not theoretical considerations of operational definitions of terms and clarification of thought--these, for him, are in the domain of dialectic.

Aristotle's treatise on rhetoric is an attempt to systematically describe civic rhetoric as a human art or skill (techne). His definition of rhetoric as a mode of discovery seems to limit the art to the inventional process, and Aristotle heavily emphasizes the logical aspect of this process. But the treatise in fact also discusses not only elements of style and (briefly) delivery, but also emotional appeals (pathos) and characterological appeals (ethos). He thus identifies three steps or "offices" of rhetoric--invention, arrangement, and style--and three different types of rhetorical proof:

- ethos: how the character and credibility of a speaker influence an audience to consider him to be believable.
- This could be any position in which the speaker--from being a college professor of the subject, to being an acquaintance of person who experienced the matter in question--knows about the topic.
- pathos: the use of emotional appeals to alter the audience's judgment.
- This can be done through metaphor, amplification, storytelling, or presenting the topic in a way that evokes strong emotions in the audience.
- logos: the use of reasoning, either inductive or deductive, to construct an argument.

Inductive reasoning uses examples (historical, mythical, or hypothetical) to draw conclusions.

Deductive or "enthymematic" reasoning uses generally accepted propositions to derive specific conclusions. The term logic evolved from logos. Aristotle emphasized enthymematic reasoning as central to the process of rhetorical invention, though later rhetorical theorists placed much less emphasis on it. Aristotle also identifies three different types or genres of civic rhetoric: forensic (also known as judicial, was concerned with determining truth or falsity of events that took place in the past), deliberative (also known as political, was concerned with determining whether or not particular actions should or should not be taken in the future), and epideictic (also known as ceremonial, was concerned with praise and blame, demonstrating beauty and skill in the present).

One of the most fruitful of Aristotelian doctrines was the idea of topics (also referred to as common topics or commonplaces). Though the term had a wide range of application (as a memory technique or compositional exercise, for example) it most often referred to the "seats of argument"--the list of categories of thought or modes of reasoning--that a speaker could use in order to generate arguments or proofs. The topics were thus a heuristic or inventional tool designed to help speakers categorize and thus better retain and apply frequently used types of argument. For example, since we often see effects as "like" their causes, one way to invent an argument (about a future effect) is by discussing the cause (which it will be "like"). This and other rhetorical topics derive from Aristotle's belief that there are certain predictable ways in which humans (particularly non-specialists) draw conclusions from premises. Based upon and adapted from his dialectical Topics, the rhetorical topics became a central feature of later rhetorical theorizing, most famously in Cicero's work of that name.

ROMAN RHETORICIANS

The Romans, for whom oration also became an important part of public life, saw much value in Greek rhetoric, hiring Greek rhetoricians to teach in their schools and as private tutors, and imitating and adapting Greek rhetorical works in Latin and with Roman examples. Roman rhetoric thus largely extends upon and develops its Greek roots, though it tends to prefer practical advice to the theoretical speculations of Greek rhetoricians. Cicero (106-43 BC) and Quintilian (35-100 AD) were chief among Roman rhetoricians, and their work is an extension of sophistic, Isocratean, Platonic and Aristotelian rhetorical theory. Latin rhetoric was developed out of the Rhodian schools of rhetoric. In the second century BC, Rhodes became an important educational center, particularly of rhetoric, and the sons of noble Roman families studied there.

Although not widely read in Roman times, the Rhetorica ad Herennium (sometimes attributed to Cicero, but probably not his work) is a notable early work on Latin rhetoric. Its author was probably a Latin rhetorician in Rhodes, and for the first time we see a systematic treatment of Latin elocutio. The Ad Herennium provides a glimpse into the early development of Latin rhetoric, and in the Middle Ages and Renaissance, it achieved wide publication as one of the basic school texts on rhetoric.

Whether or not he wrote the Rhetorica ad Herennium, Cicero, along with Quintilian (the most influential Roman teacher of rhetoric), is considered one of the most important Roman rhetoricians. His works include the early and very influential De Inventione (On Invention, often read alongside the Ad Herennium as the two basic texts of rhetorical theory throughout the Middle Ages and into the Renaissance), De Oratore (a fuller statement of rhetorical principles in dialague form), Topics (a rhetorical treatment of common topics, highly influential through the Renaissance), Brutus (a discussion of famous orators)and Orator (a defense of Cicero's style). Cicero also left a large body of speeches and letters which would establish the outlines of Latin eloquence and style for generations to come. It was the rediscovery of Cicero's speeches (such as the defence of Archias) and letters (to Atticus) by Italians like Petrach that, in part, ignited the cultural innovations that we know as the Rennaisance.

Quintilian's career began as a pleader in the courts of law; his reputation grew so great that Vespasian created a chair of rhetoric for him in Rome. The culmination of his life's work was the Institutio oratoria (or Institutes of Oratory), a lengthy treatise on the training of the orator in which he discusses the training of the "perfect" orator from birth to old age and, in the process, reviews the doctrines and opinions of many influential rhetoricians who preceeded him.

In the Institutes, Quintilian organizes rhetorical study through the stages of education that an aspiring orator would undergo, beginning with the selection of a nurse. Aspects of elementary education (training in reading and writing, grammar, and literary criticism) are followed by preliminary rhetorical exercises in composition (the progymnasmata) that include maxims and fables, narratives and comparisons, and finally full legal or political speeches. The delivery of speeches within the context of education or for entertainment purposes became widespread and popular under the term "declamation." Rhetorical training proper was categorized under five canons that would persist for centuries in academic circles:

- Inventio (invention) is the process that leads to the development and refinement of an argument.
- Once arguments are developed, dispositio (disposition, or arrangement) is used to determine how it should be organized for greatest effect, usually beginning with the exordium.
- Once the speech content is known and the structure is

determined, the next steps involve elocutio (style) and pronuntiatio (presentation).

- Memoria (memory) comes to play as the speaker recalls each of these elements during the speech.
- Actio (delivery) is the final step as the speech is presented in a gracious and pleasing way to the audience-the Grand Style.

This work was available only in fragments in medieval times, but the discovery of a complete copy at Abbey of St. Gall in 1416 led to its emergence as one of the most influential works on rhetoric during the Renaissance.

Quintilian's work attempts to describe not just the art of rhetoric, but the formation of the perfect orator as a politically active, virtuous, publically minded citizen. His emphasis on the real life application of rhetorical training was in part nostalgia for the days when rhetoric was an important political tool, and in part a reaction against the growing tendency in Roman schools toward standarization of themes and techniques and increasing separation between school exercises and actual legal practice, a tendency equally powerful today in public schools and law schools alike.

At the same time that rhetoric was becoming divorced from political decision making, rhetoric rose as a culturally vibrant and important mode of entertainment and cultural criticism in a movement known as the "second sophistic," a development which gave rise to the charge (made by Quintilian and others) that teachers were emphasizing ornamentation over substance in rhetoric.

Quintilian's masterful work was not enough to curb this movement, but his dismayed response cemented the scholarly opinion that 2nd Century C.E. rhetoric fell into decadence and political irrelevance, despite its wide popularity and cultural importance.

Although he is not commonly regarded as a rhetorician, St. Augustine (354-430) was trained in rhetoric and was at one time a teacher of Latin rhetoric. After his conversion to Christianity, he became interested in using these "pagan" arts for spreading his religion. This new use of rhetoric is explored in the Fourth Book of his De Doctrina Christiana, which laid the foundation of what would become homiletics, the rhetoric of the sermon.

A valuable collection of studies can be found in Stanley E. Porter, ed., Handbook of Classical Rhetoric in the Hellenistic Period 330 B.C.-A.D. 400 (Brill, 1997).

RHETORIC FROM THE RENAISSANCE TO THE ENLIGHTENMENT

After the Roman Empire, the study of rhetoric continued to be central to the study of the verbal arts; but the study of the verbal arts went into decline for several centuries, followed eventually by a gradual rise in formal education, culminating in the rise of medieval universities. But rhetoric transmuted during this period in the arts of letter writing (ars dictaminis) and writing sermons (ars praedicandi). As part of the trivium, rhetoric was secondary to the study of logic, and its study was highly scholastic: students were given repetitive exercises in the creation of discourses on historical subjects (suasoriae) or on classic legal questions (controversiae).

In his 1943 Cambridge University doctoral dissertation in English, Marshall McLuhan (1911-1980) surveys the verbal arts from approximately the time of Cicero down to the time of Thomas Nashe (1567-1600). His dissertation is still noteworthy for undertaking to study the history of the verbal arts together as the trivium, even though the developments that he surveys have been studied in greater detail since he undertook his study. As noted below, McLuhan became one of the most widely publicized thinkers in the 20th century, so it is important to note his scholarly roots in the study of the history of rhetoric and dialectic.

Sixteenth Century

Walter J. Ong's encyclopedia article "Humanism" in the 1967 New Catholic Encyclopedia provides a well-informed survey of Renaissance humanism, which defined itself broadly as disfavoring medieval scholastic logic and dialectic and as favoring instead the study of classical Latin style and grammar and philology and rhetoric. (Reprinted in Ong's Faith and Contexts (Scholars Press, 1999; 4: 69-91.)

One influential figure in the rebirth of interest in classical rhetoric was Erasmus (c.1466-1536). His work, De Duplici Copia Verborum et Rerum (1512), was widely published (it went through more than 150 editions throughout Europe) and became one of the basic school texts on the subject. Its treatment of rhetoric is less comprehensive than the classic works of antiquity, but provides a traditional treatment of res-verba (matter and form): its first book treats the subject of elocutio, showing the student how to use schemes and tropes; the second book covers inventio. Much of the emphasis is on abundance of variation (copia means "plenty" or "abundance", as in copious or cornucopia), so both books focus on ways to introduce the maximum amount of variety into discourse. For instance, in one section of the De Copia, Erasmus presents two hundred variations of the sentence "Semper, dum vivam, tui meminero". Another of his works, the extremely popular The Praise of Folly also had considerable influence on the teaching of rhetoric in the later sixteenth century. Its orations in favour of qualities such as madness spawned a type of exercise popular in Elizabethan grammar schools, later called adoxography, which required pupils to compose passages in praise of useless things.

Juan Luis Vives (1492-1540) also helped shape the study of rhetoric in England. A Spaniard, he was appointed in 1523 to the Lectureship of Rhetoric at Oxford by Cardinal Wolsey, and was entrusted by Henry VIII to be one of the tutors of Mary. Vives fell into disfavor when Henry VIII divorced Catherine of Aragon and left England in 1528. His best-known work was a book on education, De Disciplinis, published in 1531, and his writings on rhetoric included Rhetoricae, sive De Ratione Dicendi, Libri Tres (1533), De Consultatione (1533), and a rhetoric on letter writing, De Conscribendis Epistolas (1536).

It is likely that many well-known English writers would have been exposed to the works of Erasmus and Vives (as well as those of the Classical rhetoricians) in their schooling, which was conducted in Latin (not English) and often included some study of Greek and placed considerable emphasis on rhetoric. See, for example, T.W. Baldwin's William Shakspere's Small Latine and Lesse Greeke, 2 vols. (University of Illinois Press, 1944).

The mid-1500s saw the rise of vernacular rhetorics-those written in English rather than in the Classical languages; adoption of works in English was slow, however, due to the strong orientation toward Latin and Greek. A successful early text was Thomas Wilson's The Arte of Rhetorique (1553), which presents a traditional treatment of rhetoric.

For instance, Wilson presents the five canons of rhetoric (Invention, Disposition, Elocutio, Memoria, and Utterance or Actio). Other notable works included Angel Day's The English Secretorie (1586, 1592), George Puttenham's The Arte of English Poesie (1589), and Richard Rainholde's Foundacion of Rhetorike (1563).

During this same period, a movement began that would change the organization of the school curriculum in Protestant and especially Puritan circles and lead to rhetoric losing its central place. A French scholar, Petrus Ramus (1515-1572), dissatisfied with what he saw as the overly broad and redundant organization of the trivium, proposed a new curriculum.

In his scheme of things, the five components of rhetoric no longer lived under the common heading of rhetoric. Instead, invention and disposition were determined to fall exclusively under the heading of dialectic, while style, delivery, and memory were all that remained for rhetoric. See Walter J. Ong, Ramus, Method, and the Decay of Dialogue: From the Art of Discourse to the Art of Reason (Harvard University Press, 1958; reissued by the University of Chicago Press, 2004, with a new foreword by Adrian Johns). One of Ramus' followers, Audomarus Talaeus (Omer Talon) published his rhetoric, Institutiones Oratoriae, in 1544. This work provided a simple presentation of rhetoric that emphasized the treatment of style, and became so popular that it was mentioned in John Brinsley's (1612) Ludus literarius; or The Grammar Schoole as being the "most used in the best schooles."

Many other Ramist rhetorics followed in the next half-century, and by the 1600s, their approach became the primary method of teaching rhetoric in Protestant and especially Puritan circles. See Walter J. Ong, Ramus and Talon Inventory (Harvard University Press, 1958); Joseph S. Freedman, Philosophy and the Arts in Central Europe, 1500-1700: Teaching and Texts at Schools and Universities (Ashgate, 1999).

John Milton (1608-1674) wrote a textbook in logic or dialectic in Latin based on Ramus' work, which has now been translated into English by Walter J. Ong and Charles J. Ermatinger in The Complete Prose Works of John Milton (Yale University Press, 1982; 8: 206-407), with a lengthy introduction by Ong (144-205). The introduction is reprinted in Ong's Faith and Contexts (Scholars Press, 1999; 4: 111-41).

But Ramism did not strongly influence the established Catholic schools and universities or the new Catholic schools and universities founded by members of the religious order known as the Society of Jesus, as can be seen in the Jesuit document known as the Ratio Studiorum that Claude Pavur, S.J., has recently translated into English, with the Latin text in the parallel column on each page (St. Louis: Institute of Jesuit Sources, 2005). The influence of Cicero and Quintilian permeates the Ratio Studiorum.

Seventeenth Century

In New England and at Harvard College (founded 1636), Ramus and his followers dominated, as Perry Miller shows in The New England Mind: The Seventeenth Century (Harvard University Press, 1939). However, in England, several writers influenced the course of rhetoric during the seventeenth century, many of them carrying forward the dichotomy that had been set forth by Ramus and his followers during the preceding decades. Of greater importance is that this century saw the development of a modern, vernacular style that looked to English, rather than to Greek, Latin, or French models.

Francis Bacon (1561-1626), although not a rhetorician, contributed to the field in his writings. One of the concerns of the age was to find a suitable style for the discussion of scientific topics, which needed above all a clear exposition of facts and arguments, rather than the ornate style favored at the time. Bacon in his The Advancement of Learning criticized those who are preoccupied with style rather than "the weight of matter, worth of subject, soundness of argument, life of invention, or depth of judgment." On matters of style, he proposed that the style conform to the subject matter and to the audience, that simple words be employed whenever possible, and that the style should be agreeable. See Lisa Jardine, Francis Bacon: Discovery and the Art of Discourse (Camb e University Press, 1975).

Thomas Hobbes (1588-1679) also wrote on rhetoric. Along with a shortened translation of Aristotle's Rhetoric, Hobbes also produced a number of other works on the subject. Sharply contrarian on many subjects, Hobbes, like Bacon, also promoted a simpl nd more natural style that used figures of speech sparingly.

Perhaps the most influential development in English style came out of the work of the Royal Society (founded in 1660), which in 1664 set up a committee to improve the English language. Am ttee's members were John Evelyn (1620-1706), Thomas Sprat (1635-1713), and John Dryden (1631-1700). Sprat regarded "fine speaking" as a disease, and thought that a proper style should "reject all amplifications, digressions, and swellings of style" and instead "return back to a primitive purity and shortness" (History of the Royal Society, 1667).

While the work of this committee never went beyond planning, John Dryden is often credited with creating and exemplifying a new and modern English style. His central tenet was that the style should be proper "to the occasion, the subject, and the persons." As such, he advocated the use of English words whenever possible instead of foreign ones, as well as vernacular, rather than Latinate, syntax. His own prose (and his poetry) became exemplars of this new style.

MODERN DEVELOPMENTS

Walter Jost has examined Rhetorical Thought in John Henry Newman (1989). (John Henry Newman lived from 1801-1890.)

The Canadian Jesuit philosopher and theologian Bernard Lonergan (1904-1984), who was deeply influenced by Newman's An Essay in Aid of a Grammar of Assent (1870), worked out what he styles the generalized empirical method in Insight: A Study of Human Understanding (1957) and elsewhere. In a review article originally published in the Quarterly Journal of Speech (1985: 476-88), John Angus Campbell has characterized Lonergan's generalized empirical method as his rhetoric, an astute observation that has not yet been widely noted. Even so, Lonergan's generalized empirical method holds enormous potential for taking the theory of rhetoric to the next level of significance. (Campbell's essay is reprinted in Communication and Lonergan (Sheed & Ward, 1991: 3-22).

At the turn of the twentieth century, there was a revival of rhetorical study manifested in the establishment of departments of rhetoric and speech at academic institutions, as well as the formation of national and international professional organizations. Theorists generally agree that a significant reason for the revival of the study of rhetoric was the renewed importance of language and persuasion in the increasingly mediated environment of the twentieth century. The rise of advertising and of mass media such as photography, telegraphy, radio, and film brought rhetoric more prominently into people's lives.

For example, when McLuhan was working on his 1943 Cambridge University doctoral dissertation on the verbal arts and Nashe, mentioned above, he was also preparing the materials that were eventually published as the book The Mechanical Bride: The Folklore of Industrial Man (Vanguard Press, 1951). This book is a compilation of exhibits of ads and other materials from popular culture with short essays about them by McLuhan. The essays involve rhetorical analyses of the ways in which the material in an item aims to persuade, and commentary on the persuasive strategies in each item.

After studying the persuasive strategies involved in such an array of items in popular culture, McLuhan shifted the focus of his rhetorical analysis and began to consider how communication media themselves have an impact on us as persuasive, in a manner of speaking. In other words, the communication media as such embody and carry a persuasive dimension. McLuhan uses hyperbole to express this insight when he says "the medium is the message." This shift in focus from his 1951 book led to his two most widely known books, The Gutenberg Galaxy: The Making of Typographic Man (University of Toronto Press, 1962) and Understanding Media: The Extensions of Man (McGraw-Hill, 1964). These two books led McLuhan to become one of the most publicized thinkers in the 20th century. No other scholar of the history and theory of rhetoric was as widely publicized in the 20th century as McLuhan.

McLuhan read Lonergan's Insight, mentioned above, in 1957 (see Letters of Marshall McLuhan, 1987: 251). Lonergan's book is an elaborate guidebook to cultivate one's inwardness and on attending to and reflecting on one's inward consciousness. McLuhan's 1962 and 1964 books represent an inward turn to attending to one's consciousness that is far more pronounced than anything found in his 1951 book or in his 1943 dissertation. By contrast, many other thinkers in the study of rhetoric are more outward oriented toward sociological considerations and symbolic interaction.

McLuhan's famous dictum "the medium is the message" can be paraphrased with terminology from Lonergan. At the empirical level of consciousness, the medium is the message, whereas at the intelligent and rational levels of consciousness, the content is the message. McLuhan is thus ordering us to pay attention to the empirical level of consciousness.

CURRENT STATE

Rhetorical theory today is as much influenced by the research results and research methods of the behavioral sciences and by theories of literary criticism as by ancient rhetorical theory. Early rhetorical theorists attempted to turn the study of rhetoric into a social science that allowed predictive analyses of human behavior. Interdisciplinary scholars of symbol systems, such as Ernst Cassirer (1874-1945), Hugh Duncan, and most notably Kenneth Burke (1897-1993), influenced a new generation of rhetorical scholars who drew from various disciplines to more fully comprehend the phenomenon of human communication in all its aspects. While ancient rhetorical scholarship had focused primarily on rhetoric as speech, contemporary rhetorical theorists are interested in the panoply of human symbolic behavior-both the spoken and written word as well as music, film, radio, television, etc. Thus Kenneth Burke, who defined the human being as the "symbol-using animal," defined rhetoric as "the use of symbols to induce cooperation in those who by nature respond to symbols." Current rhetorical theory also draws heavily from cultural studies, performance studies, and design studies. Topics of interest to contemporary scholars include the relationships between rhetoric and gender, studies of non-traditional or alternative rhetorics, and rhetorics of science, technology, and new media.

Other notable 20th-century authors in the study of the history and theory of rhetoric include Herbert Wichelns, Edwin Black, Ernest Wrage, Wayne C. Booth, Cleanth Brooks, Karlyn Kohrs Campbell, Barbara Biesecker, Dana L. Cloud, Celeste M. Condit, Edward P.J. Corbett, James Darsey, Paul de Man, Raymie McKerrow, Dilip Parameshwar Gaonkar, G. Thomas Goodnight, Susan Jarrett, James Kinneavy, Ernesto Laclau, Richard A. Lanham, Michael Leff, Andrea Lunsford, Michael Calvin McGee, Martin Medhurst, Marie Hochmuth Nichols, Lucy Olbrechts-Tyteca, Chaim Perelman, I.A. Richards, Edward Schiappa, Stephen Toulmin, Mark Turner, Victor J. Vitanza, Robert Penn Warren, and Richard M. Weaver.

Contemporary scholars in rhetoric come from diverse academic backgrounds, and are often housed in departments of English,

Communication Studies, Rhetoric, Education, or Speech Communication. Rhetorical scholars meet at conferences such as the Conference on College Composition and Communication, the National Communication Association conference, and the Rhetoric Society of America conference. They publish research in journals including the Quarterly Journal of Speech, College Composition and Communication, the Rhetoric Society Quarterly, Rhetoric Review, Rhetoric and Public Affairs, and Philosophy and Rhetoric.

POETRY

Poetry (from the Greek, poiesis, "making" or "creating") is a form of art in which language is used for its aesthetic qualities in addition to, or in lieu of, its ostensible meaning. Poetry may be written independently, as discrete poems, or may be used in conjunction with other arts, as in poetic drama, hymns or lyrics.

Poetry has a long history. Early attempts to define it, such as Aristotle's Poetics, focused on the uses of speech in rhetoric, drama, song and comedy. Later attempts focused on features such as repetition and rhyme, and emphasised the aesthetics which distinguish poetry from prose. From the mid-20th century, poetry has sometimes been more loosely defined as a fundamental creative act using language.

Poetry often uses particular forms and conventions to expand the literal meaning of the words, or to invoke emotional or sensual responses. Devices such as assonance, alliteration and rhythm are sometimes used to achieve musical or incantatory effects. Poetry's use of ambiguity, symbolism, irony and other stylistic elements of poetic diction often leaves a poem open to multiple interpretations. Similarly, metaphor and simile create a resonance between otherwise disparate images-a layering of meanings, forming connections previously not perceived. Kindred forms of resonance may exist, between individual verses, in their patterns of rhyme or rhythm.

Some forms of poetry are specific to particular cultures and genres, responding to the characteristics of the language in which the poet writes. While readers accustomed to identifying poetry with Dante, Shakespeare, Goethe and Mickiewicz may think of it as being written in rhyming lines and regular meter, there are other traditions, such as those of Du Fu and Beowulf, that use other approaches to achieve rhythm and euphony.

In today's globalized world, poets often borrow styles, techniques and forms from diverse cultures and languages.

Poetry as an art form may predate literacy. Thus many ancient works, from the Vedas (1800-1500 BC) to the Odyssey (700-500 BC), appear to have been composed in poetic form to aid memorization and oral transmission, in prehistoric and ancient societies. Poetry appears among the earliest records of most literate cultures, with poetic fragments found on early monoliths, rune stones and stelae.

The oldest surviving poem is the Epic of Gilgamesh, from the 3rd millennium BC in Sumer (in Iraq/Mesopotamia), which was written in cuneiform script on clay tablets and, later, papyrus. The Epic of Gilgamesh is based on the historical king Gilgamesh. The oldest love poem, found on a clay tablet now known as Istanbul #2461, was also a Sumerian poem. It was recited by a bride of the Sumerian king Shu-Sin, who ruled 2037-2029 BC. The oldest epic poetry besides the Epic of Gilgamesh are the Greek epics, Iliad and Odyssey, and the Indian epics, Ramayana and Mahabharata. The longest epic poems ever written were the Mahabharata and the Tibetan Epic of King Gesar.

The efforts of ancient thinkers to determine what makes poetry distinctive as a form, and what distinguishes good poetry from bad, resulted in "poetics"-the study of the aesthetics of poetry. Some ancient societies, such as the Chinese through the Shi Jing, one of the Five Classics of Confucianism, developed canons of poetic works that had ritual as well as aesthetic importance. More recently, thinkers have struggled to find a definition that could encompass formal differences as great as those between Chaucer's Canterbury Tales and Matsuo Basho's Oku no Hosomichi, as well as differences in context spanning Tanakh religious poetry, love poetry, and rap. Context can be critical to poetics and to the development of poetic genres and forms.

Poetry that records historic events in epics, such as Gilgamesh or Ferdowsi's Shahnameh, will necessarily be lengthy and narrative, while poetry used for liturgical purposes (hymns, psalms, suras and hadiths) is likely to have an inspirational tone, whereas elegy and tragedy are meant to evoke deep emotional responses. Other contexts include Gregorian chants, formal or diplomatic speech, political rhetoric and invective, light-hearted nursery and nonsense rhymes, and even medical texts.

The Polish historian of aesthetics, Wladyslaw Tatarkiewicz, in a paper on "The Concept of Poetry," traces the evolution of what is in fact two concepts of poetry. Tatarkiewicz points out that the term is applied to two distinct things that, as the poet Paul Valéry observes, "at a certain point find union. Poetry [...] is an art based on language. But poetry also has a more general meaning [...] that is difficult to define because it is less determinate: poetry expresses a certain state of mind."

TWENTIETH-CENTURY DISPUTES

Some 20th-century literary theorists, relying less on the opposition of prose and poetry, focused on the poet as simply one who creates using language, and poetry as what the poet creates. The underlying concept of the poet as creator is not uncommon, and some modernist poets essentially do not distinguish between the creation of a poem with words, and creative acts in other media such as carpentry. Yet other modernists challenge the very attempt to define poetry as misguided, as when Archibald MacLeish concludes his paradoxical poem, "Ars Poetica," with the lines: "A poem should not mean "but be."

Disputes over the definition of poetry, and over poetry's distinction from other genres of literature, have been inextricably intertwined with the debate over the role of poetic form. The rejection of traditional forms and structures for poetry that began in the first half of the twentieth century, coincided with a questioning of the purpose and meaning of traditional definitions of poetry and of distinctions between poetry and prose, particularly given examples of poetic prose and prosaic "poetry." Numerous modernist poets have written in non-traditional forms or in what traditionally would have been considered prose, although their writing was generally infused with poetic diction and often with rhythm and tone established by non-metrical means. While there was a substantial formalist reaction within the modernist schools to the breakdown of structure, this reaction focused as much on the development of new formal structures and syntheses as on the revival of older forms and structures. More recently, postmodernism has fully embraced MacLeish's concept and come to regard boundaries between prose and poetry, and also among genres of poetry, as having meaning only as cultural artifacts. Postmodernism goes beyond modernism's emphasis on the creative role of the poet, to emphasize the role of the reader of a text, and to highlight the complex cultural web within which a poem is read. Today, throughout the world, poetry often incorporates poetic form and diction from other cultures and from the past, further confounding attempts at definition and classification that were once sensible within a tradition such as the Western canon.

BASIC ELEMENTS

Prosody

Prosody is the study of the meter, rhythm, and intonation of a poem. Rhythm and meter, although closely related, should be distinguished. Meter is the definitive pattern established for a verse (such as iambic pentameter), while rhythm is the actual sound that results from a line of poetry. Thus, the meter of a line may be described as being "iambic", but a full description of the rhythm would require noting where the language causes one to pause or accelerate and how the meter interacts with other elements of the language. Prosody also may be used more specifically to refer to the scanning of poetic lines to show meter.

Rhythm

The methods for creating poetic rhythm vary across languages and between poetic traditions. Languages are often described as having timing set primarily by accents, syllables, or moras, depending on how rhythm is established, though a language can be influenced by multiple approaches. Japanese is a mora-timed language. Syllable-timed languages include Latin, Catalan, French and Spanish. English, Russian and, generally, German are stress-timed languages. Varying intonation also affects how rhythm is perceived. Languages also can rely on either pitch, such as in Vedic or ancient Greek, or tone. Tonal languages include Chinese, Vietnamese, Lithuanian, and most subsaharan languages.

Metrical rhythm generally involves precise arrangements of stresses or syllables into repeated patterns called feet within a line. In Modern English verse the pattern of stresses primarily differentiate feet, so rhythm based on meter in Modern English is most often founded on the pattern of stressed and unstressed syllables (alone or elided). In the classical languages, on the other hand, while the metrical units are similar, vowel length rather than stresses define the meter. Old English poetry used a metrical pattern involving varied numbers of syllables but a fixed number of strong stresses in each line. The chief device of ancient Hebrew Biblical poetry, including many of the psalms, was parallelism, a rhetorical structure in which successive lines reflected each other in grammatical structure, sound structure, notional content, or all three. Parallelism lent itself to antiphonal or call-and-response performance, which could also be reinforced by intonation. Thus, Biblical poetry relies much less on metrical feet to create rhythm, but instead creates rhythm based on much larger sound units of lines, phrases and sentences. Some classical poetry forms, such as Venpa of the Tamil language, had rigid grammars (to the point that they could be expressed as a context-free grammar) which ensured a rhythm. In Chinese poetry, tones as well as stresses create rhythm. Classical Chinese poetics identifies four tones: the level tone, rising tone, falling tone, and entering tone. Note that other classifications may have as many as eight tones for Chinese and six for Vietnamese.

The formal patterns of meter used developed in Modern English verse to create rhythm no longer dominate contemporary English poetry. In the case of free verse, rhythm is often organized based on looser units of cadence than a regular meter. Robinson Jeffers, Marianne Moore, and William Carlos Williams are three notable poets who reject the idea that regular accentual meter is critical to English poetry. Jeffers experimented with sprung rhythm as an alternative to accentual rhythm.

Meter

In the Western poetic tradition, meters are customarily grouped according to a characteristic metrical foot and the number of feet per line. Thus, "iambic pentameter" is a meter comprising five feet per line, in which the predominant kind of foot is the "iamb." This metric system originated in ancient Greek poetry, and was used by poets such as Homer, Pindar, Hesiod and Sappho, and by the great tragedians of Athens.

Meter is often scanned based on the arrangement of "poetic feet" into lines. In English, each foot usually includes one syllable with a stress and one or two without a stress. In other languages, it may be a combination of the number of syllables and the length of the vowel that determines how the foot is parsed. For example, in Greek, one syllable with a long unstressed vowel may be treated as the equivalent of two syllables with short vowels. In Anglo-Saxon meter, the unit on which lines are built is a half-line containing two stresses rather than a foot. Scanning meter can often show the basic or fundamental pattern underlying a verse, but does not show the v ng re f stress, as well as the differing pitches and lengths of syllables.

As an example of how a line of meter is defined, in English-language iambic pentameter, each line has five metrical feet, and each foot is an iamb, or an unstressed syllable followed by a stressed syllable. When a particular line is scanned, there may be variations upon the basic pattern of the meter; for example, the first foot of English iambic pentameters is quite often inverted, meaning that the stress falls on the first syllable. The generally accepted names for some of the most commonly used kinds of feet include:

- spondee-two stressed syllables together
- iamb-unstressed syllable followed by a stressed syllable
- trochee-one stressed syllable followed by an unstressed syllable
- dactyl-one stressed syllable followed by two unstressed syllables
- anapest-two unstressed syllables followed by one stressed syllable

The number of metrical feet in a line are described in Greek terminology as follows:

- dimeter-two feet
- trimeter-three feet
- tetrameter-four feet
- pentameter-five feet
- hexameter-six feet
- heptameter-seven feet
- octameter-eight feet

There are a wide range of names for other types of feet, right up to a choriamb of four syllable metric foot with a stressed syllable followed by two unstressed syllables and closing with a stressed syllable. The choriamb is derived from some ancient Greek and Latin poetry. Languages which utilize vowel length or intonation rather than or in addition to syllabic accents in determining meter, such as Ottoman Turkish or Vedic, often have concepts similar to the iamb and dactyl to describe common combinations of long and short sounds.

Each of these types of feet has a certain "feel," whether alone or in combination with other feet. The iamb, for example, is the most natural form of rhythm in the English language, and generally produces a subtle but stable verse. The dactyl, on the other hand, almost gallops along. And, as readers of The Night Before Christmas or Dr. Seuss realize, the anapest is perfect for a light-hearted, comic feel.

There is debate over how useful a multiplicity of different "feet" is in describing meter. For example, Robert Pinsky has argued that while dactyls are important in classical verse, English dactylic verse uses dactyls very irregularly and can be better described based on patterns of iambs and anapests, feet which he considers natural to the language.

Actual rhythm is significantly more complex than the basic scanned meter described above, and many scholars have sought to develop systems that would scan such complexity. Vladimir Nabokov noted that overlaid on top of the regular pattern of stressed and unstressed syllables in a line of verse was a separate pattern of accents resulting from the natural pitch of the spoken words, and suggested that the term "scud" be used to distinguish an unaccented stress from an accented stress.

Metrical Patterns

Different traditions and genres of poetry tend to use different meters, ranging from the Shakespearian iambic pentameter and the Homerian dactylic hexameter to the Anapestic tetrameter used in many nursery rhymes. However, a number of variations to the established meter are common, both to provide emphasis or attention to a given foot or line and to avoid boring repetition. For example, the stress in a foot may be inverted, a caesura (or pause) may be added (sometimes in place of a foot or stress), or the final foot in a line may be given a feminine ending to soften it or be replaced by a spondee to emphasize it and create a hard stop.

Some patterns (such as iambic pentameter) tend to be fairly regular, while other patterns, such as dactylic hexameter, tend to be highly irregular. Regularity can vary between language. In addition, different patterns often develop distinctively in different languages, so that, for example, iambic tetrameter in Russian will generally reflect a regularity in the use of accents to reinforce the meter, which does not occur or occurs to a much lesser extent in English.

Some common metrical patterns, with notable examples of poets and poems who use them, include:

- Iambic pentameter (John Milton, Paradise Lost)
- Dactylic hexameter (Homer, Iliad; Ovid, The Metamorphoses)
- Iambic tetrameter (Andrew Marvell, "To His Coy Mistress")
- Iambic tetrameter (Aleksandr Pushkin, Eugene Onegin)
- Trochaic octameter (Edgar Allan Poe, "The Raven")
- Anapestic tetrameter (Lewis Carroll, "The Hunting of the Snark"; Lord Byron, Don Juan)
- Alexandrine, also known as iambic hexameter (Jean Racine, Phèdre)

Rhyme, Alliteration, Assonance

Rhyme, alliteration, assonance and consonance are ways of creating repetitive patterns of sound. They may be used as an independent structural element in a poem, to reinforce rhythmic patterns, or as an ornamental element.

Rhyme consists of identical ("hard-rhyme") or similar ("soft-rhyme") sounds placed at the ends of lines or at predictable locations within lines ("internal rhyme"). Languages vary in the richness of their rhyming structures; Italian, for example, has a rich rhyming structure permitting maintenance of a limited set of rhymes throughout a lengthy poem. The richness results from word endings that follow regular forms. English, with its irregular word endings adopted from other languages, is less rich in rhyme. The degree of richness of a language's rhyming structures plays a substantial role in determining what poetic forms are commonly used in that language. Alliteration and assonance played a key role in structuring early Germanic, Norse and Old English forms of poetry. The alliterative patterns of early Germanic poetry interweave meter and alliteration as a key part of their structure, so that the metrical pattern determines when the listener expects instances of alliteration to occur. This can be compared to an ornamental use of alliteration in most Modern European poetry, where alliterative patterns are not formal or carried through full stanzas. Alliteration is particularly useful in languages with less rich rhyming structures. Assonance, where the use of similar vowel sounds within a word rather than similar sounds at the beginning or end of a word, was widely used in skaldic poetry, but goes back to the Homeric epic. Because verbs carry much of the pitch in the English language, assonance can loosely evoke the tonal elements of Chinese poetry and so is useful in translating Chinese poetry. Consonance occurs where a consonant sound is repeated throughout a sentence without putting the sound only at the front of a word. Consonance provokes a more subtle effect than alliteration and so is less useful as a structural element.

Rhyming Schemes

In many languages, including modern European languages and Arabic, poets use rhyme in set patterns as a structural element for specific poet forms, such as ballads, sonnets and rhyming couplets. However, the use of structural rhyme is not universal even within the European tradition. Much modern poetry avoids traditional rhyme schemes. Classical Greek and Latin poetry did not use rhyme. Rhyme entered European poetry in the High Middle Ages, in part under the influence of the Arabic language in Al Andalus (modern Spain).

Arabic language poets have always used rhyme extensively, most notably in their long, rhyming qasidas. Some rhyming schemes have become associated with a specific language, culture or period, while other rhyming schemes have achieved use across languages, cultures or time periods. Some forms of poetry carry a consistent and well-defined rhyming scheme, such as the chant royal or the rubaiyat, while other poetic forms have variable rhyme schemes.

Most rhyme schemes are described using letters that correspond to sets of rhymes, so if the first, second and fourth lines of a quatrain rhyme with each other and the third line does not rhyme, the quatrain is said to have an "a-a-b-a" rhyme scheme. This rhyme scheme is the one used, for example, in the rubaiyat form. Similarly, an "a-b-b-a" quatrain (what is known as "enclosed rhyme") is used in such forms as the Petrarchan sonnet. Some types of more complicated rhyming schemes have developed names of their own, separate from the "a-b-c" convention, such as the ottava rima and terza rima. The types and use of differing rhyming schemes is discussed further in the main article.

The ottava rima is a poem with a stanza of eight lines with an alternating a-b rhyming scheme for the first six lines followed by a closing couplet first used by Boccaccio. This rhyming scheme was developed for heroic epics but has also been used for mock-heroic poetry.

Dante and Terza Rima

Dante's Divine Comed is written in terza rima, where each stanza has three lines, with the first and third rhyming, and the second line rhyming with the first and third lines of the next stanza (thus, a-b-a / b-c-b / c-d-c, etc.) in a chain rhyme. The terza rima provides a flowing, progressive sense to the poem, and used skillfully it can evoke a sense of motion, both forward and backward. Terza rima is appropriately used in lengthy poems in languages with rich rhyming schemes (such as Italian, with its many common word endings).

POETIC FORM

Poetic form is very much more flexible nowadays than ever before. Many modern poets eschew recognisable structures or forms, and write in 'free verse'. However, major structural elements often used in poetry are the line, the stanza or verse paragraph, and larger combinations of stanzas or lines such as cantos. The broader visual presentation of words and calligraphy can also be utilized. These basic units of poetic form are often combined into larger structures, called poetic forms or poetic modes, such as in the sonnet or haiku.

LINES

Poetry is often separated into lines on a page. These lines may be based on the number of metrical feet, or may emphasize a rhyming pattern at the ends of lines. Lines may serve other functions, particularly where the poem is not written in a formal metrical pattern. Lines can separate, compare or contrast thoughts expressed in different units, or can highlight a change in tone.

Lines may be combined into couplets, a combination of two lines which may or may not relate to each other by rhyme or rhythm. For example, a couplet may be two lines with identical meters which rhyme or two lines held together by a common meter alone. Lines also may be combined into triplets, or sets of three lines. Lines are often grouped into verses or stanzas, which often have related couplets or triplets within them.

STANZAS AND PARAGRAPHS

Related lines of poems are often organized into stanzas, which are denominated by the number of lines included. Thus a collection of two lines is a couplet (or distich), three lines a triplet (or tercet), four lines a quatrain, five lines a quintain (or cinquain), six lines a sestet, and eight lines an octet.

Other poems may be organized into verse paragraphs, in which regular rhymes with established rhythms are not used, but the poetic tone is instead established by a collection of rhythms, alliterations, and rhymes established in paragraph form. Many medieval poems were written in verse paragraphs, even where regular rhymes and rhythms were used.

In many forms of poetry, stanzas are interlocking, so that the rhyming scheme or other structural elements of one stanza determine those of succeeding stanzas. Examples of such interlocking stanzas include, for example, the ghazal and the villanelle, where a refrain (or, in the case of the villanelle, refrains) is established in the first stanza which then repeats in subsequent stanzas. Related to the use of interlocking stanzas is their use to separate thematic parts of a poem. For example, the strophe, antistrophe and epode of the ode form are often separated into one or more stanzas. In such cases, or where structures are meant to be highly formal, a stanza will usually form a complete thought, consisting of full sentences and cohesive thoughts.

In some cases, particularly lengthier formal poetry such as some forms of epic poetry, stanzas themselves are constructed according to strict rules and then combined. In skaldic poetry, the dróttkvætt stanza had eight lines, each having three "lifts" produced with alliteration or assonance. In addition to two or three alliterations, the odd numbered lines had partial rhyme of consonants with dissimilar vowels, not necessarily at the beginning of the word; the even lines contained internal rhyme in set syllables (not necessarily at the end of the word). Each half-line had exactly six syllables, and each line ended in a trochee. The arrangement of dróttkvætts followed far less rigid rules than the construction of the individual dróttkvætts.

VISUAL PRESENTATION

Even before the advent of printing, the appearance of written poetry often added significant meaning or depth. Acrostic poems included clues or meanings in the letters beginning lines or in other specific places in a poem. In Arabic, Hebrew, and Chinese poetry, the presentation of the poems in fine calligraphy has always been an important part of the overall artistic and poetic effect for many poems.

With the advent of printing, poets gained greater control over the mass produced visual presentation of their work. As a result, the use of visual elements became an important part of the poet's toolbox, and many poets have sought to use visual presentation for a wide range of purposes. Some Modernist poetry takes this to an extreme, with the placement of individual lines or groups of lines on the page forming an integral part of the poem's composition, whether to complement the poem's rhythm through various lengthed visual caesuras, to create juxtapositions to accentuate meaning, ambiguity or irony, or simply to create an aesthetically pleasing form. In its most extreme form, this can lead to concrete poetry or asemic writing.

POETIC DICTION

Poetic diction describes the manner in which language is used and refers not only to the sound but also to the underlying meaning and its interaction with sound and form. Many languages and poetic forms have very specific poetic dictions, to the point where separate grammars and dialects are used specifically for poetry. Poetic diction can include rhetorical devices such as simile and metaphor, as well as tones of voice, such as irony. Aristotle wrote in the Poetics that "the greatest thing by far is to be a master of metaphor". Since the rise of Modernism, some poets have opted for a poetic diction that deemphasizes rhetorical devices, attempting the direct presentation of things and experiences and the exploration of tone. On the other hand, Surrealists have pushed rhetorical devices to their limits, making frequent use of catachresis.

Allegorical stories are central to the poetic diction of many cultures, and were prominent in the west during classical times, the late Middle Ages and Renaisance. Rather than being fully allegorical, a poem may contain symbols or allusion that deepens the meaning or impact of its words without constructing a full allegory. Another strong element of poetic diction can be the use of vivid imagery for effect. The juxtaposition of unexpected or impossible images is, for example, a particularly strong element in surrealist poetry and haiku. Vivid images are often endowed with symbolism as well.

Many poetic dictions will use repetitive phrases for effect, either a short phrase (such as Homer's "rosy-fingered dawn") or a longer refrain. Such repetition can add a somber tone to a poem, as in many odes, or can be laced with irony as the contexts of the words change. For example, in Antony's famous eulogy to in Shakespeare's Julius Caesar, Anthony's repetition of the words, "for Brutus is an honorable man," moves from a sincere tone to one that exudes irony.

SPECIFIC POETIC FORMS

Specific poetic forms have been developed by many cultures. In more developed, closed or "received" poetic forms, the rhyming scheme, meter and other elements of a poem are based on sets of rules, ranging from the relatively loose rules that govern the construction of an elegy to the highly formalized structure of the ghazal or villanelle.

Sonnets

Among the most common form of poetry through the ages is the sonnet, which, by the thirteenth century, was a poem of fourteen lines following a set rhyme scheme and logical structure. The conventions associated with the sonnet have changed during its history, and so there are several different sonnet forms. Traditionally, English poets use iambic pentameter when writing sonnets, with the Spenserian and Shakespearean sonnets being especially notable. In the Romance languages, the hendecasyllable and Alexandrines are the most widely used meters, although the Petrarchan sonnet has been used in Italy since the 14th century. Sonnets are particularly associated with love poetry, and often use a poetic diction heavily based on vivid imagery, but the twists and turns associated with the move from octave to sestet and to final couplet make them a useful and dynamic form for many subjects. Shakespeare's sonnets are among the most famous in English poetry, with 20 being included in the Oxford Book of English Verse.

Jintishi

The jintishi is a Chinese poetic form based on a series of set tonal patterns using the four tones of the classical Chinese language in each couplet: the level, rising, falling and entering tones. The basic form of the jintishi has eight lines in four couplets, with parallelism between the lines in the second and third couplets. The couplets with parallel lines contain contrasting content but an identical grammatical relationship between words. Jintishi often have a rich poetic diction, full of allusion, and can have a wide range of subject, including history and politics. One of the masters of the form was Du Fu, who wrote during the Tang Dynasty (8th century). There are several variations on the basic form of the jintishi.

Villanelle

The Villanelle is a nineteen-line poem made up of five triplets with a closing quatrain; the poem is characterized by having two refrains, initially used in the first and third lines of the first stanza, and then alternately used at the close of each subsequent stanza until the final quatrain, which is concluded by the two refrains. The remaining lines of the poem have an a-b alternating rhyme. The villanelle has been used regularly in the English language since the late nineteenth century by such poets as Dylan Thomas, W.H. Auden, and Elizabeth Bishop. It is a form that has gained heavier use at a time when the use of received forms of poetry has generally been declining.

Tanka

The Tanka is a form of Japanese poetry, generally not possessing rhyme, with five lines structured in a 5-7-5 7-7 patterns. The 5-7-5 phrase (the "upper phrase") and the 7-7 phrase (the "lower phrase") generally show a shift in tone and subject matter. Tanka were written as early as the Nara period by such poets as Kakinomoto no Hitomaro, at a time when Japan was emerging from a period where much of its poetry followed Chinese form. Tanka was originally the shorter form of Japanese formal poetry, and was used more heavily to explore personal rather than public themes. It thus had a more informal poetic diction. By the 13th century, Tanka had become the dominant form of Japanese poetry, and it is still widely written today.

Ode

Odes were first developed by poets writing in ancient Greek, such as Pindar, and Latin, such as Horace, and forms of odes appear in many of the cultures influenced by the Greeks and Latins. The ode generally has three parts: a strophe, an antistrophe, and an epode. The antistrophes of the ode possess similar metrical structures and, depending on the tradition, similar rhyme structures. In contrast, the epode is written with a different scheme and structure. Odes have a formal poetic diction, and general dealing with a serious subject. The strophe and antistrophe look at the subject from different, often conflicting, perspectives, with the epode moving to a higher level to either view or resolve the underlying issues. Odes are often intended to be recited or sung by two choruses (or individuals), with the first reciting the strophe, the second the antistrophe, and both together the epode. Over time, differing forms for odes have developed with considerable variations in form and structure, but generally showing the original influence of the Pindaric or Horatian ode. One non-Western form which resembles the ode is the qasida in Persian poetry.

Ghazal

The ghazal is a form of poetry common in Arabic, Persian, Urdu and Bengali poetry. In classic form, the ghazal has from five to fifteen rhyming couplets that share a refrain at the end of the second line (which need be of only a few syllables). Each line has an identical meter, and there is a set pattern of rhymes in the first couplet and among the refrains. Each couplet forms a complete thought and stands alone, and the overall ghazal often reflects on a theme of unattainable love or divinity. The last couplet generally includes the signature of the author.

As with other forms with a long history in many languages, many variations have been developed, including forms with a quasi-musical poetic diction in Urdu. Ghazals have a classical affinity with Sufism, and a number of major Sufi religious works are written in ghazal form. The relatively steady meter and the use of the refrain produce an incantatory effect, which complements Sufi mystical themes well. Among the masters of the form is the Persian poet Rumi.

POETIC GENRES

Narrative Poetry

Narrative poetry is a genre of poetry that tells a story. Broadly it subsumes epic poetry, but the term "narrative poetry" is often reserved for smaller works, generally with more direct appeal than the epic to human interest.

Narrative poetry may be the oldest genre of poetry. Many scholars of Homer have concluded that his Iliad and Odyssey were composed from compilations of shorter narrative poems that related individual episodes and were more suitable for an evening's entertainment. Much narrative poetry-such as Scots and English ballads, and Baltic and Slavic heroic poems-is performance poetry with roots in a preliterate oral tradition. It has been speculated that some features that distinguish poetry from prose, such as meter, alliteration and kennings, once served as memory aids for bards who recited traditional tales. Notable narrative poets have included Ovid, Dante, Chaucer, William Langland, Shakespeare, Alexander Pope, Robert Burns, Adam Mickiewicz, Alexander Pushkin, Tennyson and Poe.

Epic Poetry

Epic poetry is a genre of poetry, and a major form of narrative literature. It recounts, in a continuous narrative, the life and works of a heroic or mythological person or group of persons. Western epic poems include Homer's Iliad and Odyssey, Vergil's Aeneid and the Nibelungenlied. Eastern examples are the Epic of Gilgamesh, the Mahabharata, Valmiki's Ramayana, Ferdowsi's Shahnama, and the Epic of King Gesar. The composition of epic poetry, and of long poems generally, became uncommon in the west after the early 20th century, while the meaning of the term "epic" evolved to refer also to prose writings, films and similar works that are characterized by great length, multiple settings, large numbers of characters, or long span of time involved.

Dramatic Poetry

Dramatic poetry is drama written in verse to be spoken. Verse drama was long the dominant form of drama in Europe, and was also important in non-European cultures. Greek tragedy and Racine's plays are written in verse, as are almost all of Shakespeare's dramas, and Goethe's Faust.

A practical reason to write drama in verse was that verse lines are easier for actors to memorize exactly. In the latter half of the 20th century, verse drama fell almost completely out of favor with English-language dramatists. Christopher Fry and T.S. Eliot may have been its last practitioners in that language.

Lyric Poetry

Lyric poetry is a genre that, unlike epic poetry and dramatic poetry, does not attempt to tell a story but instead is of a more personal nature. Rather than depicting characters and actions, it portrays the poet's own feelings, states of mind, and perceptions. While the genre's name, derived from "lyre," implies that it is intended to be sung, much lyric poetry is meant purely for reading. Though lyric poetry has long celebrated love, many courtly-love poets also wrote lyric poems about war and peace, nature and nostalgia, grief and loss. Notable among these are the 15th-century French lyric poets, Christine de Pizan and Charles, Duke of Orléans. Spiritual and religious themes were addressed by such medieval lyric poets as St. John of the Cross and Teresa of Ávila. The tradition of lyric poetry based on spiritual experience was continued by later poets such as John Donne, Gerard Manley Hopkins and T.S. Eliot. Although the most popular form of western lyric poetry may be the 14-line sonnet-Petrarchan or Shakespearean-lyric poetry has shown a bewildering variety of forms, including increasingly, in the 20th century, unrhymed ones.

Verse Fable

The fable is an ancient and near-ubiquitous literary genre, often (though not invariably) set in verse form. Notable verse fabulists have included Aesop (mid-6th century BCE), Vishnu Sarma (ca. 200 BCE), Phaedrus (15 BCE-50 CE), Marie de France (12th century), Biernat of Lublin (1465-after 1529), Jean de la Fontaine (1621-95), Ignacy Krasicki (1735-1801), Ivan Krylov (1769-1844) and Ambrose Bierce (1842-1914). All of the semi-legendary Aesop's successors, translators and imitators have owed him a fundamental debt. Verse fables have been written in a variety of meter and rhyme patterns. Ignacy Krasicki, for example, in his Fables and Parables, used 13-syllable lines, in couplets rhyming aa, bb...

Prose Poetry

Prose poetry is a hybrid genre that demonstrates attributes of both prose and poetry. It may be indistinguishable from the micro-story (aka the "short short story," "flash fiction"). Most critics argue that it qualifies as poetry because of its conciseness, use of metaphor, and special care for language. While some examples of earlier prose strike modern readers as poetic, prose poetry is commonly regarded as having originated in 19th-century France, where its practitioners included Aloysius Bertrand, Charles Baudelaire, Arthur Rimbaud and Stéphane Mallarmé. The genre has subsequently found notable exemplars in French (Francis Ponge); English (Oscar Wilde, T.S. Eliot, Gertrude Stein, Sherwood Anderson, Allen Ginsberg, Russell Edson, Charles Simic, Robert Bly, James Wright); Spanish (Octavio Paz, Ángel Crespo); Polish (Boleslaw Prus); Russian; and Japanese. Since the late 1980s especially, prose poetry has gained increasing popularity, with journals devoted solely to that genre.

PROSODY

Prosody may refer to:

- Prosody (linguistics) includes intonation and vocal stress in speech.
- Meter (poetry) includes the scansion and metrical shape of the lines.
- Prosody (music) refers to the way the composer sets the text of a vocal composition in the assignment of syllables to notes in the melody to which the text is sung; this is particularly a function of rhythm and pitch, and is not to be confused with musical form.

METER (POETRY)

Meter (British English spelling: metre) describes the linguistic sound patterns of a verse. Scansion is the analysis of poetry's metrical and rhythmic patterns. Prosody is sometimes used to describe poetic meter, and indicates the analysis of similar aspects of language in linguistics. Meter is part of many formal verse forms.

Fundamentals

The units of poetic meter, like rhyme, vary from language to any language and between poetic traditions. They can involve arrangements of syllables into repeated patterns called feet within a line. English meter is traditionally conceived as being founded on the patterns of stressed and unstressed syllables. In Latin verse, on the other hand, while the metrical units are similar, not syllable stresses but syllable lengths are the component parts of meter. Old English poetry used alliterative verse, a metrical pattern involving varied numbers of syllables but a fixed number of strong stresses in each line. Meters in English verse, and in the classical Western poetic tradition on which it is founded, are named by the characteristic foot and the number of feet per line. Thus, for example, blank verse is unrhymed "iambic pentameter," a meter composed of five feet per line in which the kind of feet called iambs predominate. This tradition of metrics originated from the ancient Greek poetry of Homer, Pindar, Hesiod, Sappho, and the great tragedians of Athens.

Technical Terms

- caesura: (literally, a cut or cutting) refers to a particular kind of break within a poetic line. In Latin and Greek meter, caesura refers to a break within a foot caused by the end of a word. In English poetry, a caesura refers to a sense of a break within a line. Caesurae play a particularly important role in Old English poetry.
- Headless: a meter where the first foot is missing its first syllable.
- Quantitative: Use in prosody and poetry.

Meter in Various Languages

Greek and Latin

The metrical "feet" in the classical languages were based on the length of time taken to pronounce each syllable, which were categorized as either "long" syllables or "short" syllables (also known as "heavy" and "light" syllables, respectively, to distinguish from long and short vowels). The foot is often compared to a musical measure and the long and short syllables to whole notes and half notes. In English poetry, feet are determined by emphasis rather than length, with stressed and unstressed syllables serving the same function as long and short syllables in classical meter. The basic unit in Greek and Latin prosody is a mora, which is defined as a single short syllable. A long syllable is equivalent to two moras.

A long syllable contains either a long vowel, a diphthong, or a short vowel followed by two or more consonants. Various rules of elision sometimes prevent a grammatical syllable from making a full syllable, and certain other lengthening and shortening rules (such as correption) can create long or short syllables in contexts where one would expect the opposite.

The most important Classical meter is the dactylic hexameter, the meter of Homer and Virgil. This form uses verses of six feet. The first four feet are dactyls, but can be spondees. The fifth foot is almost always a dactyl.

The sixth foot is either a spondee or a trochee. The initial syllable of either foot is called the ictus, the basic "beat" of the verse. There is usually a caesura after the ictus of the third foot. The opening line of the Æneid is a typical line of dactylic hexameter:

Árma virumque cano, // Troi? qui prímus ab óris

("I sing of arms and the man, who first from the shores of Troy...")

The first and second feet are dactyls; their vowels are grammatically short, but long in poetry because both are followed by two consonants. The third and fourth feet are spondees, with two long vowels, one on either side of the caesura. The fifth foot is a dactyl, as it must be, with the ictus this time falling on a grammatically long vowel. The final foot is a spondee with two grammatically long vowels.

The dactylic hexameter was imitated in English by Henry Wadsworth Longfellow in his poem Evangeline:

This is the forest primeval. The murmuring pines and the hemlocks,
Bearded with moss, and in garments green, indistinct in the twilight,
Stand like Druids of old, with voices sad and prophetic,
Stand like harpers hoar, with beards that rest on their bosoms.

Also important in Greek and Latin poetry is the dactylic pentameter. This was a line of verse, made up of two equal parts, each of which contains two dactyls followed by a long syllable. Spondees can take the place of the dactyls in the first half, but never in the second. The long syllable at the close of the first half of the verse always ends a word, giving rise to a caesura.

Dactylic pentameter is never used in isolation. Rather, a line of dactylic pentameter follows a line of dactylic hexameter in the elegiac distich or elegiac couplet, a form of verse that was used for the composition of elegies and other tragic and solemn verse in the Greek and Latin world, as well as love poetry that was sometimes light and cheerful. An example from Ovid's Tristia:

("I only saw Vergil, greedy Fate gave Tibullus no time for me.")

The Greeks and Romans also used a number of lyric meters, which were typically used for shorter poems than elegiacs or hexameter. One important line was called the hendecasyllabic, a line of eleven syllables. This meter was used most often in the Sapphic stanza, named after the Greek poet Sappho, who wrote many of her poems in the form.

A hendecasyllabic is a line with a never-varying structure: two trochees, followed by a dactyl, then two more trochees. In the Sapphic stanza, three hendecasyllabics are followed by an "Adonic" line, made up of a dactyl and a trochee. This is the form of Catullus 51 (itself a translation of Sappho 31):

/ x / x / x x/ x / x

Ille mi par esse deo videtur;

/ x / x / x x / x / x

ille, si fas est, superare divos,

/ x / x / x x / x / x

qui sedens adversus identidem te

/ x x / x

spectat et audit...

("He seems to me to be like a god; if it is permitted, he seems above the gods, he who sitting across from you gazes at you and listens to you.")

The Sapphic stanza was imitated in English by Algernon Charles Swinburne in a poem he simply called Sapphics:

Saw the white implacable Aphrodite,

Saw the hair unbound and the feet unsandalled

Shine as fire of sunset on western waters;

Saw the reluctant...

English

Old English

Old English poetry has a different metrical system from modern English. In Old English poetry, each line must contain four fully stressed syllables, which often alliterate. The unstressed syllables are less important. Old English poetry is an example of the alliterative verse found in most of the older Germanic languages.

Modern English

Most English meter is classified according to the same system as Classical meter with an important difference. English is an accentual language, and therefore beats and offbeats (stressed and unstressed syllables) take the place of the long and short syllables of classical systems. In most English verse, the meter can be considered as a sort of back beat, against which natural speech rhythms vary expressively.

The most common characteristic feet of English verse are the iamb in two syllables and the anapest in three.

Metrical Systems

The number of metrical systems in English is not agreed. The major four types are: accentual verse, accentual-syllabic verse, syllabic verse and quantitative verse. The alliterative verse of Old English could also be added to this list, or included as a special type of accentual verse.

Accentual verse focuses on the number of stresses in a line, while ignoring the number of offbeats and syllables; accentual-syllabic verse focuses on regulating both the number of stresses and the total number of syllables in a line; syllabic verse only counts the number of syllables in a line; quantitative verse regulates the patterns of long and short syllables, this sort of verse is often considered alien to English. It is to be noted, however, that the use of foreign metres in English is all but exceptional.

Frequently-used Meters

The most frequently encountered line of English verse is the iambic pentameter, in which the metrical norm is five iambic feet per line, though metrical substitution is common and rhythmic variations practically inexhaustible. John Milton's Paradise Lost, most sonnets, and much else besides in English are written in iambic pentameter. Lines of unrhymed iambic pentameter are commonly known as blank verse. Blank verse in the English language is most famously represented in the plays of William Shakespeare, although it is also notable in the work of Milton and Tennyson (e.g. Ulysses, The Princess).

A rhymed pair of lines of iambic pentameter make a heroic couplet, a verse form which was used so often in the eighteenth century that it is now used mostly for humorous effect. The most famous writers of heroic couplets are Dryden and Pope.

Another important meter in English is the ballad meter, also called the "common meter", which is a four line stanza, with two pairs of a line of iambic tetrameter followed by a line of iambic trimeter; the rhymes usually fall on the lines of trimeter, although in many instances the tetrameter also rhymes. This is the meter of most of the Border and Scots or English ballads. It is called the "common meter" in hymnody (as it is the most common of the named hymn meters used to pair lyrics with melodies) and provides the meter for a great many hymns, such as Amazing Grace:

Amazing Grace! how sweet the sound
That saved a wretch like me;
I once was lost, but now am found;
Was blind, but now I see.

Emily Dickinson is famous for her frequent use of ballad meter:

Great streets of silence led away
To neighborhoods of pause;
Here was no notice-no dissent-
No universe-no laws.

A number of different Hymn meters are also in use.

French

In French poetry, meter is determined solely by the number of syllables in a line. A silent 'e' counts as a syllable before a consonant, but is elided before a vowel (where "h aspiré" counts as a consonant). At the end of a line, the "e" remains unelided but is hypermetrical (outside the count of syllables, like a feminine ending in English verse). The most frequently encountered meter in French is the alexandrine, composed of two hemistichs of six syllables each. Classical French poetry also had a complex set of rules for rhymes that goes beyond how words merely sound. These are usually taken into account when describing the meter of a poem.

Spanish

In Spanish poetry, meter is determined mainly by the position of the last accent in a line. Interestingly, a line whose last accent falls in the seventh syllable is invariably called an "octosyllable", regardless of whether it contains seven, eight or nine syllables. Syllables in Spanish metrics are determined by consonant breaks, not word boundaries; thus a single syllable may span multiple words. For example, the line De armas y hombres canto consists of 6 syllables: "Dear" "ma" "syhom" "bres" "can" "to." Note how the vowel sounds in adjacent words combine into a single unit, as in the third syllable of the line: De armas y hombres canto. Some common meters in Spanish verse are:

- Septenary: A line with the last accent on the sixth syllable.
- Octosyllable: A line with its last accent on the seventh syllable. This meter is commonly used in romances, narrative poems similar to English ballads, and in most proverbs.
- Hendecasyllable: A line with its last accent in the tenth and accents either in the sixth, or the fourth and the eighth. This meter plays a similar role to pentameter in English verse. It is commonly used in sonnets, among other things.
- Alexandrines: A line consisting of two heptasyllables.

Italian

In Italian poetry, meter is determined solely by the position of the last accent in a line. Syllables are enumerated with respect to a verse which ends with a paroxytone, so that a Septenary (literally, 'having seven syllables') is defined as a verse whose last accent falls on the sixth syllable: it may so contain eight syllables (Ei fu. Siccome immobile) or just six (la terra al nunzio sta). Moreover, when a word ends with a vowel and the next one starts with a vowel, they are considered to be in the same syllable: so Gli anni e i giorni consists of only four syllables ("Gli an" "ni e i" "gior" "ni"). Because of the mostly trochaic nature of the Italian language, verses with an even number of syllables are far easier to compose, and the Novenary is usually regarded as the most difficult verse. Some common meters in Italian verse are:

- Septenary: A line whose last stressed syllable is the sixth one.
- Octosyllable: A line whose last accent falls on the seventh syllable. More often than not, the secondary accents fall on the first, third and fifth syllable, especially in nursery rhymes for which this meter is particularly well-suited.
- Hendecasyllable: A line whose last accent falls on the tenth syllable. It therefore usually consists of eleven syllables; there are various kinds of possible accentations. It is used in sonnets, in ottava rima, and in many other works. The Divine Comedy, in particular, is composed entirely of hendecasyllables.

CONSTRAINED WRITING

Constrained writing is a literary technique in which the writer is bound by some condition that forbids certain things or imposes a pattern. Constraints are very common in poetry, which often requires the writer to use a particular verse form. The most common constrained forms of writing are strict restrictions in vocabulary, e.g. Basic English, E-Prime, defining vocabulary for dictionaries, and other limited vocabularies for teaching English as a Second Language or to children. This is not generally what is meant by "constrained writing" in the literary sense, which is motivated by more aesthetic concerns. For example:

- Lipogram, a letter (commonly e or o) is outlawed
- Palindromes, such as the word "radar," read the same both ways
- Alliteratives, in which every word must start with the same letter (or subset of letters; see Alphabetical Africa)
- Acrostics
- Reverse-lipograms (each word must contain a particular letter)
- Anglish
- Anagrams
- Aleatory (where the reader supplies a random input)
- Univocalic poetry

The Oulipo group is a gathering of writers who use such techniques. The Outrapo group use theatrical constraints.

Gadsby is an English-language novel consisting of 50,100 words, none of which contain the letter "e."

In 1969, French writer Georges Perec published La Disparition, a novel that did not include the letter "e." It was translated into English in 1995 by Gilbert Adair as "A Void." Perec subsequently joked that he incorporated the "e"s not used in La Disparition in the novella Les Revenentes (1972), which uses no vowels other than "e". Les Revenentes was translated into English by Ian Monk as The Exeter Text: Jewels, Secrets, Sex. In 2004, a new marvel from France: a novel, entirely without verbs: Le Train de Nulle Part ("The Train from Nowhere") by Michel Thaler.

Experimental Canadian poet Christian Bök's Eunoia is a lipogram that uses only one vowel in each of its five chapters

One famous constrained writing in the Chinese language is the Lion-Eating Poet in the Stone Den which consists of 92 characters, all with the sound shi. Another is the Thousand Character Classic in which all 1000 characters are unique without any repetition. Cadaeic Cadenza is a short book by Mike Keith using the digits of pi as the length of words. Never Again is a novel by Doug Nufer in which no word is used more than once. Ella Minnow Pea is a book by Mark Dunn where certain letters become unusable throughout the novel.

POETICS

Poetics refers generally to the theory of literary discourse and specifically to the theory of poetry, although some speakers use the term so broadly as to denote the concept of "theory" itself. The word originated with Aristotle's Poetics, a work on the definition of poetry that laid the foundation for Western thought on the subject.

History

Leading poetics scholar T.V.F. Brogan identifies three major movements in Western poetics over the past 3000 years, beginning with the formalist, objectivist Aristotelian tradition. During the romantic era, poetics tended toward expressionism and emphasized the perceiving subject. The 20th century witnessed a return to the Aristotelian paradigm, followed by trends toward metacriticality, or the establishment of a theory of poetics.

Eastern poetics developed primarily with reference to the lyric, as opposed to the mimetic.

HISTORY OF POETRY

The poetry as an art form predates literacy.

Early History

Poetry was employed as a means of recording oral history, storytelling (epic poetry), genealogy, and law. Poetry is often closely identified with liturgy in pre-literate societies. Many of the scriptures currently held to be sacred by contemporary religious traditions with their roots in antiquity were composed as poetry rather than prose to aid memorization and help guarantee the accuracy of oral transmission in pre-literate societies. As a result many of the poems surviving from the ancient world are a form of recorded cultural information about the people of the past, and their poems are prayers or stories about religious subject matter, histories about their politics and wars, and the important organizing myths of their societies.

Poetry as an art form may predate literacy Thus many ancient works, from the Vedas (2500-500 BC) to the Odyssey (700-500 BC), appear to have been composed in poetic form to aid memorization and oral transmission, in prehistoric and ancient societies. Poetry appears among the earliest records of most literate cultures, with poetic fragments found on early monoliths, rune stones and stelae.

The oldest surviving poem is the Epic of Gilgamesh, from the 3rd millennium BC in Sumer (in Iraq/Mesopotamia), which was written in cuneiform script on clay tablets and, later, papyrus. The Epic of Gilgamesh is based on the historical king Gilgamesh. The oldest love poem, found on a clay tablet now known as Istanbul #2461, was also a Sumerian poem.

It was recited by a bride of the Sumerian king Shu-Sin, who ruled from 2037-2029 BC. The oldest epic poetry besides the Epic of Gilgamesh are the Greek epics Iliad and Odyssey and the Indian Sanskrit epics Ramayana and Mahabharata. The longest epic poems ever written were the Mahabharata and the Tibetan Epic of King Gesar.

Ancient thinkers sought to determine what makes poetry distinctive as a form and what distinguishes good poetry from bad, resulting in the development of "poetics", or the study of the aesthetics of poetry. Some ancient societies, such as the Chinese through the Shi Jing, one of the Five Classics of Confucianism, developed canons of poetic works that had ritual as well as aesthetic importance. More recently, thinkers struggled to find a definition that could encompass formal differences as great as those between Chaucer's The Canterbury Tales and Matsuo Basho's Oku no Hosomichi, as well as differences in context that span from the religious poetry of the Tanakh to love poetry to rap.

Context can be critical to poetics and to the development of poetic genres and forms. For example, poetry employed to record historical events in epics, such as Gilgamesh or Ferdowsi's Shahnameh, will necessarily be lengthy and narrative, while poetry used for liturgical purposes in hymns, psalms, suras and hadiths is likely to have an inspirational tone, whereas elegies and tragedy are intended to invoke deep internal emotional responses.

Other contexts include music such as Gregorian chants, and formal or diplomatic speech political rhetoric and invective, light-hearted nursery and nonsense rhymes, and even medical texts. The Polish historian of aesthetics, Wladyslaw Tatarkiewicz, in a paper on "The Concept of Poetry," traces the evolution of what is in fact two concepts of poetry. Tatarkiewicz points out that the term is applied to two distinct things that, as the poet Paul Valéry observes, "at a certain point find union. Poetry [...] is an art based on language. But poetry also has a more general meaning [...] that is difficult to define because it is less determinate: poetry expresses a certain state of mind."

Classical and Early Modern Western Traditions

Classical thinkers employed classification as a way to define and assess the quality of poetry. Notably, Aristotle's Poetics describes the three genres of poetry: the epic, comic, and tragic, and develops rules to distinguish the highest-quality poetry of each genre, based on the underlying purposes of that genre. Later aestheticians identified three major genres: epic poetry, lyric poetry and dramatic poetry, treating comedy and tragedy as subgenres of dramatic poetry. Aristotle's work was influential throughout the Middle East during the Islamic Golden Age, as well as in Europe during the Renaissance. Later poets and aestheticians often distinguished poetry from, and defined it in opposition to, prose, which was generally understood as writing with a proclivity to logical explication and a linear narrative structure.

This does not imply that poetry is illogical or lacks narration, but rather that poetry is an attempt to render the beautiful or sublime without the burden of engaging the logical or narrative thought process. English Romantic poet John Keats termed this escape from logic, "Negative Capability." This "romantic" approach views form as a key element of successful poetry because form is abstract and distinct from the underlying notional logic. This approach remained influential into the twentieth century. During this period, there was also substantially more interaction among the various poetic traditions, in part due to the spread of European colonialism and the attendant rise in global trade. In addition to a boom in translation, during the Romantic period numerous ancient works were rediscovered.

Modern Developments

The use of verse to transmit cultural information continues today. Many Americans know that "in 1492, Columbus sailed the ocean blue". An alphabet song teaches the names and order of the letters of the alphabet; another jingle states the lengths and names of the months in the Gregorian calendar. Some writers believe poetry has its origins in song. Most of the characteristics that distinguish it from other forms of utterance-rhythm, rhyme, compression, intensity of feeling, the use of refrains-appear to have come about from efforts to fit words to musical forms. In the European tradition the earliest surviving poems, the Homeric and Hesiodic epics, identify themselves as poems to be recited or chanted to a musical accompaniment rather than as pure song. Another interpretation is that rhythm, refrains, and kennings are essentially paratactic devices that enable the reciter to reconstruct the poem from memory.

In preliterate societies, these forms of poetry were composed for, and sometimes during, performance. There was a certain degree of fluidity to the exact wording of poems. The introduction of writing fixed the content of a poem to the version that happened to be written down and survive. Written composition meant poets began to compose for an absent reader. The invention of printing accelerated these trends. Poets were now writing more for the eye than for the ear.

- Edwin Arlington Robinson's villanelle "The House on the Hill" was first published in The Globe in September 1894.

They are all gone away,

The House is shut and still,

There is nothing more to say.

Through broken walls and gray

The winds blow bleak and shrill.

They are all gone away.

Nor is there one to-day

To speak them good or ill:

There is nothing more to say.

Why is it then we stray

Around the sunken sill?

They are all gone away,

And our poor fancy-play

For them is wasted skill:

There is nothing more to say.

There is ruin and decay

In the House on the Hill:

They are all gone away,

There is nothing more to say.

- Dylan Thomas's villanelle Do not go Gentle into that Good Night

Do not go gentle into that good night,

Old age should burn and rave at close of day;

Rage, rage against the dying of the light.

Though wise men at their end know dark is right,

Because their words had forked no lightning they

Do not go gentle into that good night.

Good men, the last wave by, crying how bright
Their frail deeds might have danced in a green bay,
Rage, rage against the dying of the light.

Wild men who caught and sang the sun in flight,
And learn, too late, they grieved it on its way,
Do not go gentle into that good night.

Grave men, near death, who see with blinding sight
Blind eyes could blaze like meteors and be gay,
Rage, rage against the dying of the light.

And you, my father, there on the sad height,
Curse, bless me now with your fierce tears, I pray.
Do not go gentle into that good night.
Rage, rage against the dying of the light.

- *Theodore Roethke's villanelle "The Waking"*

I wake to sleep, and take my waking slow.
I feel my fate in what I cannot fear.
I learn by going where I have to go.

We think by feeling. What is there to know?
I hear my being dance from ear to ear.
I wake to sleep, and take my waking slow.

Of those so close beside me, which are you?
God bless the Ground! I shall walk softly there,
And learn by going where I have to go.

Light takes the Tree; but who can tell us how?
The lowly worm climbs up a winding stair;
I wake to sleep, and take my waking slow.

Great Nature has another thing to do
To you and me; so take the lively air,
And, lovely, learn by going where to go.

This shaking keeps me steady. I should know.

What falls away is always. And is near.

I wake to sleep, and take my waking slow.

I learn by going where I have to go.

BLANK VERSE

Blank verse is a type of poetry, distinguished by having a regular meter, but no rhyme. In English, the meter most commonly used with blank verse has been iambic pentameter. The first known use of blank verse in the English language was by Henry Howard, Earl of Arundel and Surrey in his interpretation of the Æneid (c. 1554). He was possibly inspired by the Latin original, as classical Latin verse (as well as Greek verse) did not use rhyme; he may have been inspired by the Italian verse form of versi sciolti, which also contained no rhyme. The unknown author of Arden of Faversham (circa 1590) is the most interesting example of end-stopped blank verse

Christopher Marlowe was the first English author to make full use of the potential of blank verse, and also established it as the dominant verse form for English drama in the age of Elizabeth I and James I. The major achievements in English blank verse were made by William Shakespeare, who wrote much of the content of his plays in unrhymed iambic pentameter, and Milton, whose Paradise Lost is written in blank verse. After Milton (in fact, during his later life), blank verse went out of fashion and for a century and a half the favored verse form in English was that of couplets. Romantic English poets such as William Wordsworth, Percy Bysshe Shelley, and John Keats revived blank verse as a major form. Following shortly afterwards, Alfred Lord Tennyson became particularly devoted to blank verse, using it for example in his long narrative poem "The Princess", as well as for one of his most famous poems: "Ulysses". Among American poets, Hart Crane and Wallace Stevens are notable for using blank verse in extended compositions at a time when many other poets were turning to free verse.

FREE VERSE

Free verse (also at times referred to as vers libre) is a term describing various styles of poetry that are not written using strict meter or rhyme, but that still are recognizable as 'poetry' by virtue of complex patterns of one sort or another that readers can perceive to be part of a coherent whole.

History

An early usage of the term appears in 1915 in the anonymous preface to the first Imagist anthology. The main author of this preface was Richard Aldington. The preface states: "We do not insist upon 'free-verse' as the only method of writing poetry. We fight for it as for a principle of liberty."

The ideal of the early practitioners of free verse was well described by Ezra Pound, who wrote: "As regarding rhythm: to compose in the sequence of the musical phrase, not in sequence of a metronome."

D. H. Lawrence wrote that Whitman "pruned away his clichés-perhaps his clichés of rhythm as well as of phrase" and that all one could do with free verse was "get rid of the stereotyped movements and the old hackneyed associations of sound and sense".

Some poets have explained that free verse, despite its freedom, must still display some elements of form. Pound's friend T. S. Eliot wrote: "No verse is free for the man who wants to do a good job." Donald Hall goes as far as to say that "the form of free verse is as binding and as liberating as the form of a rondeau." Some poets think free verse too limiting. In 1922 Robert Bridges voiced his reservations in the essay 'Humdrum and Harum-Scarum.' Robert Frost later remarked that writing free verse was like "playing tennis without a net".

Precursors

As the name vers libre suggests, this technique of using more irregular cadences is often said to derive from the practices of 19th century French poets like Gustave Kahn and especially Jules Laforgue. However, in English it can be traced back at least as far as the King James Bible. Walt Whitman, who based his verse approach on the Bible, was the major precursor for modern poets writing free verse, though they were reluctant to acknowledge his influence.

Many poets of the Victorian era experimented with form. Christina Rossetti, Coventry Patmore, and T. E. Brown all wrote examples of unpatterned rhymed verse. Matthew Arnold's poem Philomela contains some rhyme but is very free. Poems such as W. E. Henley's 'Discharged' (from his In Hospital sequence), and Robert Louis Stevenson's poems 'The Light-Keeper' and 'The Cruel Mistress' could be counted early examples of free verse.

In France, free verse was occasionally used by symbolist Arthur Rimbaud. In the Netherlands, tachtiger (i.e. member of 1880s generation of innovative poets) Frederik van Eeden also employed the form at least once in his poem Waterlelie "water lily".

3

The Anglo-saxon English

OUR FIRST POETRY

BEOWULF. Here is the story of Beowulf, the earliest and the greatest epic, or heroic poem, in our literature. It begins with a prologue, which is not an essential part of the story, but which we review gladly for the sake of the splendid poetical conception that produced Scyld, king of the Spear Danes.

At a time when the Spear Danes were without a king, a ship came sailing into their harbor. It was filled with treasures and weapons of war; and in the midst of these warlike things was a baby sleeping. No man sailed the ship; it came of itself, bringing the child, whose name was Scyld.

Now Scyld grew and became a mighty warriot, and led the Spear Danes for many years, and was their king. When his son Beowulf had become strong and wise enough to rule, then Wyrd (Fate), who speaks but once to any man, came and stood at hand; and it was time for Scyld to go. This is how they buried him:

Then Scyld departed, at word of Wyrd spoken,
The hero to go to the home of the gods.
Sadly they bore him to brink of the ocean,
Comrades, still heeding his word of command.
There rode in the harbor the prince's ship, ready,
With prow curving proudly and shining sails set.
Shipward they bore him, their hero beloved;
The mighty they laid at the foot of the mast.

Treasures were there from far and near gathered,
Byrnies of battle, armor and swords;
Never a keel sailed out of a harbor
So splendidly tricked with the trappings of war.
They heaped on his bosom a hoard of bright jewels
To fare with him forth on the flood's great breast.
No less gift they gave than the Unknown provided,
When alone, as a child, he came in from the mere.
High o'er his head waved a bright golden standard--
Now let the waves bear their wealth to the holm.
Sad-souled they gave back its gift to the ocean,
Mournful their mood as he sailed out to sea.

"And no man," says the poet, "neither counselor nor hero, can tell who received that lading."

One of Scyld's descendants was Hrothgar, king of the Danes; and with him the story of our Beowulf begins. Hrothgar in his old age had built near the sea a mead hall called Heorot, the most splendid hall in the whole world, where the king and his thanes gathered nightly to feast and to listen to the songs of his gleemen. One night, as they were all sleeping, a frightful monster, Grendel, broke into the hall, killed thirty of the sleeping warriors, and carried off their bodies to devour them in his lair under the sea. The appalling visit was speedily repeated, and fear and death reigned in the great hall. The warriors fought at first; but fled when they discovered that no weapon could harm the monster. Heorot was left deserted and silent. For twelve winters Grendel's horrible raids continued, and joy was changed to mourning among the Spear Danes.

At last the rumor of Grendel crossed over the sea to the land of the Geats, where a young hero dwelt in the house of his uncle, King Hygelac. Beowulf was his name, a man of immense strength and courage, and a mighty swimmer who had developed his powers fighting the "nickers," whales, walruses and seals, in the icebound northern ocean. When he heard the story, Beowulf was stirred to go and fight the monster and free the Danes, who were his father's friends.

With fourteen companions he crosses the sea. There is an excellent bit of ocean poetry here (ll. 210-224), and we get a vivid idea of the hospitality of a brave people by following the poet's description of Beowulf's meeting with King Hrothgar and Queen Wealhtheow, and of the joy and feasting and story-telling in Heorot. The picture of Wealhtheow passing the mead cup to the warriors with her own hand is a noble one, and plainly indicates the reverence paid by these strong men to their wives and mothers. Night comes on; the fear of Grendel is again upon the Danes, and all withdraw after the king has warned Beowulf of the frightful danger of sleeping in the hall. But Beowulf lies down with his warriors, saying proudly that, since weapons will not avail against the monster, he will grapple with him bare handed and trust to a warrior's strength.

Forth from the fens, from the misty moorlands,
Grendel came gliding--God's wrath he bore--
Came under clouds, until he saw clearly,
Glittering with gold plates, the mead hall of men.
Down fell the door, though fastened with fire bands;
Open it sprang at the stroke of his paw.
Swollen with rage burst in the bale-bringer;
Flamed in his eyes a fierce light, likest fire.

At the sight of men again sleeping in the hall, Grendel laughs in his heart, thinking of his feast. He seizes the nearest sleeper, crushes his "bone case" with a bite, tears him limb from limb, and swallows him. Then he creeps to the couch of Beowulf and stretches out a claw, only to find it clutched in a grip of steel. A sudden terror strikes the monster's heart. He roars, struggles, tries to jerk his arm free; but Beowulf leaps to his feet and grapples his enemy bare handed. To and fro they surge. Tables are overturned; golden benches ripped from their fastenings; the whole building quakes, and only its iron bands keep it from falling to pieces. Beowulf's companions are on their feet now, hacking vainly at the monster with swords and battle-axes, adding their shouts to the crashing of furniture and the howling "war song" of Grendel. Outside in the town the Danes stand shivering at the uproar. Slowly the monster struggles to the door, dragging Beowulf, whose fingers crack with the strain, but who never relaxes his first grip.

Suddenly a wide wound opens in the monster's side; the sinews snap; the whole arm is wrenched off at the shoulder; and Grendel escapes shrieking across the moor, and plunges into the sea to die.

Beowulf first exults in his night's work; then he hangs the huge arm with its terrible claws from a cross-beam over the king's seat, as one would hang up a bear's skin after a hunt. At daylight came the Danes; and all day long, in the intervals of singing, story-telling, speech making, and gift giving, they return to wonder at the mighty "grip of Grendel" and to rejoice in Beowulf's victory.

When night falls a great feast is spread in Heorot, and the Danes sleep once more in the great hall. At midnight comes another monster, a horrible, half-human creature, mother of Grendel, raging to avenge her offspring. She thunders at the door; the Danes leap up and grasp their weapons; but the monster enters, seizes Aeschere, who is friend and adviser of the king, and rushes away with him over the fens.

The old scenes of sorrow are reviewed in the morning; but Beowulf says simply:

Sorrow not, wise man. It is better for each
That his friend he avenge than that he mourn much.
Each of us shall the end await
Of worldly life: let him who may gain
Honor ere death. That is for a warrior,
When he is dead, afterwards best.
Arise, kingdom's guardian! Let us quickly go
To view the track of Grendel's kinsman.
I promise it thee: he will not escape,
Nor in earth's bosom, nor in mountain-wood,
Nor in ocean's depths, go where he will.

Then he girds himself for the new fight and follows the track of the second enemy across the fens. Here is Hrothgar's description of the place where live the monsters, "spirits of elsewhere," as he calls them:

They inhabit
The dim land that gives shelter to the wolf,

The windy headlands, perilous fen paths,
Where, under mountain mist, the stream flows down
And floods the ground. Not far hence, but a mile,
The mere stands, over which hang death-chill groves,
A wood fast-rooted overshades the flood;
There every night a ghastly miracle
Is seen, fire in the water. No man knows,
Not the most wise, the bottom of that mere.
The firm-horned heath-stalker, the hart, when pressed,
Wearied by hounds, and hunted from afar,
Will rather die of thirst upon its bank
Than bend his head to it. It is unholy.
Dark to the clouds its yeasty waves mount up
When wind stirs hateful tempest, till the air
Grows dreary, and the heavens pour down tears.

Beowulf plunges into the horrible place, while his companions wait for him oh the shore. For a long time he sinks through the flood; then, as he reaches bottom, Grendel's mother rushes out upon him and drags him into a cave, where sea monsters swarm at him from behind and gnash his armor with their tusks. The edge of his sword is turned with the mighty blow he deals the merewif; but it harms not the monster. Casting the weapon aside, he grips her and tries to hurl her down, while her claws and teeth clash upon his corslet but cannot penetrate the steel rings. She throws her bulk upon him, crushes him down, draws a short sword and plunges it at him; but again his splendid byrnie saves him. He is wearied now, and oppressed. Suddenly, as his eye sweeps the cave, he catches sight of a magic sword, made by the giants long ago, too heavy for warriors to wield. Struggling up he seizes the weapon, whirls it and brings down a crashing blow upon the monster's neck. It smashes through the ring bones; the merewif falls, and the fight is won.

The cave is full of treasures; but Beowulf heeds them not, for near him lies Grendel, dead from the wound received the previous night. Again Beowulf swings the great sword and strikes off his enemy's head; and lo, as the venomous blood touches the sword blade, the steel melts like ice before the fire, and only the hilt is left in Beowulf's hand. Taking the hilt and the head, the hero enters the ocean and mounts up to the shore.

Only his own faithful band were waiting there; for the Danes, seeing the ocean bubble with fresh blood, thought it was all over with the hero and had gone home. And there they were, mourning in Heorot, when Beowulf returned with the monstrous head of Grendel carried on a spear shaft by four of his stoutest followers.

In the last part of the poem there is another great fight. Beowulf is now an old man; he has reigned for fifty years, beloved by all his people. He has overcome every enemy but one, a fire dragon keeping watch over an enormous treasure hidden among the mountains. One day a wanderer stumbles upon the enchanted cave and, entering, takes a jeweled cup while the firedrake sleeps heavily. That same night the dragon, in a frightful rage, belching forth fire and smoke, rushes down upon the nearest villages, leaving a trail of death and terror behind him.

Again Beowulf goes forth to champion his people. As he approaches the dragon's cave, he has a presentiment that death lurks within:

Sat on the headland there the warrior king;
Farewell he said to hearth-companions true,
The gold-friend of the Geats; his mind was sad,
Death-ready, restless. And Wyrd was drawing nigh,
Who now must meet and touch the aged man,
To seek the treasure that his soul had saved
And separate his body from his life.

There is a flash of illumination, like that which comes to a dying man, in which his mind runs back over his long life and sees something of profound meaning in the elemental sorrow moving side by side with magnificent courage. Then follows the fight with the firedrake, in which Beowulf, wrapped in fire and smoke, is helped by the heroism of Wiglaf, one of his companions. The dragon is slain, but the fire has entered Beowulf's lungs and he knows that Wyrd is at hand. This is his thought, while Wiglaf removes his battered armor:

"One deep regret I have: that to a son
I may not give the armor I have worn,

To bear it after me. For fifty years
I ruled these people well, and not a king
Of those who dwell around me, dared oppress
Or meet me with his hosts. At home I waited
For the time that Wyrd controls. Mine own I kept,
Nor quarrels sought, nor ever falsely swore.
Now, wounded sore, I wait for joy to come."

He sends Wiglaf into the firedrake's cave, who finds it filled with rare treasures and, most wonderful of all, a golden banner from which light proceeds and illumines all the darkness. But Wiglaf cares little for the treasures; his mind is full of his dying chief. He fills his hands with costly ornaments and hurries to throw them at his hero's feet. The old man looks with sorrow at the gold, thanks the "Lord of all" that by death he has gained more riches for his people, and tells his faithful thane how his body shall be burned on the Whale ness, or headland:

"My life is well paid for this hoard; and now
Care for the people's needs. I may no more
Be with them. Bid the warriors raise a barrow
After the burning, on the ness by the sea,
On Hronesness, which shall rise high and be
For a remembrance to my people. Seafarers
Who from afar over the mists of waters
Drive foamy keels may call it Beowulf's Mount
Hereafter." Then the hero from his neck
Put off a golden collar; to his thane,
To the young warrior, gave it with his helm,
Armlet and corslet; bade him use them well.
"Thou art the last Waegmunding of our race,
For fate has swept my kinsmen all away.
Earls in their strength are to their Maker gone,
And I must follow them."

Beowulf was still living when Wiglaf sent a messenger hurriedly to his people; when they came they found him dead, and the huge dragon dead on the sand beside him.

Then the Goth's people reared a mighty pile
With shields and armour hung, as he had asked,
And in the midst the warriors laid their lord,
Lamenting. Then the warriors on the mount
Kindled a mighty bale fire; the smoke rose
Black from the Swedish pine, the sound of flame
Mingled with sound of weeping... while smoke
Spread over heaven. Then upon the hill
The people of the Weders wrought a mound,
High, broad, and to be seen far out at sea.
In ten days they had built and walled it in
As the wise thought most worthy; placed in it
Rings, jewels, other treasures from the hoard.
They left the riches, golden joy of earls,
In dust, for earth to hold; where yet it lies,
Useless as ever. Then about the mound
The warriors rode, and raised a mournful song
For their dead king; exalted his brave deeds,
Holding it fit men honour their liege lord,
Praise him and love him when his soul is fled.
Thus the [Geat's] people, sharers of his hearth,
Mourned their chief's fall, praised him, of kings, of men
The mildest and the kindest, and to all
His people gentlest, yearning for their praise.

One is tempted to linger over the details of the magnificent ending: the unselfish heroism of Beowulf, the great prototype of King Alfred; the generous grief of his people, ignoring gold and jewels in the thought of the greater treasure they had lost; the memorial mound on the low cliff, which would cause every returning mariner to steer a straight course to harbor in the remembrance of his dead hero; and the pure poetry which marks every noble line. But the epic is great enough and simple enough to speak for itself. Search the literatures of the world, and you will find no other such picture of a brave man's death.

Concerning the history of Beowulf a whole library has been written, and scholars still differ too radically for us to express a positive judgment. This much, however, is clear,--that there existed, at the time the poem was composed, various northern legends of Beowa, a half-divine hero, and the monster Grendel. The latter has been interpreted in various ways,--sometimes as a bear, and again as the malaria of the marsh lands. For those interested in symbols the simplest interpretation of these myths is to regard Beowulf's successive fights with the three dragons as the overcoming, first, of the overwhelming danger of the sea, which was beaten back by the dykes; second, the conquering of the sea itself, when men learned to sail upon it; and third, the conflict with the hostile forces of nature, which are overcome at last by man's indomitable will and perseverance.

All this is purely mythical; but there are historical incidents to reckon with. About the year 520 a certain northern chief, called by the chronicler Chochilaicus (who is generally identified with the Hygelac of the epic), led a huge plundering expedition up the Rhine. After a succession of battles he was overcome by the Franks, but--and now we enter a legendary region once more--not until a gigantic nephew of Hygelac had performed heroic feats of valor, and had saved the remnants of the host by a marvelous feat of swimming. The majority of scholars now hold that these historical events and personages were celebrated in the epic; but some still assert that the events which gave a foundation for Beowulf occurred wholly on English soil, where the poem itself was undoubtedly written.

The rhythm of Beowulf and indeed of all our earliest poetry depended upon accent and alliteration; that is, the beginning of two or more words in the same line with the same sound or letter. The lines were made up of two short halves, separated by a pause. No rime was used; but a musical effect was produced by giving each half line two strongly accented syllables. Each full line, therefore, had four accents, three of which (i.e. two in the first half, and one in the second) usually began with the same sound or letter. The musical effect was heightened by the harp with which the gleeman accompanied his singing.. The poetical form will be seen clearly in the following selection from the wonderfully realistic description of the fens haunted by Grendel. It will need only one or two readings aloud to show that many of these strange-looking words are practically the same as those we still use, though many of the vowel sounds were pronounced differently by our ancestors.

... Hie dygel lond
Warigeath, wulf-hleothu, windige naessas,
Frecne fen-gelad, thaer fyrgen-stream
Under naessa genipu nither gewiteth,
Flod under foldan. Nis thaet feor heonon,
Mil-gemearces, thaet se mere standeth,
Ofer thaem hongiath hrinde bearwas
... They (a) darksome land
Ward (inhabit), wolf cliffs, windy nesses,
Frightful fen paths where mountain stream
Under nesses' mists nether (downward) wanders,
A flood under earth. It is not far hence,
By mile measure, that the mere stands,
Over which hang rimy groves.

WIDSITH. The poem "Widsith," the wide goer or wanderer, is in part, at least, probably the oldest in our language. The author and the date of its composition are unknown; but the personal account of the minstrel's life belongs to the time before the Saxons first came to England. It expresses the wandering life of the gleeman, who goes forth into the world to abide here or there, according as he is rewarded for his singing. From the numerous references to rings and rewards, and from the praise given to generous givers, it would seem that literature as a paying profession began very early in our history, and also that the pay was barely sufficient to hold soul and body together. Of all our modern poets, Goldsmith wandering over Europe paying for his lodging with his songs is most suggestive of this first recorded singer of our race. His last lines read:

Thus wandering, they who shape songs for men
Pass over many lands, and tell their need,
And speak their thanks, and ever, south or north,
Meet someone skilled in songs and free in gifts,
Who would be raised among his friends to fame
And do brave deeds till light and life are gone.
He who has thus wrought himself praise shall have
A settled glory underneath the stars.

DEOR'S LAMENT. In "Deor" we have another picture of the Saxon scop, or minstrel, not in glad wandering, but in manly sorrow. It seems that the scop's living depended entirely upon his power to please his chief, and that at any time he might be supplanted by a better poet. Deor had this experience, and comforts himself in a grim way by recalling various examples of men who have suffered more than himself. The poem is arranged in strophes, each one telling of some afflicted hero and ending with the same refrain: His sorrow passed away; so will mine. "Deor" is much more poetic than "Widsith," and is the one perfect lyric of the Anglo-Saxon period.

Weland for a woman knew too well exile.
Strong of soul that earl, sorrow sharp he bore;
To companionship he had care and weary longing,
Winter-freezing wretchedness. Woe he found again, again,
After that Nithhad in a need had laid him--
Staggering sinew-wounds--sorrow-smitten man!
That he overwent; this also may I.

THE SEAFARER. The wonderful poem of "The Seafarer" seems to be in two distinct parts. The first shows the hardships of ocean life; but stronger than hardships is the subtle call of the sea. The second part is an allegory, in which the troubles of the seaman are symbols of the troubles of this life, and the call of the ocean is the call in the soul to be up and away to its true home with God. Whether the last was added by some monk who saw the allegorical possibilities of the first part, or whether some sea-loving Christian scop wrote both, is uncertain. Following are a few selected lines to show the spirit of the poem:

The hail flew in showers about me; and there I heard only
The roar of the sea, ice-cold waves, and the song of the swan;
For pastime the gannets' cry served me; the kittiwakes' chatter
For laughter of men; and for mead drink the call of the sea mews.
When storms on the rocky cliffs beat, then the terns, icy-feathered,
Made answer; full oft the sea eagle forebodingly screamed,
The eagle with pinions wave-wet....
The shadows of night became darker, it snowed from the north;
The world was enchained by the frost; hail fell upon earth;
'T was the coldest of grain. Yet the thoughts of my heart now are throbbing
To test the high streams, the salt waves in tumultuous play.
Desire in my heart ever urges my spirit to wander,
To seek out the home of the stranger in lands afar off.
There is no one that dwells upon earth, so exalted in mind,
But that he has always a longing, a sea-faring passion
For what the Lord God shall bestow, be it honor or death.
No heart for the harp has he, nor for acceptance of treasure,
No pleasure has he in a wife, no delight in the world,
Nor in aught save the roll of the billows; but always a longing,
A yearning uneasiness, hastens him on to the sea.
The woodlands are captured by blossoms, the hamlets grow fair,
Broad meadows are beautiful, earth again bursts into life,
And all stir the heart of the wanderer eager to journey,
So he meditates going afar on the pathway of tides.
The cuckoo, moreover, gives warning with sorrowful note,
Summer's harbinger sings, and forebodes to the heart bitter sorrow.
Now my spirit uneasily turns in the heart's narrow chamber,

Now wanders forth over the tide, o'er the home of the whale,
To the ends of the earth--and comes back to me.
Eager and greedy,
The lone wanderer screams, and resistlessly drives my soul onward,
Over the whale-path, over the tracts of the sea.

THE FIGHT AT FINNSBURGH AND WALDERE. Two other of our oldest poems well deserve mention. The "Fight at Finnsburgh" is a fragment of fifty lines, discovered on the inside of a piece of parchment drawn over the wooden covers of a book of homilies. It is a magnificent war song, describing with Homeric power the defense of a hall by Hnaef with sixty warriors, against the attack of Finn and his army. At midnight, when Hnaef and his men are sleeping, they are surrounded by an army rushing in with fire and sword. Hnaef springs to his feet at the first alarm and wakens his warriors with a call to action that rings like a bugle blast:

This no eastward dawning is, nor is here a dragon flying,
Nor of this high hall are the horns a burning;
But they rush upon us here--now the ravens sing,
Growling is the gray wolf, grim the war-wood rattles,
Shield to shaft is answering.

The fight lasts five days, but the fragment ends before we learn the outcome: The same fight is celebrated by Hrothgar's gleeman at the feast in Heorot, after the slaying of Grendel.

"Waldere" is a fragment of two leaves, from which we get only a glimpse of the story of Waldere (Walter of Aquitaine) and his betrothed bride Hildgund, who were hostages at the court of Attila. They escaped with a great treasure, and in crossing the mountains were attacked by Gunther and his warriors, among whom was Walter's former comrade, Hagen. Walter fights them all and escapes. The same story was written in Latin in the tenth century, and is also part of the old German Nibelungenlied. Though the saga did not originate with the Anglo-Saxons, their version of it is the oldest that has come down to us. The chief significance of these "Waldere" fragments lies in the evidence they afford that our ancestors were familiar with the legends and poetry of other Germanic peoples.

ANGLO-SAXON LIFE

We have now read some of our earliest records, and have been surprised, perhaps, that men who are generally described in the histories as savage fighters and freebooters could produce such excellent poetry. It is the object of the study of all literature to make us better acquainted with men,--not simply with their deeds, which is the function of history, but with the dreams and ideals which underlie all their actions. So a reading of this early Anglo-Saxon poetry not only makes us acquainted, but also leads to a profound respect for the men who were our ancestors. Before we study more of their literature it is well to glance briefly at their life and language.

THE NAME. Originally the name Anglo-Saxon denotes two of the three Germanic tribes,--Jutes, Angles, and Saxons,--who in the middle of the fifth century left their homes on the shores of the North Sea and the Baltic to conquer and colonize distant Britain. Angeln was the home of one tribe, and the name still clings to the spot whence some of our forefathers sailed on their momentous voyage. The old Saxon word angul or ongul means a hook, and the English verb angle is used invariably by Walton and older writers in the sense of fishing. We may still think, therefore, of the first Angles as hook-men, possibly because of their fishing, more probably because the shore where they lived, at the foot of the peninsula of Jutland, was bent in the shape of a fishhook. The name Saxon from seax, sax, a short sword, means the sword-man, and from the name we may judge something of the temper of the hardy fighters who preceded the Angles into Britain. The Angles were the most numerous of the conquering tribes, and from them the new home was called Anglalond. By gradual changes this became first Englelond and then England.

More than five hundred years after the landing of these tribes, and while they called themselves Englishmen, we find the Latin writers of the Middle Ages speaking of the inhabitants of Britain as Anglisaxones,--that is, Saxons of England,--to distinguish them from the Saxons of the Continent. In the Latin charters of King Alfred the same name appears; but it is never seen or heard in his native speech. There he always speaks of his beloved "Englelond" and of his brave "Englisc" people. In the sixteenth century, when the old name of Englishmen clung to the new people resulting from the union of Saxon and Norman, the name Anglo-Saxon was first used in the national sense by the scholar Camden in his History of Britain; and since then it has been in general use among English writers. In recent years the name has gained a wider significance, until it is now used to denote a spirit rather than a nation, the brave, vigorous, enlarging spirit that characterizes the English-speaking races everywhere, and that has already put a broad belt of English law and English liberty around the whole world.

THE LIFE. If the literature of a people springs directly out of its life, then the stern, barbarous life of our Saxon forefathers would seem, at first glance, to promise little of good literature. Outwardly their life was a constant hardship, a perpetual struggle against savage nature and savage men. Behind them were gloomy forests inhabited by wild beasts and still wilder men, and peopled in their imagination with dragons and evil shapes.

In front of them, thundering at the very dikes for entrance, was the treacherous North Sea, with its fogs and storms and ice, but with that indefinable call of the deep that all men hear who live long beneath its influence. Here they lived, a big, blond, powerful race, and hunted and fought and sailed, and drank and feasted when their labor was done. Almost the first thing we notice about these big, fearless, childish men is that they love the sea; and because they love it they hear and answer its call:

... No delight has he in the world,

Nor in aught save the roll of the billows; but always a longing,

A yearning uneasiness, hastens him on to the sea.

As might be expected, this love of the ocean finds expression in all their poetry. In Beowulf alone there are fifteen names for the sea, from the holm, that is, the horizon sea, the "upmounding," to the brim, which is the ocean flinging its welter of sand and creamy foam upon the beach at your feet. And the figures used to describe or glorify it--"the swan road, the whale path, the heaving battle plain"--are almost as numerous. In all their poetry there is a magnificent sense of lordship over the wild sea even in its hour of tempest and fury:

Often it befalls us, on the ocean's highways,

In the boats our boatmen, when the storm is roaring,

Leap the billows over, on our stallions of the foam.

THE INNER LIFE. A man's life is more than his work; his dream is ever greater than his achievement; and literature reflects not so much man's deed as the spirit which animates him; not the poor thing that he does, but rather the splendid thing that he ever hopes to do. In no place is this more evident than in the age we are now studying. Those early sea kings were a marvelous mixture of savagery and sentiment, of rough living and of deep feeling, of splendid courage and the deep melancholy of men who know their limitations and have faced the unanswered problem of death. They were not simply fearless freebooters who harried every coast in their war galleys. If that were all, they would have no more history or literature than the Barbary pirates, of whom the same thing could be said. These strong fathers of ours were men of profound emotions. In all their fighting the love of an untarnished glory was uppermost; and under the warrior's savage exterior was hidden a great love of home and homely virtues, and a reverence for the one woman to whom he would presently return in triumph. So when the wolf hunt was over, or the desperate fight was won, these mighty men would gather in the banquet hall, and lay their weapons aside where the open fire would flash upon them, and there listen to the songs of Scop and Gleeman,--men who could put into adequate words the emotions and aspirations that all men feel but that only a few can ever express:

Music and song where the heroes sat--

The glee-wood rang, a song uprose

When Hrothgar's scop gave the hall good cheer.

It is this great and hidden life of the Anglo-Saxons that finds expression in all their literature. Briefly, it is summed up in five great principles,--their love of personal freedom, their responsiveness to nature, their religion, their reverence for womanhood, and their struggle for glory as a ruling motive in every noble life.

In reading Anglo-Saxon poetry it is well to remember these five principles, for they are like the little springs at the head of a great river,--clear, pure springs of poetry, and out of them the best of our literature has always flowed. Thus when we read,

Blast of the tempest--it aids our oars;

Rolling of thunder--it hurts us not;

Rush of the hurricane--bending its neck

To speed us whither our wills are bent,

we realize that these sea rovers had the spirit of kinship with the mighty life of nature; and kinship with nature invariably expresses itself in poetry. Again, when we read,

Now hath the man

O'ercome his troubles. No pleasure does he lack,

Nor steeds, nor jewels, nor the joys of mead;

Nor any treasure that the earth can give,

O royal woman, if he have but thee,

we know we are dealing with an essentially noble man, not a savage; we are face to face with that profound reverence for womanhood which inspires the greater part of all good poetry, and we begin to honor as well as understand our ancestors. So in the matter of glory or honor; it was, apparently, not the love of fighting, but rather the love of honor resulting from fighting well, which animated our forefathers in every campaign. "He was a man deserving of remembrance" was the highest thing that could be said of a dead warrior; and "He is a man deserving of praise" was the highest tribute to the living. The whole secret of Beowulf's mighty life is summed up in the last line, "Ever yearning for his people's praise." So every tribe had its scop, or poet, more important than any warrior, who put the deeds of its heroes into the expressive words that constitute literature; and every banquet hall had its gleeman, who sang the scop's poetry in order that the deed and the man might be remembered. Oriental peoples built monuments to perpetuate the memory of their dead; but our ancestors made poems, which should live and stir men's souls long after monuments of brick and stone had crumbled away. It is to this intense love of glory and the desire to be remembered that we are indebted for Anglo-Saxon literature.

OUR FIRST SPEECH. Our first recorded speech begins with the songs of Widsith and Deor, which the Anglo-Saxons may have brought with them when they first conquered Britain. At first glance these songs in their native dress look strange as a foreign tongue; but when we examine them carefully we find many words that have been familiar since childhood. We have seen this in Beowulf; but in prose the resemblance of this old speech to our own is even more striking.

Here, for instance, is a fragment of the simple story of the conquest of Britain by our Anglo-Saxon ancestors:

Her Hengest and AEsc his sunu gefuhton with Bryttas, on thaere stowe the is gecweden Creccanford, and thaer ofslogon feower thusenda wera. And tha Bryttas tha forleton Cent-lond, and mid myclum ege flugon to Lundenbyrig. (At this time Hengest and Aesc, his son, fought against the Britons at the place which is called Crayford and there slew four thousand men. And then the Britons forsook Kentland, and with much fear fled to London town.)

The reader who utters these words aloud a few times will speedily recognize his own tongue, not simply in the words but also in the whole structure of the sentences.

From such records we see that our speech is Teutonic in its origin; and when we examine any Teutonic language we learn that it is only a branch of the great Aryan or Indo-European family of languages. In life and language, therefore, we are related first to the Teutonic races, and through them to all the nations of this Indo-European family, which, starting with enormous vigor from their original home (probably in central Europe) spread southward and westward, driving out the native tribes and slowly developing the mighty civilizations of India, Persia, Greece, Rome, and the wilder but more vigorous life of the Celts and Teutons. In all these languages--Sanskrit, Iranian, Greek, Latin, Celtic, Teutonic--we recognize the same root words for father and mother, for God and man, for the common needs and the common relations of life; and since words are windows through which we see the soul of this old people, we find certain ideals of love, home, faith, heroism, liberty, which seem to have been the very life of our forefathers, and which were inherited by them from their old heroic and conquering ancestors. It was on the borders of the North Sea that our fathers halted for unnumbered centuries on their westward journey, and slowly developed the national life and language which we now call Anglo-Saxon.

It is this old vigorous Anglo-Saxon language which forms the basis of our modern English. If we read a paragraph from any good English book, and then analyze it, as we would a flower, to see what it contains, we find two distinct classes of words. The first class, containing simple words expressing the common things of life, makes up the strong framework of our language. These words are like the stem and bare branches of a mighty oak, and if we look them up in the dictionary we find that almost invariably they come to us from our Anglo-Saxon ancestors. The second and larger class of words is made up of those that give grace, variety, ornament, to our speech. They are like the leaves and blossoms of the same tree, and when we examine their history we find that they come to us from the Celts, Romans, Normans, and other peoples with whom we have been in contact in the long years of our development. The most prominent characteristic of our present language, therefore, is its dual character. Its best qualities--strength, simplicity, directness--come from Anglo-Saxon sources; its enormous added wealth of expression, its comprehensiveness, its plastic adaptability to new conditions and ideas, are largely the result of additions from other languages, and especially of its gradual absorption of the French language after the Norman Conquest. It is this dual character, this combination of native and foreign, of innate and exotic elements, which accounts for the wealth of our English language and literature. To see it in concrete form, we should read in succession Beowulf and Paradise Lost, the two great epics which show the root and the flower of our literary development.

CHRISTIAN WRITERS OF THE ANGLO-SAXON PERIOD

The literature of this period falls naturally into two divisions,--pagan and Christian. The former represents the poetry which the Anglo-Saxons probably brought with them in the form of oral sagas,--the crude material out of which literature was slowly developed on English soil; the latter represents the writings developed under teaching of the monks, after the old pagan religion had vanished, but while it still retained its hold on the life and language of the people. In reading our earliest poetry it is well to remember that all of it was copied by the monks, and seems to have been more or less altered to give it a religious coloring.

The coming of Christianity meant not simply a new life and leader for England; it meant also the wealth of a new language. The scop is now replaced by the literary monk; and that monk, though he lives among common people and speaks with the English tongue, has behind him all the culture and literary resources of the Latin language. The effect is seen instantly in our early prose and poetry.

NORTHUMBRIAN LITERATURE. In general, two great schools of Christian influence came into England, and speedily put an end to the frightful wars that had waged continually among the various petty kingdoms of the Anglo-Saxons. The first of these, under the leadership of Augustine, came from Rome. It spread in the south and center of England, especially in the kingdom of Essex. It founded schools and partially educated the rough people, but it produced no lasting literature. The other, under the leadership of the saintly Aidan, came from Ireland, which country had been for centuries a center of religion and education for all western Europe. The monks of this school labored chiefly in Northumbria, and to their influence we owe all that is best in Anglo-Saxon literature. It is called the Northumbrian School; its center was the monasteries and abbeys, such as Jarrow and Whitby, and its three greatest names are Bede, Caedmon, and Cynewulf.

BEDE (673-735)

The Venerable Bede, as he is generally called, our first great scholar and "the father of our English learning," wrote almost exclusively in Latin, his last work, the translation of the Gospel of John into Anglo-Saxon, having been unfortunately lost. Much to our regret, therefore, his books and the story of his gentle, heroic life must be excluded from this history of our literature. His works, over forty in number, covered the whole field of human knowledge in his day, and were so admirably written that they were widely copied as text-books, or rather manuscripts, in nearly all the monastery schools of Europe.

The work most important to us is the Ecclesiastical History of the English People. It is a fascinating history to read even now, with its curious combination of accurate scholarship and immense credulity. In all strictly historical matters Bede is a model. Every known authority on the subject, from Pliny to Gildas, was carefully considered; every learned pilgrim to Rome was commissioned by Bede to ransack the archives and to make copies of papal decrees and royal letters; and to these were added the testimony of abbots who could speak from personal knowledge of events or repeat the traditions of their several monasteries.

Side by side with this historical exactness are marvelous stories of saints and missionaries. It was an age of credulity, and miracles were in men's minds continually. The men of whom he wrote lived lives more wonderful than any romance, and their courage and gentleness made a tremendous impression on the rough, warlike people to whom they came with open hands and hearts. It is the natural way of all primitive peoples to magnify the works of their heroes, and so deeds of heroism and kindness, which were part of the daily life of the Irish missionaries, were soon transformed into the miracles of the saints. Bede believed these things, as all other men did, and records them with charming simplicity, just as he received them from bishop or abbot. Notwithstanding its errors, we owe to this work nearly all our knowledge of the eight centuries of our history following the landing of Caesar in Britain.

CAEDMON (SEVENTH CENTURY)

Now must we hymn the Master of heaven,

The might of the Maker, the deeds of the Father,

The thought of His heart. He, Lord everlasting,

Established of old the source of all wonders:

Creator all-holy, He hung the bright heaven,

A roof high upreared, o'er the children of men;

The King of mankind then created for mortals

The world in its beauty, the earth spread beneath them,

He, Lord everlasting, omnipotent God.

If Beowulf and the fragments of our earliest poetry were brought into England, then the hymn given above is the first verse of all native English song that has come down to us, and Caedmon is the first poet to whom we can give a definite name and date. The words were written about 665 A.D. and are found copied at the end of a manuscript of Bede's Ecclesiastical History.

LIFE OF CaeDMON. What little we know of Caedmon, the Anglo-Saxon Milton, as he is properly called, is taken from Bede's account of the Abbess Hilda and of her monastery at Whitby. Here is a free and condensed translation of Bede's story:

There was, in the monastery of the Abbess Hilda, a brother distinguished by the grace of God, for that he could make poems treating of goodness and religion. Whatever was translated to him (for he could not read) of Sacred Scripture he shortly reproduced in poetic form of great sweetness and beauty. None of all the English poets could equal him, for he learned not the art of song from men, nor sang by the arts of men. Rather did he receive all his poetry as a free gift from God, and for this reason he did never compose poetry of a vain or worldly kind.

Until of mature age he lived as a layman and had never learned any poetry. Indeed, so ignorant of singing was he that sometimes, at a feast, where it was the custom that for the pleasure of all each guest should sing in turn, he would rise from the table when he saw the harp coming to him and go home ashamed. Now it happened once that he did this thing at a certain festivity, and went out to the stall to care for the horses, this duty being assigned to him for that night. As he slept at the usual time, one stood by him saying: "Caedmon, sing me something." "I cannot sing," he answered, "and that is why I came hither from the feast." But he who spake unto him said again, "Caedmon, sing to me." And he said, "What shall I sing?" and he said, "Sing the beginning of created things." Thereupon Caedmon began to sing verses that he had never heard before, of this import: "Now should we praise the power and wisdom of the Creator, the works of the Father." This is the sense but not the form of the hymn that he sang while sleeping.

When he awakened, Caedmon remembered the words of the hymn and added to them many more. In the morning he went to the steward of the monastery lands and showed him the gift he had received in sleep. The steward brought him to Hilda, who made him repeat to the monks the hymn he had composed, and all agreed that the grace of God was upon Caedmon. To test him they expounded to him a bit of Scripture from the Latin and bade him, if he could, to turn it into poetry. He went away humbly and returned in the morning with an excellent poem. Thereupon Hilda received him and his family into the monastery, made him one of the brethren, and commanded that the whole course of Bible history be expounded to him. He in turn, reflecting upon what he had heard, transformed it into most delightful poetry, and by echoing it back to the monks in more melodious sounds made his teachers his listeners. In all this his aim was to turn men from wickedness and to help them to the love and practice of well doing.

[Then follows a brief record of Caedmon's life and an exquisite picture of his death amidst the brethren.] And so it came to pass [says the simple record] that as he served God while living in purity of mind and serenity of spirit, so by a peaceful death he left the world and went to look upon His face.

CaeDMON'S WORKS. The greatest work attributed to Caedmon is the so-called Paraphrase. It is the story of Genesis, Exodus, and a part of Daniel, told in glowing, poetic language, with a power of insight and imagination which often raises it from paraphrase into the realm of true poetry. Though we have Bede's assurance that Caedmon "transformed the whole course of Bible history into most delightful poetry," no work known certainly to have been composed by him has come down to us. In the seventeenth century this Anglo-Saxon Paraphrase was discovered and attributed to Caedmon, and his name is still associated with it, though it is now almost certain that the Paraphrase is the work of more than one writer.

Aside from the doubtful question of authorship, even a casual reading of the poem brings us into the presence of a poet rude indeed, but with a genius strongly suggestive at times of the matchless Milton. The book opens with a hymn of praise, and then tells of the fall of Satan and his rebel angels from heaven, which is familiar to us in Milton's Paradise Lost. Then follows the creation of the world, and the Paraphrase begins to thrill with the old Anglo-Saxon love of nature.

Here first the Eternal Father, guard of all,
Of heaven and earth, raised up the firmament,
The Almighty Lord set firm by His strong power
This roomy land; grass greened not yet the plain,
Ocean far spread hid the wan ways in gloom.
Then was the Spirit gloriously bright
Of Heaven's Keeper borne over the deep
Swiftly. The Life-giver, the Angel's Lord,
Over the ample ground bade come forth Light.
Quickly the High King's bidding was obeyed,
Over the waste there shone light's holy ray.
Then parted He, Lord of triumphant might,
Shadow from shining, darkness from the light.

Light, by the Word of God, was first named day.

After recounting the story of Paradise, the Fall, and the Deluge, the Paraphrase is continued in the Exodus, of which the poet makes a noble epic, rushing on with the sweep of a Saxon army to battle. A single selection is given here to show how the poet adapted the story to his hearers:

Then they saw,

Forth and forward faring, Pharaoh's war array

Gliding on, a grove of spears;--glittering the hosts!

Fluttered there the banners, there the folk the march trod.

Onwards surged the war, strode the spears along,

Blickered the broad shields; blew aloud the trumpets....

Wheeling round in gyres, yelled the fowls of war,

Of the battle greedy; hoarsely barked the raven,

Dew upon his feathers, o'er the fallen corpses--

Swart that chooser of the slain! Sang aloud the wolves

At eve their horrid song, hoping for the carrion.

Besides the Paraphrase we have a few fragments of the same general character which are attributed to the school of Caedmon. The longest of these is Judith, in which the story of an apocryphal book of the Old Testament is done into vigorous poetry. Holofernes is represented as a savage and cruel Viking, reveling in his mead hall; and when the heroic Judith cuts off his head with his own sword and throws it down before the warriors of her people, rousing them to battle and victory, we reach perhaps the most dramatic and brilliant point of Anglo-Saxon literature.

CYNEWULF (EIGHTH CENTURY)

Of Cynewulf, greatest of the Anglo-Saxon poets, excepting only the unknown author of Beowulf, we know very little. Indeed, it was not till 1840, more than a thousand years after his death, that even his name became known. Though he is the only one of our early poets who signed his works, the name was never plainly written, but woven into the verses in the form of secret runes, suggesting a modern charade, but more difficult of interpretation until one has found the key to the poet's signature.

WORKS OF CYNEWULF. The only signed poems of Cynewulf are The Christ, Juliana, The Fates of the Apostles, and Elene. Unsigned poems attributed to him or his school are Andreas, the Phoenix, the Dream of the Rood, the Descent into Hell, Guthlac, the Wanderer, and some of the Riddles. The last are simply literary conundrums in which some well-known object, like the bow or drinking horn, is described in poetic language, and the hearer must guess the name. Some of them, like "The Swan" and "The Storm Spirit," are unusually beautiful.

Of all these works the most characteristic is undoubtedly The Christ, a didactic poem in three parts: the first celebrating the Nativity; the second, the Ascension; and the third, "Doomsday," telling the torments of the wicked and the unending joy of the redeemed. Cynewulf takes his subject-matter partly from the Church liturgy, but more largely from the homilies of Gregory the Great. The whole is well woven together, and contains some hymns of great beauty and many passages of intense dramatic force. Throughout the poem a deep love for Christ and a reverence for the Virgin Mary are manifest. More than any other poem in any language, The Christ reflects the spirit of early Latin Christianity.

Here is a fragment comparing life to a sea voyage,--a comparison which occurs sooner or later to every thoughtful person, and which finds perfect expression in Tennyson's "Crossing the Bar."

Now 'tis most like as if we fare in ships

On the ocean flood, over the water cold,

Driving our vessels through the spacious seas

With horses of the deep. A perilous way is this

Of boundless waves, and there are stormy seas

On which we toss here in this (reeling) world

O'er the deep paths. Ours was a sorry plight

Until at last we sailed unto the land,

Over the troubled main. Help came to us

That brought us to the haven of salvation,

God's Spirit-Son, and granted grace to us
That we might know e'en from the vessel's deck
Where we must bind with anchorage secure
Our ocean steeds, old stallions of the waves.

In the two epic poems of Andreas and Elene Cynewulf (if he be the author) reaches the very summit of his poetical art. Andreas, an unsigned poem, records the story of St. Andrew, who crosses the sea to rescue his comrade St. Matthew from the cannibals. A young ship-master who sails the boat turns out to be Christ in disguise, Matthew is set free, and the savages are converted by a miracle. It is a spirited poem, full of rush and incident, and the descriptions of the sea are the best in Anglo-Saxon poetry.

Elene has for its subject-matter the finding of the true cross. It tells of Constantine's vision of the Rood, on the eve of battle. After his victory under the new emblem he sends his mother Helena (Elene) to Jerusalem in search of the original cross and the nails. The poem, which is of very uneven quality, might properly be put at the end of Cynewulf's works. He adds to the poem a personal note, signing his name in runes; and, if we accept the wonderful "Vision of the Rood" as Cynewulf's work, we learn how he found the cross at last in his own heart. There is a suggestion here of the future Sir Launfal and the search for the Holy Grail.

DECLINE OF NORTHUMBRIAN LITERATURE. The same northern energy which had built up learning and literature so rapidly in Northumbria was instrumental in pulling it down again. Toward the end of the century in which Cynewulf lived, the Danes swept down on the English coasts and overwhelmed Northumbria. Monasteries and schools were destroyed; scholars and teachers alike were put to the sword, and libraries that had been gathered leaf by leaf with the toil of centuries were scattered to the four winds. So all true Northumbrian literature perished, with the exception of a few fragments, and that which we now possess is largely a translation in the dialect of the West Saxons. This translation was made by Alfred's scholars, after he had driven back the Danes in an effort to preserve the ideals and the civilization that had been so hardly won. With the conquest of Northumbria ends the poetic period of Anglo-Saxon literature. With

Alfred the Great of Wessex our prose literature makes a beginning.

ALFRED (848-901)

> *"Every craft and every power soon grows old and is passed over and forgotten, if it be without wisdom.... This is now to be said, that whilst I live I wish to live nobly, and after life to leave to the men who come after me a memory of good works."*

So wrote the great Alfred, looking back over his heroic life. That he lived nobly none can doubt who reads the history of the greatest of Anglo-Saxon kings; and his good works include, among others, the education of half a country, the salvage of a noble native literature, and the creation of the first English prose.

LIFE AND TIMES OF ALFRED. For the history of Alfred's times, and details of the terrific struggle with the Northmen, the reader must be referred to the histories. The struggle ended with the Treaty of Wedmore, in 878, with the establishment of Alfred not only as king of Wessex, but as overlord of the whole northern country. Then the hero laid down his sword, and set himself as a little child to learn to read and write Latin, so that he might lead his people in peace as he had led them in war. It is then that Alfred began to be the heroic figure in literature that he had formerly been in the wars against the Northmen.

With the same patience and heroism that had marked the long struggle for freedom, Alfred set himself to the task of educating his people. First he gave them laws, beginning with the Ten Commandments and ending with the Golden Rule, and then established courts where laws could be faithfully administered. Safe from the Danes by land, he created a navy, almost the first of the English fleets, to drive them from the coast. Then, with peace and justice established within his borders, he sent to Europe for scholars and teachers, and set them over schools that he established. Hitherto all education had been in Latin; now he set himself the task, first, of teaching every free-born Englishman to read and write his own language, and second, of translating into English the best books for their instruction. Every poor scholar was honored at his court and was speedily set to work at teaching or translating; every wanderer bringing a book or a leaf of manuscript from the pillaged monasteries of Northumbria was sure of his reward. In this way the few fragments of native Northumbrian literature, which we have been studying, were saved to the world. Alfred and his scholars treasured the rare fragments and copied them in the West-Saxon dialect. With the exception of Caedmon's Hymn, we have hardly a single leaf from the great literature of Northumbria in the dialect in which it was first written.

WORKS OF ALFRED. Aside from his educational work, Alfred is known chiefly as a translator. After fighting his country's battles, and at a time when most men were content with military honor, he began to learn Latin, that he might translate the works that would be most helpful to his people. His important translations are four in number: Orosius's Universal History and Geography, the leading work in general history for several centuries; Bede's History, the first great historical work written on English soil; Pope Gregory's Shepherds' Book, intended especially for the clergy; and Boethius's Consolations of Philosophy, the favorite philosophical work of the Middle Ages.

More important than any translation is the English or Saxon Chronicle. This was probably at first a dry record, especially of important births and deaths in the West-Saxon kingdom. Alfred enlarged this scant record, beginning the story with Caesar's conquest. When it touches his own reign the dry chronicle becomes an interesting and connected story, the oldest history belonging to any modern nation in its own language. The record of Alfred's reign, probably by himself, is a splendid bit of writing and shows clearly his claim to a place in literature as well as in history. The Chronicle was continued after Alfred's death, and is the best monument of early English prose that is left to us. Here and there stirring songs are included in the narrative, like "The Battle of Brunanburh" and "The Battle of Maldon." The last, entered 991, seventy-five years before the Norman Conquest, is the swan song of Anglo-Saxon poetry. The Chronicle was continued for a century after the Norman Conquest, and is extremely valuable not only as a record of events but as a literary monument showing the development of our language.

CLOSE OF THE ANGLO-SAXON PERIOD. After Alfred's death there is little to record, except the loss of the two supreme objects of his heroic struggle, namely, a national life and a national literature. It was at once the strength and the weakness of the Saxon that he lived apart as a free man and never joined efforts willingly with any large body of his fellows. The tribe was his largest idea of nationality, and, with all our admiration, we must confess as we first meet him that he has not enough sense of unity to make a great nation, nor enough culture to produce a great literature. A few noble political ideals repeated in a score of petty kingdoms, and a few literary ideals copied but never increased,--that is the summary of his literary history. For a full century after Alfred literature was practically at a standstill, having produced the best of which it was capable, and England waited for the national impulse and for the culture necessary for a new and greater art. Both of these came speedily, by way of the sea, in the Norman Conquest.

SUMMARY OF ANGLO-SAXON PERIOD. Our literature begins with songs and stories of a time when our Teutonic ancestors were living on the borders of the North Sea. Three tribes of these ancestors, the Jutes, Angles, and Saxons, conquered Britain in the latter half of the fifth century, and laid the foundation of the English nation. The first landing was probably by a tribe of Jutes, under chiefs called by the chronicle Hengist and Horsa. The date is doubtful; but the year 449 is accepted by most historians. These old ancestors were hardy warriors and sea rovers, yet were capable of profound and noble emotions. Their poetry reflects this double nature. Its subjects were chiefly the sea and the plunging boats, battles, adventure, brave deeds, the glory of warriors, and the love of home. Accent, alliteration, and an abrupt break in the middle of each line gave their poetry a kind of martial rhythm. In general the poetry is earnest and somber, and pervaded by fatalism and religious feeling. A careful reading of the few remaining fragments of Anglo-Saxon literature reveals five striking characteristics: the love of freedom; responsiveness to nature, especially in her sterner moods; strong religious convictions, and a belief in Wyrd, or Fate; reverence for womanhood; and a devotion to glory as the ruling motive in every warrior's life.

In our study we have noted: (1) the great epic or heroic poem Beowulf, and a few fragments of our first poetry, such as "Widsith," "Deor's Lament," and "The Seafarer." (2) Characteristics of Anglo-Saxon life; the form of our first speech. (3) The Northumbrian school of writers. Bede, our first historian, belongs to this school; but all his extant works are in Latin. The two great poets are Caedmon and Cynewulf. Northumbrian literature flourished between 650 and 850. In the year 867 Northumbria was conquered by the Danes, who destroyed the monasteries and the libraries containing our earliest literature. (4) The beginnings of English prose writing under Alfred (848-901). Our most important prose work of this age is the Anglo-Saxon Chronicle, which was revised and enlarged by Alfred, and which was continued for more than two centuries. It is the oldest historical record known to any European nation in its own tongue.

4

The Anglo-norman English

INTRODUCTION

THE NORMANS. The name Norman, which is a softened form of Northman, tells its own story. The men who bore the name came originally from Scandinavia,--bands of big, blond, fearless men cruising after plunder and adventure in their Viking ships, and bringing terror wherever they appeared. It was these same "Children of Woden" who, under the Danes' raven flag, had blotted out Northumbrian civilization in the ninth century. Later the same race of men came plundering along the French coast and conquered the whole northern country; but here the results were altogether different. Instead of blotting out a superior civilization, as the Danes had done, they promptly abandoned their own.

Their name of Normandy still clings to the new home; but all else that was Norse disappeared as the conquerors intermarried with the native Franks and accepted French ideals and spoke the French language. So rapidly did they adopt and improve the Roman civilization of the natives that, from a rude tribe of heathen Vikings, they had developed within a single century into the most polished and intellectual people in all Europe. The union of Norse and French (i.e. Roman-Gallic) blood had here produced a race having the best qualities of both,--the will power and energy of the one, the eager curiosity and vivid imagination of the other. When these Norman-French people appeared in Anglo-Saxon England they brought with them three noteworthy things: a lively Celtic disposition, a vigorous and progressive Latin civilization, and a Romance language. We are to think of the conquerors, therefore, as they thought and spoke of themselves in the Domesday Book and all their contemporary literature, not as Normans but as Franci, that is, Frenchmen.

THE CONQUEST. At the battle of Hastings (1066) the power of Harold, last of the Saxon kings, was broken, and William, duke of Normandy, became master of England. Of the completion of that stupendous Conquest which began at Hastings, and which changed the civilization of a whole nation, this is not the place to speak. We simply point out three great results of the Conquest which have a direct bearing on our literature. First, notwithstanding Caesar's legions and Augustine's monks, the Normans were the first to bring the culture and the practical ideals of Roman civilization home to the English people; and this at a critical time, when England had produced her best, and her own literature and civilization had already begun to decay. Second, they forced upon England the national idea, that is, a strong, centralized government to replace the loose authority of a Saxon chief over his tribesmen. And the world's history shows that without a great nationality a great literature is impossible. Third, they brought to England the wealth of a new language and literature, and our English gradually absorbed both. For three centuries after Hastings French was the language of the upper classes, of courts and schools and literature; yet so tenaciously did the common people cling to their own strong speech that in the end English absorbed almost the whole body of French words and became the language of the land. It was the welding of Saxon and French into one speech that produced the wealth of our modern English.

Naturally such momentous changes in a nation were not brought about suddenly. At first Normans and Saxons lived apart in the relation of masters and servants, with more or less contempt on one side and hatred on the other; but in an astonishingly short time these two races were drawn powerfully together, like two men of different dispositions who are often led into a steadfast friendship by the attraction of opposite qualities, each supplying what the other lacks. The Anglo-Saxon Chronicle, which was continued for a century after Hastings, finds much to praise in the conquerors; on the other hand the Normans, even before the Conquest, had no great love for the French nation. After conquering England they began to regard it as home and speedily developed a new sense of nationality. Geoffrey's popular History, written less than a century after the Conquest, made conquerors and conquered alike proud of their country by its stories of heroes who, curiously enough, were neither Norman nor Saxon, but creations of the native Celts. Thus does literature, whether in a battle song or a history, often play the chief role in the development of nationality. Once the mutual distrust was overcome the two races gradually united, and out of this union of Saxons and Normans came the new English life and literature.

LITERARY IDEALS OF THE NORMANS. The change in the life of the conquerors from Norsemen to Normans, from Vikings to Frenchmen, is shown most clearly in the literature which they brought with them to England. The old Norse strength and grandeur, the magnificent sagas telling of the tragic struggles of men and gods, which still stir us profoundly,--these have all disappeared. In their place is a bright, varied, talkative literature, which runs to endless verses, and which makes a wonderful romance out of every subject it touches. The theme may be religion or love or chivalry or history, the deeds of Alexander or the misdeeds of a monk; but the author's purpose never varies. He must tell a romantic story and amuse his audience; and the more wonders and impossibilities he relates, the more surely is he believed. We are reminded, in reading, of the native Gauls, who would stop every traveler and compel him to tell a story ere he passed on. There was more of the Gaul than of the Norseman in the conquerors, and far more of fancy than of thought or feeling in their literature. If you would see this in concrete form, read the Chanson de Roland, the French national epic (which the Normans first put into literary form), in contrast with Beowulf, which voices the Saxon's thought and feeling before the profound mystery of human life. It is not our purpose to discuss the evident merits or the serious defects of Norman-French literature, but only to point out two facts which impress the student, namely, that Anglo-Saxon literature was at one time enormously superior to the French, and that the latter, with its evident inferiority, absolutely replaced the former. "The fact is too often ignored," says Professor Schofield, "that before 1066 the Anglo-Saxons had a body of native literature distinctly superior to any which the Normans or French could boast at that time; their prose especially was unparalleled for extent and power in any European vernacular." Why, then, does this superior literature disappear and for nearly three centuries French remain supreme, so much so that writers on English soil, even when they do not use the French language, still slavishly copy the French models?

To understand this curious phenomenon it is necessary only to remember the relative conditions of the two races who lived side by side in England. On the one hand the Anglo-Saxons were a conquered people, and without liberty a great literature is impossible. The inroads of the Danes and their own tribal wars had already destroyed much of their writings, and in their new condition of servitude they could hardly preserve what remained. The conquering Normans, on the other hand, represented the civilization of France, which country, during the early Middle Ages, was the literary and educational center of all Europe. They came to England at a time when the idea of nationality was dead, when culture had almost vanished, when Englishmen lived apart in narrow isolation; and they brought with them law, culture, the prestige of success, and above all the strong impulse to share in the great world's work and to join in the moving currents of the world's history. Small wonder, then, that the young Anglo-Saxons felt the quickening of this new life and turned naturally to the cultured and progressive Normans as their literary models.

LITERATURE OF THE NORMAN PERIOD

In the Advocates' Library at Edinburgh there is a beautifully illuminated manuscript, written about 1330, which gives us an excellent picture of the literature of the Norman period. In examining it we are to remember that literature was in the hands of the clergy and nobles; that the common people could not read, and had only a few songs and ballads for their literary portion. We are to remember also that parchments were scarce and very expensive, and that a single manuscript often contained all the reading matter of a castle or a village. Hence this old manuscript is as suggestive as a modern library. It contains over forty distinct works, the great bulk of them being romances. There are metrical or verse romances of French and Celtic and English heroes, like Roland, Arthur and Tristram, and Bevis of Hampton. There are stories of Alexander, the Greek romance of "Flores and Blanchefleur," and a collection of Oriental tales called "The Seven Wise Masters." There are legends of the Virgin and the saints, a paraphrase of Scripture, a treatise on the seven deadly sins, some Bible history, a dispute among birds concerning women, a love song or two, a vision of Purgatory, a vulgar story with a Gallic flavor, a chronicle of English kings and

Norman barons, and a political satire. There are a few other works, similarly incongruous, crowded together in this typical manuscript, which now gives mute testimony to the literary taste of the times.

Obviously it is impossible to classify such a variety. We note simply that it is mediaeval in spirit, and French in style and expression; and that sums up the age. All the scholarly works of the period, like William of Malmesbury's History, and Anselm's Cur Deus Homo, and Roger Bacon's Opus Majus, the beginning of modern experimental science, were written in Latin; while nearly all other works were written in French, or else were English copies or translations of French originals. Except for the advanced student, therefore, they hardly belong to the story of English literature. We shall note here only one or two marked literary types, like the Riming Chronicle (or verse history) and the Metrical Romance, and a few writers whose work has especial significance.

GEOFFREY OF MONMOUTH. (d. 1154). Geoffrey's Historia Regum Britanniae is noteworthy, not as literature, but rather as a source book from which many later writers drew their literary materials. Among the native Celtic tribes an immense number of legends, many of them of exquisite beauty, had been preserved through four successive conquests of Britain. Geoffrey, a Welsh monk, collected some of these legends and, aided chiefly by his imagination, wrote a complete history of the Britons. His alleged authority was an ancient manuscript in the native Welsh tongue containing the lives and deeds of all their kings, from Brutus, the alleged founder of Britain, down to the coming of Julius Caesar. From this Geoffrey wrote his history, down to the death of Cadwalader in 689.

The "History" is a curious medley of pagan and Christian legends, of chronicle, comment, and pure invention,--all recorded in minute detail and with a gravity which makes it clear that Geoffrey had no conscience, or else was a great joker. As history the whole thing is rubbish; but it was extraordinarily successful at the time and made all who heard it, whether Normans or Saxons, proud of their own country. It is interesting to us because it gave a new direction to the literature of England by showing the wealth of poetry and romance that lay in its own traditions of Arthur and his knights. Shakespeare's King Lear, Malory's Morte d'Arthur, and Tennyson's Idylls of the King were founded on the work of this monk, who had the genius to put unwritten Celtic tradition in the enduring form of Latin prose.

WORK OF THE FRENCH WRITERS. The French literature of the Norman period is interesting chiefly because of the avidity with which foreign writers seized upon the native legends and made them popular in England. Until Geoffrey's preposterous chronicle appeared, these legends had not been used to any extent as literary material. Indeed, they were scarcely known in England, though familiar to French and Italian minstrels. Legends of Arthur and his court were probably first taken to Brittany by Welsh emigrants in the fifth and sixth centuries. They became immensely popular wherever they were told, and they were slowly carried by minstrels and story-tellers all over Europe. That they had never received literary form or recognition was due to a peculiarity of mediaeval literature, which required that every tale should have some ancient authority behind it. Geoffrey met this demand by creating an historical manuscript of Welsh history. That was enough for the age. With Geoffrey and his alleged manuscript to rest upon, the Norman-French writers were free to use the fascinating stories which had been-for centuries in the possession of their wandering minstrels. Geoffrey's Latin history was put into French verse by Gaimar (c. 1150) and by Wace (c. 1155), and from these French versions the work was first translated into English. From about 1200 onward Arthur and Guinevere and the matchless band of Celtic heroes that we meet later (1470) in Malory's Morte d' Arthur became the permanent possession of our literature.

LAYAMON'S BRUT (c. 1200). This is the most important of the English riming chronicles, that is, history related in the form of doggerel verse, probably because poetry is more easily memorized than prose. We give here a free rendering of selected lines at the beginning of the poem, which tell us all we know of Layamon, the first who ever wrote as an Englishman for Englishmen, including in the term all who loved England and called it home, no matter where their ancestors were born.

Now there was a priest in the land named Layamon. He was son of Leovenath--may God be gracious unto him. He dwelt at Ernley, at a noble church on Severn's bank. He read many books, and it came to his mind to tell the noble deeds of the English. Then he began to journey far and wide over the land to procure noble books for authority. He took the English book that Saint Bede made, another in Latin that Saint Albin made, and a third book that a French clerk made, named Wace. Layamon laid these works before him and turned the leaves;

lovingly he beheld them. Pen he took, and wrote on book-skin, and made the three books into one.

The poem begins with the destruction of Troy and the flight of "AEneas the duke" into Italy. Brutus, a great-grandson of AEneas, gathers his people and sets out to find a new land in the West. Then follows the founding of the Briton kingdom, and the last third of the poem, which is over thirty thousand lines in length, is taken up with the history of Arthur and his knights. If the Brut had no merits of its own, it would still interest us, for it marks the first appearance of the Arthurian legends in our own tongue. A single selection is given here from Arthur's dying speech, familiar to us in Tennyson's Morte d'Arthur. The reader will notice here two things: first, that though the poem is almost pure Anglo-Saxon, our first speech has already dropped many inflections and is more easily read than Beowulf; second, that French influence is already at work in Layamon's rimes and assonances, that is, the harmony resulting from using the same vowel sound in several successive lines:

And ich wulle varen to Avalun: And I will fare to Avalun,

To vairest alre maidene, To fairest of all maidens,

To Argante there quene, To Argante the queen,

Alven swithe sceone. An elf very beautiful.

And heo seal mine wunden And she shall my wounds

Makien alle isunde, Make all sound;

Al hal me makien All whole me make

Mid haleweiye drenchen. With healing drinks.

And seothe ich cumen wulle And again will I come

To mine kiueriche To my kingdom

And wunien mid Brutten And dwell with Britons

Mid muchelere wunne. With mickle joy.

Aefne than worden Even (with) these words

Ther com of se wenden There came from the sea

That wes an sceort bat lithen, A short little boat gliding,

Sceoven mid uthen, Shoved by the waves;

And twa wimmen ther inne, And two women therein,

Wunderliche idihte. Wondrously attired.
And heo nomen Arthur anan And they took Arthur anon
And an eovste hine vereden And bore him hurriedly,
And softe hine adun leiden, And softly laid him down,
And forth gunnen lithen. And forth gan glide.

METRICAL ROMANCES. Love, chivalry, and religion, all pervaded by the spirit of romance,--these are the three great literary ideals which find expression in the metrical romances. Read these romances now, with their knights and fair ladies, their perilous adventures and tender love-making, their minstrelsy and tournaments and gorgeous cavalcades,--as if humanity were on parade, and life itself were one tumultuous holiday in the open air,--and you have an epitome of the whole childish, credulous soul of the Middle Ages. The Normans first brought this type of romance into England, and so popular did it become, so thoroughly did it express the romantic spirit of the time, that it speedily overshadowed all other forms of literary expression.

Though the metrical romances varied much in form and subject-matter, the general type remains the same,--a long rambling poem or series of poems treating of love or knightly adventure or both. Its hero is a knight; its characters are fair ladies in distress, warriors in armor, giants, dragons, enchanters, and various enemies of Church and State; and its emphasis is almost invariably on love, religion, and duty as defined by chivalry. In the French originals of these romances the lines were a definite length, the meter exact, and rimes and assonances were both used to give melody. In England this metrical system came in contact with the uneven lines, the strong accent and alliteration of the native songs; and it is due to the gradual union of the two systems, French and Saxon, that our English became capable of the melody and amazing variety of verse forms which first find expression in Chaucer's poetry. In the enormous number of these verse romances we note three main divisions, according to subject, into the romances (or the so-called matter) of France, Rome, and Britain. The matter of France deals largely with the exploits of Charlemagne and his peers, and the chief of these Carlovingian cycles is the Chanson de Roland, the national epic, which celebrates the heroism of Roland in his last fight against the Saracens at Ronceval. Originally these romances were called Chansons de Geste; and the name is significant as indicating that the poems were originally short songs celebrating the deeds (gesta) of well-known heroes. Later the various songs concerning one hero were gathered together and the Geste became an epic, like the Chanson de Roland, or a kind of continued ballad story, hardly deserving the name of epic, like the Geste of Robin Hood.

The matter of Rome consisted largely of tales from Greek and Roman sources; and the two great cycles of these romances deal with the deeds of Alexander, a favorite hero, and the siege of Troy, with which the Britons thought they had some historic connection. To these were added a large number of tales from Oriental sources; and in the exuberant imagination of the latter we see the influence which the Saracens--those nimble wits who gave us our first modern sciences and who still reveled in the Arabian Nights--had begun to exercise on the literature of Europe.

To the English reader, at least, the most interesting of the romances are those which deal with the exploits of Arthur and his Knights of the Round Table,--the richest storehouse of romance which our literature has ever found. There were many cycles of Arthurian romances, chief of which are those of Gawain, Launcelot, Merlin, the Quest of the Holy Grail, and the Death of Arthur. In preceding sections we have seen how these fascinating romances were used by Geoffrey and the French writers, and how, through the French, they found their way into English, appearing first in our speech in Layamon's Brut. The point to remember is that, while the legends are Celtic in origin, their literary form is due to French poets, who originated the metrical romance. All our early English romances are either copies or translations of the French; and this is true not only of the matter of France and Rome, but of Celtic heroes like Arthur, and English heroes like Guy of Warwick and Robin Hood.

The most interesting of all Arthurian romances are those of the Gawain cycle, and of these the story of Sir Gawain and the Green Knight is best worth reading, for many reasons. First, though the material is taken from French sources, the English workmanship is the finest of our early romances. Second, the unknown author of this romance probably wrote also "The Pearl," and is the greatest English poet of the Norman period. Third, the poem itself with its dramatic interest, its vivid descriptions, and its moral purity, is one of the most delightful old romances in any language.

In form Sir Gawain is an interesting combination of French and Saxon elements. It is written in an elaborate stanza combining meter and alliteration. At the end of each stanza is a rimed refrain, called by the French a "tail rime." We give here a brief outline of the story; but if the reader desires the poem itself, he is advised to begin with a modern version, as the original is in the West Midland dialect and is exceedingly difficult to follow.

On New Year's day, while Arthur and his knights are keeping the Yuletide feast at Camelot, a gigantic knight in green enters the banquet hall on horseback and challenges the bravest knight present to an exchange of blows; that is, he will expose his neck to a blow of his own big battle-ax, if any knight will agree to abide a blow in return. After some natural consternation and a fine speech by Arthur, Gawain accepts the challenge, takes the battle-ax, and with one blow sends the giant's head rolling through the hall. The Green Knight, who is evidently a terrible magician, picks up his head and mounts his horse. He holds out his head and the ghastly lips speak, warning Gawain to be faithful to his promise and to seek through the world till he finds the Green Chapel. There, on next New Year's day, the Green Knight will meet him and return the blow.

The second canto of the poem describes Gawain's long journey through the wilderness on his steed Gringolet, and his adventures with storm and cold, with, wild beasts and monsters, as he seeks in vain for the Green Chapel. On Christmas eve, in the midst of a vast forest, he offers a prayer to "Mary, mildest mother so dear," and is rewarded by sight of a great castle. He enters and is royally entertained by the host, an aged hero, and by his wife, who is the most beautiful woman the knight ever beheld. Gawain learns that he is at last near the Green Chapel, and settles down for a little comfort after his long quest.

The next canto shows the life in the castle, and describes a curious compact between the host, who goes hunting daily, and the knight, who remains in the castle to entertain the young wife. The compact is that at night each man shall give the other whatever good thing he obtains during the day. While the host is hunting, the young woman tries in vain to induce Gawain to make love to her, and ends by giving him a kiss. When the host returns and gives his guest the game he has killed Gawain returns the kiss. On the third day, her temptations having twice failed, the lady offers Gawain a ring, which he refuses; but when she offers a magic green girdle that will preserve the wearer from death, Gawain, who remembers the giant's ax so soon to fall on his neck, accepts the girdle as a "jewel for the jeopardy" and promises the lady to keep the gift secret. Here, then, are two conflicting compacts. When the host returns and offers his game, Gawain returns the kiss but says nothing of the green girdle.

The last canto brings our knight to the Green Chapel, after he is repeatedly warned to turn back in the face of certain death. The Chapel is a terrible place in the midst of desolation; and as Gawain approaches he hears a terrifying sound, the grating of steel on stone, where the giant is sharpening a new battle-ax. The Green Knight appears, and Gawain, true to his compact, offers his neck for the blow. Twice the ax swings harmlessly; the third time it falls on his shoulder and wounds him. Whereupon Gawain jumps for his armor, draws his sword, and warns the giant that the compact calls for only one blow, and that, if another is offered, he will defend himself.

Then the Green Knight explains things. He is lord of the castle where Gawain has been entertained for days past. The first two swings of the ax were harmless because Gawain had been true to his compact and twice returned the kiss. The last blow had wounded him because he concealed the gift of the green girdle, which belongs to the Green Knight and was woven by his wife. Moreover, the whole thing has been arranged by Morgain the fay-woman (an enemy of Queen Guinevere, who appears often in the Arthurian romances). Full of shame, Gawain throws back the gift and is ready to atone for his deception; but the Green Knight thinks he has already atoned, and presents the green girdle as a free gift. Gawain returns to Arthur's court, tells the whole story frankly, and ever after that the knights of the Round Table wear a green girdle in his honor.

THE PEARL. In the same manuscript with "Sir Gawain" are found three other remarkable poems, written about 1350, and known to us, in order, as "The Pearl," "Cleanness," and "Patience." The first is the most beautiful, and received its name from the translator and editor, Richard Morris, in 1864. "Patience" is a paraphrase of the book of Jonah; "Cleanness" moralizes on the basis of Bible stories; but "The Pearl" is an intensely human and realistic picture of a father's grief for his little daughter Margaret, "My precious perle wythouten spot." It is the saddest of all our early poems.

On the grave of his little one, covered over with flowers, the father pours out his love and grief till, in the summer stillness, he falls asleep, while we hear in the sunshine the drowsy hum of insects and the faraway sound of the reapers' sickles. He dreams there, and the dream grows into a vision beautiful. His body lies still upon the grave while his spirit goes to a land, exquisite beyond all words, where he comes suddenly upon a stream that he cannot cross. As he wanders along the bank, seeking in vain for a ford, a marvel rises before his eyes, a crystal cliff, and seated beneath it a little maiden who raises a happy, shining face,--the face of his little Margaret.

More then me lyste my drede aros,
I stod full stylle and dorste not calle;
Wyth yghen open and mouth ful clos,
I stod as hende as hawk in halle.

He dares not speak for fear of breaking the spell; but sweet as a lily she comes down the crystal stream's bank to meet and speak with him, and tell him of the happy life of heaven and how to live to be worthy of it. In his joy he listens, forgetting all his grief; then the heart of the man cries out for its own, and he struggles to cross the stream to join her. In the struggle the dream vanishes; he wakens to find his eyes wet and his head on the little mound that marks the spot where his heart is buried.

From the ideals of these three poems, and from peculiarities of style and meter, it is probable that their author wrote also Sir Gawain and the Green Knight. If so, the unknown author is the one genius of the age whose poetry of itself has power to interest us, and who stands between Cynewulf and Chaucer as a worthy follower of the one and forerunner of the other.

MISCELLANEOUS LITERATURE OF THE NORMAN PERIOD. It is well-nigh impossible to classify the remaining literature of this period, and very little of it is now read, except by advanced students. Those interested in the development of "transition" English will find in the Ancren Riwle, i.e. "Rule of the Anchoresses" (c. 1225), the most beautiful bit of old English prose ever written. It is a book of excellent religious advice and comfort, written for three ladies who wished to live a religious life, without, however, becoming nuns or entering any religious orders. The author was Bishop Poore of Salisbury, according to Morton, who first edited this old classic in 1853. Orm's Ormulum, written soon after the Brut, is a paraphrase of the gospel lessons for the year, somewhat after the manner of Caedmon's Paraphrase, but without any of Caedmon's poetic fire and originality. Cursor Mundi (c. 1320) is a very long poem which makes a kind of metrical romance out of Bible history and shows the whole dealing of God with man from Creation to Domesday. It is interesting as showing a parallel to the cycles of miracle plays, which attempt to cover the same vast ground. They were forming in this age; but we will study them later, when we try to understand the rise of the drama in England. Besides these greater works, an enormous number of fables and satires appeared in this age, copied or translated from the French, like the metrical romances. The most famous of these are "The Owl and the Nightingale,"--a long debate between the two birds, one representing the gay side of life, the other the sterner side of law and morals,--and "Land of Cockaygne," i.e. "Luxury Land," a keen satire on monks and monastic religion.

While most of the literature of the time was a copy of the French and was intended only for the upper classes, here and there were singers who made ballads for the common people; and these, next to the metrical romances, are the most interesting and significant of all the works of the Norman period. On account of its obscure origin and its oral transmission, the ballad is always the most difficult of literary subjects. We make here only three suggestions, which may well be borne in mind: that ballads were produced continually in England from Anglo-Saxon times until the seventeenth century; that for centuries they were the only really popular literature; and that in the ballads alone one is able to understand the common people. Read, for instance, the ballads of the "merrie greenwood men," which gradually collected into the Geste of Robin Hood, and you will understand better, perhaps, than from reading many histories what the common people of England felt and thought while their lords and masters were busy with impossible metrical romances. In these songs speaks the heart of the English folk. There is lawlessness indeed; but this seems justified by the oppression of the times and by the barbarous severity of the game laws. An intense hatred of shams and injustice lurks in every song; but the hatred is saved from bitterness by the humor with which captives, especially rich churchmen, are solemnly lectured by the bandits, while they squirm at sight of devilish tortures prepared before their eyes in order to make them give up their golden purses; and the scene generally ends in a bit of wild horse-play. There is fighting enough, and ambush and sudden death lurk at every turn of the lonely roads; but there is also a rough, honest chivalry for women, and a generous sharing of plunder with the poor and needy. All literature is but a dream expressed, and "Robin Hood" is the dream of an ignorant and oppressed but essentially noble people, struggling and determined to be free.

Far more poetical than the ballads, and more interesting even than the romances, are the little lyrics of the period,--those tears and smiles of long ago that crystallized into poems, to tell us that the hearts of men are alike in all ages. Of these, the best known are the "Luve Ron" (love rune or letter) of Thomas de Hales (c. 1250); "Springtime" (c. 1300), beginning "Lenten (spring) ys come with luve to toune"; and the melodious love song "Alysoun," written at the end of the thirteenth century by some unknown poet who heralds the coming of Chaucer:

Bytuene Mersh and Averil,
When spray biginneth to springe
The lutel foul hath hire wyl
On hyre lud to synge.
Ich libbe in love longinge
For semlokest of all thinge.
She may me blisse bringe;
Icham in hire baundoun.
An hendy hap ichabbe yhent,
Ichot from hevene it is me sent,
From alle wymmen mi love is lent
And lyht on Alysoun.

SUMMARY OF THE NORMAN PERIOD. The Normans were originally a hardy race of sea rovers inhabiting Scandinavia. In the tenth century they conquered a part of northern France, which is still called Normandy, and rapidly adopted French civilization and the French language. Their conquest of Anglo-Saxon England under William, Duke of Normandy, began with the battle of Hastings in 1066. The literature which they brought to England is remarkable for its bright, romantic tales of love and adventure, in marked contrast with the strength and somberness of Anglo-Saxon poetry. During the three centuries following Hastings, Normans and Saxons gradually united. The Anglo-Saxon speech simplified itself by dropping most of its Teutonic inflections, absorbed eventually a large part of the French vocabulary, and became our English language. English literature is also a combination of French and Saxon elements. The three chief effects of the conquest were (1) the bringing of Roman civilization to England; (2) the growth of nationality, i.e. a strong centralized government, instead of the loose union of Saxon tribes; (3) the new language and literature, which were proclaimed in Chaucer.

At first the new literature was remarkably varied, but of small intrinsic worth; and very little of it is now read. In our study we have noted: (1) Geoffrey's History, which is valuable as a source book of literature, since it contains the native Celtic legends of Arthur. (2) The work of the French writers, who made the Arthurian legends popular. (3) Riming Chronicles, i.e. history in doggerel verse, like Layamon's Brut. (4) Metrical Romances, or tales in verse. These were numerous, and of four classes: (a) the Matter of France, tales centering about Charlemagne and his peers, chief of which is the Chanson de Roland; (b) Matter of Greece and Rome, an endless series of fabulous tales about Alexander, and about the Fall of Troy; (c) Matter of England, stories of Bevis of Hampton, Guy of Warwick, Robin Hood, etc.; (d) Matter of Britain, tales having for their heroes Arthur and his knights of the Round Table. The best of these romances is Sir Gawain and the Green Knight. (5) Miscellaneous literature,--the Ancren Riwle, our best piece of early English prose; Orm's Ormulum; Cursor Mundi, with its suggestive parallel to the Miracle plays; and ballads, like King Horn and the Robin Hood songs, which were the only poetry of the common people.

5

The Revival in Literature

HISTORY OF THE PERIOD

POLITICAL CHANGES. The century and a half following the death of Chaucer (1400-1550) is the most volcanic period of English history. The land is swept by vast changes, inseparable from the rapid accumulation of national power; but since power is the most dangerous of gifts until men have learned to control it, these changes seem at first to have no specific aim or direction. Henry V--whose erratic yet vigorous life, as depicted by Shakespeare, was typical of the life of his times--first let Europe feel the might of the new national spirit. To divert that growing and unruly spirit from rebellion at home, Henry led his army abroad, in the apparently impossible attempt to gain for himself three things: a French wife, a French revenue, and the French crown itself. The battle of Agincourt was fought in 1415, and five years later, by the Treaty of Troyes, France acknowledged his right to all his outrageous demands.

The uselessness of the terrific struggle on French soil is shown by the rapidity with which all its results were swept away. When Henry died in 1422, leaving his son heir to the crowns of France and England, a magnificent recumbent statue with head of pure silver was placed in Westminster Abbey to commemorate his victories. The silver head was presently stolen, and the loss is typical of all that he had struggled for. His son, Henry VI, was but the shadow of a king, a puppet in the hands of powerful nobles, who seized the power of England and turned it to self-destruction. Meanwhile all his foreign possessions were won back by the French under the magic leadership of Joan of Arç. Cade's Rebellion (1450) and the bloody Wars of the Roses (1455-1485) are names to show how the energy of England was violently destroying itself, like a great engine that has lost its balance wheel. The frightful reign of Richard III followed, which had, however, this redeeming quality, that it marked the end of civil wars and the self-destruction of feudalism, and made possible a new growth of English national sentiment under the popular Tudors.

In the long reign of Henry VIII the changes are less violent, but have more purpose and significance. His age is marked by a steady increase in the national power at home and abroad, by the entrance of the Reformation "by a side door," and by the final separation of England from all ecclesiastical bondage in Parliament's famous Act of Supremacy. In previous reigns chivalry and the old feudal system had practically been banished; now monasticism, the third mediaeval institution with its mixed evil and good, received its death-blow in the wholesale suppression of the monasteries and the removal of abbots from the House of Lords. Notwithstanding the evil character of the king and the hypocrisy of proclaiming such a creature the head of any church or the defender of any faith, we acquiesce silently in Stubb's declaration[105] that "the world owes some of its greatest debts to men from whose memory the world recoils."

While England during this period was in constant political strife, yet rising slowly, like the spiral flight of an eagle, to heights of national greatness, intellectually it moved forward with bewildering rapidity. Printing was brought to England by Caxton (c. 1476), and for the first time in history it was possible for a book or an idea to reach the whole nation. Schools and universities were established in place of the old monasteries; Greek ideas and Greek culture came to England in the Renaissance, and man's spiritual freedom was proclaimed in the Reformation. The great names of the period are numerous and significant, but literature is strangely silent. Probably the very turmoil of the age prevented any literary development, for literature is one of the arts of peace; it requires quiet and meditation rather than activity, and the stirring life of the Renaissance had first to be lived before it could express itself in the new literature of the Elizabethan period.

THE REVIVAL OF LEARNING. The Revival of Learning denotes, in its broadest sense, that gradual enlightenment of the human mind after the darkness of the Middle Ages. The names Renaissance and Humanism, which are often applied to the same movement, have properly a narrower significance. The term Renaissance, though used by many writers "to denote the whole transition from the Middle Ages to the modern world," is more correctly applied to the revival of art resulting from the discovery and imitation of classic models in the fourteenth and fifteenth centuries. Humanism applies to the revival of classic literature, and was so called by its leaders, following the example of Petrarch, because they held that the study of the classics, literae humaniores,--i.e. the "more human writings," rather than the old theology,--was the best means of promoting the largest human interests. We use the term Revival of Learning to cover the whole movement, whose essence was, according to Lamartine, that "man discovered himself and the universe," and, according to Taine, that man, so long blinded, "had suddenly opened his eyes and seen."

We shall understand this better if we remember that in the Middle Ages man's whole world consisted of the narrow Mediterranean and the nations that clustered about it; and that this little world seemed bounded by impassable barriers, as if God had said to their sailors, "Hitherto shalt thou come, but no farther." Man's mind also was bounded by the same narrow lines. His culture as measured by the great deductive system of Scholasticism consisted not in discovery, but rather in accepting certain principles and traditions established by divine and ecclesiastical authority as the basis of all truth. These were his Pillars of Hercules, his mental and spiritual bounds that he must not pass, and within these, like a child playing with lettered blocks, he proceeded to build his intellectual system. Only as we remember their limitations can we appreciate the heroism of these toilers of the Middle Ages, giants in intellect, yet playing with children's toys; ignorant of the laws and forces of the universe, while debating the essence and locomotion of angels; eager to learn, yet forbidden to enter fresh fields in the right of free exploration and the joy of individual discovery.

The Revival stirred these men as the voyages of Da Gama and Columbus stirred the mariners of the Mediterranean. First came the sciences and inventions of the Arabs, making their way slowly against the prejudice of the authorities, and opening men's eyes to the unexplored realms of nature. Then came the flood of Greek literature which the new art of printing carried swiftly to every school in Europe, revealing a new world of poetry and philosophy. Scholars flocked to the universities, as adventurers to the new world of America, and there the old authority received a deathblow. Truth only was authority; to search for truth everywhere, as men sought for new lands and gold and the fountain of youth,--that was the new spirit which awoke in Europe with the Revival of Learning.

LITERATURE OF THE REVIVAL

The hundred and fifty years of the Revival period are singularly destitute of good literature. Men's minds were too much occupied with religious and political changes and with the rapid enlargement of the mental horizon to find time for that peace and leisure which are essential for literary results. Perhaps, also, the floods of newly discovered classics, which occupied scholars and the new printing presses alike, were by their very power and abundance a discouragement of native talent. Roger Ascham (1515-1568), a famous classical scholar, who published a book called Toxophilus (School of Shooting) in 1545, expresses in his preface, or "apology," a very widespread dissatisfaction over the neglect of native literature when he says, "And as for ye Latin or greke tongue, every thing is so excellently done in them, that none can do better: In the Englysh tonge contrary, every thinge in a maner so meanly, both for the matter and handelynge, that no man can do worse."

On the Continent, also, this new interest in the classics served to check the growth of native literatures. In Italy especially, for a full century after the brilliant age of Dante and Petrarch, no great literature was produced, and the Italian language itself seemed to go backward. The truth is that these great writers were, like Chaucer, far in advance of their age, and that the mediaeval mind was too narrow, too scantily furnished with ideas to produce a varied literature. The fifteenth century was an age of preparation, of learning the beginnings of science, and of getting acquainted with the great ideals,--the stern law, the profound philosophy, the suggestive mythology, and the noble poetry of the Greeks and Romans. So the mind was furnished with ideas for a new literature.

With the exception of Malory's Morte d'Arthur (which is still mediaeval in spirit) the student will find little of interest in the literature of this period. We give here a brief summary of the men and the books most "worthy of remembrance"; but for the real literature of the Renaissance one must go forward a century and a half to the age of Elizabeth.

The two greatest books which appeared in England during this period are undoubtedly Erasmus's Praise of Folly (Encomium Moriae) and More's Utopia, the famous "Kingdom of Nowhere." Both were written in Latin, but were speedily translated into all European languages. The Praise of Folly is like a song of victory for the New Learning, which had driven away vice, ignorance, and superstition, the three foes of humanity. It was published in 1511 after the accession of Henry VIII. Folly is represented as donning cap and bells and mounting a pulpit, where the vice and cruelty of kings, the selfishness and ignorance of the clergy, and the foolish standards of education are satirized without mercy.

More's Utopia, published in 1516, is a powerful and original study of social conditions, unlike anything which had ever appeared in any literature. In our own day we have seen its influence in Bellamy's Looking Backward, an enormously successful book, which recently set people to thinking of the unnecessary cruelty of modern social conditions. More learns from a sailor, one of Amerigo Vespucci's companions, of a wonderful Kingdom of Nowhere, in which all questions of labor, government, society, and religion have been easily settled by simple justice and common sense. In this Utopia we find for the first time, as the foundations of civilized society, the three great words, Liberty, Fraternity, Equality, which retained their inspiration through all the violence of the French Revolution and which are still the unrealized ideal of every free government. As he hears of this wonderful country More wonders why, after fifteen centuries of Christianity, his own land is so little civilized; and as we read the book to-day we ask ourselves the same question. The splendid dream is still far from being realized; yet it seems as if any nation could become Utopia in a single generation, so simple and just are the requirements.

Greater than either of these books, in its influence upon the common people, is Tyndale's translation of the New Testament (1525), which fixed a standard of good English, and at the same time brought that standard not only to scholars but to the homes of the common people. Tyndale made his translation from the original Greek, and later translated parts of the Old Testament from the Hebrew. Much of Tyndale's work was included in Cranmer's Bible, known also as the Great Bible, in 1539, and was read in every parish church in England. It was the foundation for the Authorized Version, which appeared nearly a century later and became the standard for the whole English-speaking race.

WYATT AND SURREY. In 1557 appeared probably the first printed collection of miscellaneous English poems, known as Tottel's Miscellany. It contained the work of the so-called courtly makers, or poets, which had hitherto circulated in manuscript form for the benefit of the court. About half of these poems were the work of Sir Thomas Wyatt (1503?-1542) and of Henry Howard, Earl of Surrey (1517?-1547). Both together wrote amorous sonnets modeled after the Italians, introducing a new verse form which, although very difficult, has been a favorite ever since with our English poets. Surrey is noted, not for any especial worth or originality of his own poems, but rather for his translation of two books of Virgil "in strange meter." The strange meter was the blank verse, which had never before appeared in English. The chief literary work of these two men, therefore, is to introduce the sonnet and the blank verse,--one the most dainty, the other the most flexible and characteristic form of English poetry,--which in the hands of Shakespeare and Milton were used to make the world's masterpieces.

MALORY'S MORTE D'ARTHUR. The greatest English work of this period, measured by its effect on subsequent literature, is undoubtedly the Morte d'Arthur, a collection of the Arthurian romances told in simple and vivid prose. Of Sir Thomas Malory, the author, Caxton in his introduction says that he was a knight, and completed his work in 1470, fifteen years before Caxton printed it. The record adds that "he was the servant of Jesu both by day and night." Beyond that we know little except what may be inferred from the splendid work itself.

Malory groups the legends about the central idea of the search for the Holy Grail. Though many of the stories, like Tristram and Isolde, are purely pagan, Malory treats them all in such a way as to preserve the whole spirit of mediaeval Christianity as it has been preserved in no other work. It was to Malory rather than to Layamon or to the early French writers that Shakespeare and his contemporaries turned for their material; and in our own age he has supplied Tennyson and Matthew Arnold and Swinburne and Morris with the inspiration for the "Idylls of the King" and the "Death of Tristram" and the other exquisite poems which center about Arthur and the knights of his Round Table.

In subject-matter the book belongs to the mediaeval age; but Malory himself, with his desire to preserve the literary monuments of the past, belongs to the Renaissance; and he deserves our lasting gratitude for attempting to preserve the legends and poetry of Britain at a time when scholars were chiefly busy with the classics of Greece and Rome. As the Arthurian legends are one of the great recurring motives of English literature, Malory's work should be better known. His stories may be and should be told to every child as part of his literary inheritance. Then Malory may be read for his style and his English prose and his expression of the mediaeval spirit. And then the stories may be read again, in Tennyson's "Idylls," to show how those exquisite old fancies appeal to the minds of our modern poets.

SUMMARY OF THE REVIVAL OF LEARNING PERIOD. This transition period is at first one of decline from the Age of Chaucer, and then of intellectual preparation for the Age of Elizabeth. For a century and a half after Chaucer not a single great English work appeared, and the general standard of literature was very low. There are three chief causes to account for this: (1) the long war with France and the civil Wars of the Roses distracted attention from books and poetry, and destroyed of ruined many noble English families who had been friends and patrons of literature; (2) the Reformation in the latter part of the period filled men's minds with religious questions; (3) the Revival of Learning set scholars and literary men to an eager study of the classics, rather than to the creation of native literature. Historically the age is noticeable for its intellectual progress, for the introduction of printing, for the discovery of America, for the beginning of the Reformation, and for the growth of political power among the common people.

6

Literature in the Age of Elizabeth

HISTORY OF THE PERIOD

In the Age of Elizabeth all doubt seems to vanish from English history. After the reigns of Edward and Mary, with defeat and humiliation abroad and persecutions and rebellion at home, the accession of a popular sovereign was like the sunrise after a long night, and, in Milton's words, we suddenly see England, "a noble and puissant nation, rousing herself, like a strong man after sleep, and shaking her invincible locks." With the queen's character, a strange mingling of frivolity and strength which reminds one of that iron image with feet of clay, we have nothing whatever to do. It is the national life that concerns the literary student, since even a beginner must notice that any great development of the national life is invariably associated with a development of the national literature. It is enough for our purpose, therefore, to point out two facts: that Elizabeth, with all her vanity and inconsistency, steadily loved England and England's greatness; and that she inspired all her people with the unbounded patriotism which exults in Shakespeare, and with the personal devotion which finds a voice in the Faery Queen. Under her administration the English national life progressed by gigantic leaps rather than by slow historical process, and English literature reached the very highest point of its development. It is possible to indicate only a few general characteristics of this great age which had a direct bearing upon its literature.

CHARACTERISTICS OF THE ELIZABETHAN AGE. The most characteristic feature of the age was the comparative religious tolerance, which was due largely to the queen's influence. The frightful excesses of the religious war known as the Thirty Years' War on the

Continent found no parallel in England. Upon her accession Elizabeth found the whole kingdom divided against itself; the North was largely Catholic, while the southern counties were as strongly Protestant. Scotland had followed the Reformation in its own intense way, while Ireland remained true to its old religious traditions, and both countries were openly rebellious.

The court, made up of both parties, witnessed the rival intrigues of those who sought to gain the royal favor. It was due partly to the intense absorption of men's minds in religious questions that the preceding century, though an age of advancing learning, produced scarcely any literature worthy of the name. Elizabeth favored both religious parties, and presently the world saw with amazement Catholics and Protestants acting together as trusted counselors of a great sovereign. The defeat of the Spanish Armada established the Reformation as a fact in England, and at the same time united all Englishmen in a magnificent national enthusiasm. For the first time since the Reformation began, the fundamental question of religious toleration seemed to be settled, and the mind of man, freed from religious fears and persecutions, turned with a great creative impulse to other forms of activity. It is partly from this new freedom of the mind that the Age of Elizabeth received its great literary stimulus.

It was an age of comparative social contentment, in strong contrast with the days of Langland. The rapid increase of manufacturing towns gave employment to thousands who had before been idle and discontented. Increasing trade brought enormous wealth to England, and this wealth was shared to this extent, at least, that for the first time some systematic care for the needy was attempted. Parishes were made responsible for their own poor, and the wealthy were taxed to support them or give them employment. The increase of wealth, the improvement in living, the opportunities for labor, the new social content--these also are factors which help to account for the new literary activity. It is an age of dreams, of adventure, of unbounded enthusiasm springing from the new lands of fabulous riches revealed by English explorers. Drake sails around the world, shaping the mighty course which English colonizers shall follow through the centuries; and presently the young philosopher Bacon is saying confidently, "I have taken all knowledge for my province." The mind must search farther than the eye; with new, rich lands opened to the sight, the imagination must create new forms to people the new worlds. Hakluyt's famous Collection of Voyages, and Purchas, His Pilgrimage, were even more stimulating to the English imagination than to the English acquisitiveness. While her explorers search the new world for the Fountain of Youth, her poets are creating literary works that are young forever. Marston writes: "Why, man, all their dripping pans are pure gold.

The prisoners they take are fettered in gold; and as for rubies and diamonds, they goe forth on holydayes and gather 'hem by the seashore to hang on their children's coates." This comes nearer to being a description of Shakespeare's poetry than of the Indians in Virginia. Prospero, in The Tempest, with his control over the mighty powers and harmonies of nature, is only the literary dream of that science which had just begun to grapple with the forces of the universe. Cabot, Drake, Frobisher, Gilbert, Raleigh, Willoughby, Hawkins,--a score of explorers reveal a new earth to men's eyes, and instantly literature creates a new heaven to match it. So dreams and deeds increase side by side, and the dream is ever greater than the deed. That is the meaning of literature. To sum up, the Age of Elizabeth was a time of intellectual liberty, of growing intelligence and comfort among all classes, of unbounded patriotism, and of peace at home and abroad. For a parallel we must go back to the Age of Pericles in Athens, or of Augustus in Rome, or go forward a little to the magnificent court of Louis XIV, when Corneille, Racine, and Moliere brought the drama in France to the point where Marlowe, Shakespeare, and Jonson had left it in England half a century earlier.

Such an age of great thought and great action, appealing to the eyes as well as to the imagination and intellect, finds but one adequate literary expression; neither poetry nor the story can express the whole man,--his thought, feeling, action, and the resulting character; hence in the Age of Elizabeth literature turned instinctively to the drama and brought it rapidly to the highest stage of its development.

THE NON-DRAMATIC POETS OF THE ELIZABETHAN AGE

EDMUND SPENSER (1552-1599)

(Cuddie)

"Piers, I have piped erst so long with pain

That all mine oaten reeds been rent and wore,

And my poor Muse hath spent her spared store,

Yet little good hath got, and much less gain.

Such pleasaunce makes the grasshopper so poor,

And ligge so layd when winter doth her strain.

The dapper ditties that I wont devise,

To feed youth's fancy, and the flocking fry

Delghten much--what I the bet forthy?

They han the pleasure, I a slender prize:

I beat the bush, the birds to them do fly:

What good thereof to Cuddie can arise?

(Piers)

Cuddie, the praise is better than the price,

The glory eke much greater than the gain:..."

Shepherd's Calendar, October

In these words, with their sorrowful suggestion of Deor, Spenser reveals his own heart, unconsciously perhaps, as no biographer could possibly do. His life and work seem to center about three great influences, summed up in three names: Cambridge, where he grew acquainted with the classics and the Italian poets; London, where he experienced the glamour and the disappointment of court life; and Ireland, which steeped him in the beauty and imagery of old Celtic poetry and first gave him leisure to write his masterpiece.

LIFE. Of Spenser's early life and parentage we know little, except that he was born in East Smithfield, near the Tower of London, and was poor. His education began at the Merchant Tailors' School in London and was continued in Cambridge, where as a poor sizar and fag for wealthy students he earned a scant living. Here in the glorious world that only a poor scholar knows how to create for himself he read the classics, made acquaintance with the great Italian poets, and wrote numberless little poems of his own. Though Chaucer was his beloved master, his ambition was not to rival the Canterbury Tales, but rather to express the dream of English chivalry, much as Ariosto had done for Italy in Orlando Furioso. After leaving Cambridge (1576) Spenser went to the north of England, on some unknown work or quest. Here his chief occupation was to fall in love and to record his melancholy over the lost Rosalind in the Shepherd's Calendar. Upon his friend Harvey's advice he came to London, bringing his poems; and here he met Leicester, then at the height of royal favor, and the latter took him to live at Leicester House. Here he finished the Shepherd's Calendar, and here he met Sidney and all the queen's favorites. The court was full of intrigues, lying and flattery, and Spenser's opinion of his own uncomfortable position is best expressed in a few lines from "Mother Hubbard's Tale":

Full little knowest thou, that has not tried,

What hell it is, in suing long to bide:

To lose good days, that might be better spent;

To waste long nights in pensive discontent;

* * * * *

To fret thy soul with crosses and with cares;

To eat thy heart through comfortless despairs;

To fawn, to crouch, to wait, to ride, to run,

To spend, to give, to want, to be undone.

In 1580, through Leicester's influence, Spenser, who was utterly weary of his dependent position, was made secretary to Lord Grey, the queen's deputy in Ireland, and the third period of his life began. He accompanied his chief through one campaign of savage brutality in putting down an Irish rebellion, and was given an immense estate with the castle of Kilcolman, in Munster, which had been confiscated from Earl Desmond, one of the Irish leaders. His life here, where according to the terms of his grant he must reside as an English settler, he regarded as lonely exile:

My luckless lot,

That banished had myself, like wight forlore,

Into that waste, where I was quite forgot.

It is interesting to note here a gentle poet's view of the "unhappy island." After nearly sixteen years' residence he wrote his View of the State of Ireland (1596), his only prose work, in which he submits a plan for "pacifying the oppressed and rebellious people." This was to bring a huge force of cavalry and infantry into the country, give the Irish a brief time to submit, and after that to hunt them down like wild beasts. He calculated that cold, famine, and sickness would help the work of the sword, and that after the rebels had been well hounded for two winters the following summer would find the country peaceful. This plan, from the poet of harmony and beauty, was somewhat milder than the usual treatment of a brave people whose offense was that they loved liberty and religion. Strange as it may seem, the View was considered most statesmanlike, and was excellently well received in England.

In Kilcolman, surrounded by great natural beauty, Spenser finished the first three books of the Faery Queen. In 1589 Raleigh visited him, heard the poem with enthusiasm, hurried the poet off to London, and presented him to Elizabeth. The first three books met with instant success when published and were acclaimed as the greatest work in the English language. A yearly pension of fifty pounds was conferred by Elizabeth, but rarely paid, and the poet turned back to exile, that is, to Ireland again.

Soon after his return, Spenser fell in love with his beautiful Elizabeth, an Irish girl; wrote his Amoretti, or sonnets, in her honor; and afterwards represented her, in the Faery Queen, as the beautiful woman dancing among the Graces. In 1594 he married Elizabeth, celebrating his wedding with his "Epithalamion," one of the most beautiful wedding hymns in any language.

Spenser's next visit to London was in 1595, when he published "Astrophel," an elegy on the death of his friend Sidney, and three more books of the Faery Queen. On this visit he lived again at Leicester House, now occupied by the new favorite Essex, where he probably met Shakespeare and the other literary lights of the Elizabethan Age. Soon after his return to Ireland, Spenser was appointed Sheriff of Cork, a queer office for a poet, which probably brought about his undoing. The same year Tyrone's Rebellion broke out in Munster. Kilcolman, the ancient house of Desmond, was one of the first places attacked by the rebels, and Spenser barely escaped with his wife and two children. It is supposed that some unfinished parts of the Faery Queen were burned in the castle.

From the shock of this frightful experience Spenser never recovered. He returned to England heartbroken, and in the following year (1599) he died in an inn at Westminster. According to Ben Jonson he died "for want of bread"; but whether that is a poetic way of saying that he had lost his property or that he actually died of destitution, will probably never be known. He was buried beside his master Chaucer in Westminster Abbey, the poets of that age thronging to his funeral and, according to Camden, "casting their elegies and the pens that had written them into his tomb."

SPENSER'S WORKS. The Faery Queen is the great work upon which the poet's fame chiefly rests. The original plan of the poem included twenty-four books, each of which was to recount the adventure and triumph of a knight who represented a moral virtue. Spenser's purpose, as indicated in a letter to Raleigh which introduces the poem, is as follows:

> To pourtraict in Arthure, before he was king, the image of a brave Knight, perfected in the twelve private Morall Vertues, as Aristotle hath devised; which is the purpose of these first twelve bookes: which if I finde to be well accepted, I may be perhaps encoraged to frame the other part of Polliticke Vertues in his person, after that hee came to be king.

Each of the Virtues appears as a knight, fighting his opposing Vice, and the poem tells the story of the conflicts. It is therefore purely allegorical, not only in its personified virtues but also in its representation of life as a struggle between good and evil. In its strong moral element the poem differs radically from Orlando Furioso, upon which it was modeled. Spenser completed only six books, celebrating Holiness, Temperance, Chastity, Friendship, Justice, and Courtesy. We have also a fragment of the seventh, treating of Constancy; but the rest of this book was not written, or else was lost in the fire at Kilcolman. The first three books are by far the best; and judging by the way the interest lags and the allegory grows incomprehensible, it is perhaps as well for Spenser's reputation that the other eighteen books remained a dream.

ARGUMENT OF THE FAERY QUEEN. From the introductory letter we learn that the hero visits the queen's court in Fairy Land, while she is holding a twelve-days festival. On each day some distressed person appears unexpectedly, tells a woful story of dragons, of enchantresses, or of distressed beauty or virtue, and asks for a champion to right the wrong and to let the oppressed go free. Sometimes a knight volunteers or begs for the dangerous mission; again the duty is assigned by the queen; and the journeys and adventures of these knights are the subjects of the several books. The first recounts the adventures of the Redcross Knight, representing Holiness, and the lady Una, representing Religion. Their contests are symbolical of the world-wide struggle between virtue and faith on the one hand, and sin and heresy on the other. The second book tells the story of Sir Guyon, or Temperance; the third, of Britomartis, representing Chastity; the fourth, fifth, and sixth, of Cambel and Triamond (Friendship), Artegall (Justice), and Sir Calidore (Courtesy). Spenser's plan was a very elastic one and he filled up the measure of his narrative with everything that caught his fancy,--historical events and personages under allegorical masks, beautiful ladies, chivalrous knights, giants, monsters, dragons, sirens, enchanters, and adventures enough to stock a library of fiction. If you read Homer or Virgil, you know his subject in the first strong line; if you read Caedmon's Paraphrase or Milton's epic, the introduction gives you the theme; but Spenser's great poem--with the exception of a single line in the prologue, "Fierce warres and faithfull loves shall moralize my song"--gives hardly a hint of what is coming.

As to the meaning of the allegorical figures, one is generally in doubt. In the first three books the shadowy Faery Queen sometimes represents the glory of God and sometimes Elizabeth, who was naturally flattered by the parallel. Britomartis is also Elizabeth. The Redcross Knight is Sidney, the model Englishman. Arthur, who always appears to rescue the oppressed, is Leicester, which is another outrageous flattery. Una is sometimes religion and sometimes the Protestant Church; while Duessa represents Mary Queen of Scots, or general Catholicism. In the last three books Elizabeth appears again as Mercilla; Henry IV of France as Bourbon; the war in the Netherlands as the story of Lady Belge; Raleigh as Timias; the earls of Northumberland and Westmoreland (lovers of Mary or Duessa) as Blandamour and Paridell; and so on through the wide range of contemporary characters and events, till the allegory becomes as difficult to follow as the second part of Goethe's Faust.

POETICAL FORM. For the Faery Queen Spenser invented a new verse form, which has been called since his day the Spenserian stanza. Because of its rare beauty it has been much used by nearly all our poets in their best work. The new stanza was an improved form of Ariosto's ottava rima (i.e. eight-line stanza) and bears a close resemblance to one of Chaucer's most musical verse forms in the "Monk's Tale." Spenser's stanza is in nine lines, eight of five feet each and the last of six feet, riming ababbcbcc. A few selections from the first book, which is best worth reading, are reproduced here to show the style and melody of the verse.

A Gentle Knight was pricking on the plaine,
Ycladd in mightie armes and silver shielde,
Wherein old dints of deepe woundes did remaine
The cruell markes of many a bloody fielde;
Yet armes till that time did he never wield:
His angry steede did chide his foming bitt,
As much disdayning to the curbe to yield:
Full iolly knight he seemd, and faire did sitt,
As one for knightly giusts and fierce encounters fitt.

And on his brest a bloodie crosse he bore,
The deare remembrance of his dying Lord,
For whose sweete sake that glorious badge he wore,
And dead, as living ever, him ador'd:
Upon his shield the like was also scor'd,
For soveraine hope, which in his helpe he had,
Right faithfull true he was in deede and word;
But of his cheere did seeme too solemne sad;
Yet nothing did he dread, but ever was ydrad.

This sleepy bit, from the dwelling of Morpheus, invites us to linger:

And, more to lulle him in his slumber soft,
A trickling streame from high rock tumbling downe,
And ever-drizling raine upon the loft,
Mixt with a murmuring winde, much like the sowne
Of swarming bees, did cast him in a swowne.
No other noyse, nor peoples troublous cryes,
As still are wont t'annoy the walled towne,
Might there be heard: but carelesse Quiet lyes,

Wrapt in eternal silence farre from enimyes.

The description of Una shows the poet's sense of ideal beauty:

One day, nigh wearie of the yrkesome way,
From her unhastie beast she did alight;
And on the grasse her dainty limbs did lay
In secrete shadow, far from all mens sight;
From her fayre head her fillet she undight,
And layd her stole aside; Her angels face,
As the great eye of heaven, shyned bright,
And made a sunshine in the shady place;
Did never mortall eye behold such heavenly grace.
It fortuned, out of the thickest wood
A ramping lyon rushed suddeinly,
Hunting full greedy after salvage blood:
Soone as the royall Virgin he did spy,
With gaping mouth at her ran greedily,
To have at once devourd her tender corse:
But to the pray whenas he drew more ny,
His bloody rage aswaged with remorse,
And, with the sight amazd, forgat his furious forse.
Instead thereof he kist her wearie feet,
And lickt her lilly hands with fawning tong;
As he her wronged innocence did weet.
O how can beautie maister the most strong,
And simple truth subdue avenging wrong!

MINOR POEMS. Next to his masterpiece, the Shepherd's Calendar (1579) is the best known of Spenser's poems; though, as his first work, it is below many others in melody. It consists of twelve pastoral poems, or eclogues, one for each month of the year. The themes are generally rural life, nature, love in the fields; and the speakers are shepherds and shepherdesses. To increase the rustic effect Spenser uses strange forms of speech and obsolete words, to such an extent that Jonson complained his works are not English or any other language. Some are melancholy poems on his lost Rosalind; some are satires on the clergy; one, "The Briar and the Oak," is an allegory; one flatters Elizabeth, and others are pure fables touched with the Puritan spirit. They are written in various styles and meters, and show plainly that Spenser was practicing and preparing himself for greater work.

Other noteworthy poems are "Mother Hubbard's Tale," a satire on society; "Astrophel," an elegy on the death of Sidney; Amoretti, or sonnets, to his Elizabeth; the marriage hymn, "Epithalamion," and four "Hymns," on Love, Beauty, Heavenly Love, and Heavenly Beauty. There are numerous other poems and collections of poems, but these show the scope of his work and are best worth reading.

IMPORTANCE OF THE SHEPHERD'S CALENDAR. The publication of this work, in 1579, by an unknown writer who signed himself modestly "Immerito," marks an important epoch in our literature. We shall appreciate this better if we remember the long years during which England had been without a great poet. Chaucer and Spenser are often studied together as poets of the Renaissance period, and the idea prevails that they were almost contemporary. In fact, nearly two centuries passed after Chaucer's death,--years of enormous political and intellectual development,--and not only did Chaucer have no successor but our language had changed so rapidly that Englishmen had lost the ability to read his lines correctly.

This first published work of Spenser is noteworthy in at least four respects: first, it marks the appearance of the first national poet in two centuries; second, it shows again the variety and melody of English verse, which had been largely a tradition since Chaucer; third, it was our first pastoral, the beginning of a long series of English pastoral compositions modeled on Spenser, and as such exerted a strong influence on subsequent literature; and fourth, it marks the real beginning of the outburst of great Elizabethan poetry.

CHARACTERISTICS OF SPENSER'S POETRY. The five main qualities of Spenser's poetry are (1) a perfect melody; (2) a rare sense of beauty; (3) a splendid imagination, which could gather into one poem heroes, knights, ladies, dwarfs, demons and dragons, classic mythology, stories of chivalry, and the thronging ideals of the Renaissance,--all passing in gorgeous procession across an ever-changing and ever-beautiful landscape; (4) a lofty moral purity and seriousness; (5) a delicate idealism, which could make all nature and every common thing beautiful. In contrast with these excellent qualities the reader will probably note the strange appearance of his lines due to his fondness for obsolete words, like eyne (eyes) and shend (shame), and his tendency to coin others, like mercify, to suit his own purposes.

It is Spenser's idealism, his love of beauty, and his exquisite melody which have caused him to be known as "the poets' poet." Nearly all our subsequent singers acknowledge their delight in him and their indebtedness. Macaulay alone among critics voices a fault which all who are not poets quickly feel, namely that, with all Spenser's excellences, he is difficult to read. The modern man loses himself in the confused allegory of the Faery Queen, skips all but the marked passages, and softly closes the book in gentle weariness. Even the best of his longer poems, while of exquisite workmanship and delightfully melodious, generally fail to hold the reader's attention. The movement is languid; there is little dramatic interest, and only a suggestion of humor. The very melody of his verses sometimes grows monotonous, like a Strauss waltz too long continued. We shall best appreciate Spenser by reading at first only a few well-chosen selections from the Faery Queen and the Shepherd's Calendar, and a few of the minor poems which exemplify his wonderful melody.

COMPARISON BETWEEN CHAUCER AND SPENSER.

At the outset it is well to remember that, though Spenser regarded Chaucer as his master, two centuries intervene between them, and that their writings have almost nothing in common. We shall appreciate this better by a brief comparison between our first two modern poets.

Chaucer was a combined poet and man of affairs, with the latter predominating. Though dealing largely with ancient or mediaeval material, he has a curiously modern way of looking at life. Indeed, he is our only author preceding Shakespeare with whom we feel thoroughly at home. He threw aside the outgrown metrical romance, which was practically the only form of narrative in his day, invented the art of story-telling in verse, and brought it to a degree of perfection which has probably never since been equaled. Though a student of the classics, he lived wholly in the present, studied the men and women of his own time, painted them as they were, but added always a touch of kindly humor or romance to make them more interesting. So his mission appears to be simply to amuse himself and his readers. His mastery of various and melodious verse was marvelous and has never been surpassed in our language; but the English of his day was changing rapidly, and in a very few years men were unable to appreciate his art, so that even to Spenser and Dryden, for example, he seemed deficient in metrical skill. On this account his influence on our literature has been much less than we should expect from the quality of his work and from his position as one of the greatest of English poets.

Like Chaucer, Spenser was a busy man of affairs, but in him the poet and the scholar always predominates. He writes as the idealist, describing men not as they are but as he thinks they should be; he has no humor, and his mission is not to amuse but to reform. Like Chaucer he studies the classics and contemporary French and Italian writers; but instead of adapting his material to present-day conditions, he makes poetry, as in his Eclogues for instance, more artificial even than his foreign models. Where Chaucer looks about him and describes life as he sees it, Spenser always looks backward for his inspiration; he lives dreamily in the past, in a realm of purely imaginary emotions and adventures. His first quality is imagination, not observation, and he is the first of our poets to create a world of dreams, fancies, and illusions. His second quality is a wonderful sensitiveness to beauty, which shows itself not only in his subject-matter but also in the manner of his poetry. Like Chaucer, he is an almost perfect workman; but in reading Chaucer we think chiefly of his natural characters or his ideas, while in reading Spenser we think of the beauty of expression. The exquisite Spenserian stanza and the rich melody of Spenser's verse have made him the model of all our modern poets.

MINOR POETS

Though Spenser is the one great non-dramatic poet of the Elizabethan Age, a multitude of minor poets demand attention of the student who would understand the tremendous literary activity of the period. One needs only to read The Paradyse of Daynty Devises (1576), or A Gorgeous Gallery of Gallant Inventions (1578), or any other of the miscellaneous collections to find hundreds of songs, many of them of exquisite workmanship, by poets whose names now awaken no response. A glance is enough to assure one that over all England "the sweet spirit of song had arisen, like the first chirping of birds after a storm." Nearly two hundred poets are recorded in the short period from 1558 to 1625, and many of them were prolific writers. In a work like this, we can hardly do more than mention a few of the best known writers, and spend a moment at least with the works that suggest Marlowe's description of "infinite riches in a little room." The reader will note for himself the interesting union of action and thought in these men, so characteristic of the Elizabethan Age; for most of them were engaged chiefly in business or war or politics, and literature was to them a pleasant recreation rather than an absorbing profession.

THOMAS SACKVILLE (1536-1608). Sir Thomas Sackville, Earl of Dorset and Lord High Treasurer of England, is generally classed with Wyatt and Surrey among the predecessors of the Elizabethan Age. In imitation of Dante's Inferno, Sackville formed the design of a great poem called The Mirror for Magistrates. Under guidance of an allegorical personage called Sorrow, he meets the spirits of all the important actors in English history. The idea was to follow Lydgate's Fall of Princes and let each character tell his own story; so that the poem would be a mirror in which present rulers might see themselves and read this warning: "Who reckless rules right soon may hope to rue." Sackville finished only the "Induction" and the "Complaint of the Duke of Buckingham." These are written in the rime royal, and are marked by strong poetic feeling and expression. Unfortunately Sackville turned from poetry to politics, and the poem was carried on by two inferior poets, William Baldwin and George Ferrers.

Sackville wrote also, in connection with Thomas Norton, the first English tragedy, Ferrex and Porrex, called also Gorboduc, which will be considered in the following section on the Rise of the Drama.

PHILIP SIDNEY (1554-1586). Sidney, the ideal gentleman, the Sir Calidore of Spenser's "Legend of Courtesy," is vastly more interesting as a man than as a writer, and the student is recommended to read his biography rather than his books. His life expresses, better than any single literary work, the two ideals of the age,--personal honor and national greatness. As a writer he is known by three principal works, all published after his death, showing how little importance he attached to his own writing, even while he was encouraging Spenser. The Arcadia is a pastoral romance, interspersed with eclogues, in which shepherds and shepherdesses sing of the delights of rural life. Though the work was taken up idly as a summer's pastime, it became immensely popular and was imitated by a hundred poets. The Apologie for Poetrie (1595), generally called the Defense of Poesie, appeared in answer to a pamphlet by Stephen Gosson called The School of Abuse (1579), in which the poetry of the age and its unbridled pleasure were denounced with Puritan thoroughness and conviction. The Apologie is one of the first critical essays in English; and though its style now seems labored and unnatural,--the pernicious result of Euphues and his school,--it is still one of the best expressions of the place and meaning of poetry in any language. Astrophel and Stella is a collection of songs and sonnets addressed to Lady Penelope Devereux, to whom Sidney had once been betrothed. They abound in exquisite lines and passages, containing more poetic feeling and expression than the songs of any other minor writer of the age.

GEORGE CHAPMAN (1559?-1634). Chapman spent his long, quiet life among the dramatists, and wrote chiefly for the stage. His plays, which were for the most part merely poems in dialogue, fell far below the high dramatic standard of his time and are now almost unread. His most famous work is the metrical translation of the Iliad (1611) and of the Odyssey (1614). Chapman's Homer, though lacking the simplicity and dignity of the original, has a force and rapidity of movement which makes it superior in many respects to Pope's more familiar translation. Chapman is remembered also as the finisher of Marlowe's Hero and Leander, in which, apart from the drama, the Renaissance movement is seen at perhaps its highest point in English poetry. Out of scores of long poems of the period, Hero and Leander and the Faery Queen are the only two which are even slightly known to modern readers.

MICHAEL DRAYTON (1563-1631). Drayton is the most voluminous and, to antiquarians at least, the most interesting of the minor poets. He is the Layamon of the Elizabethan Age, and vastly more scholarly than his predecessor. His chief work is Polyolbion, an enormous poem of many thousand couplets, describing the towns, mountains, and rivers of Britain, with the interesting legends connected with each. It is an extremely valuable work and represents a lifetime of study and research. Two other long works are the Barons' Wars and the Heroic Epistle of England; and besides these were many minor poems. One of the best of these is the "Battle of Agincourt," a ballad written in the lively meter which Tennyson used with some variations in the "Charge of the Light Brigade," and which shows the old English love of brave deeds and of the songs that stir a people's heart in memory of noble ancestors.

THE FIRST ENGLISH DRAMATISTS

THE ORIGIN OF THE DRAMA. First the deed, then the story, then the play; that seems to be the natural development of the drama in its simplest form. The great deeds of a people are treasured in its literature, and later generations represent in play or pantomime certain parts of the story which appeal most powerfully to the imagination. Among primitive races the deeds of their gods and heroes are often represented at the yearly festivals; and among children, whose instincts are not yet blunted by artificial habits, one sees the story that was heard at bedtime repeated next day in vigorous action, when our boys turn scouts and our girls princesses, precisely as our first dramatists turned to the old legends and heroes of Britain for their first stage productions. To act a part seems as natural to humanity as to tell a story; and originally the drama is but an old story retold to the eye, a story put into action by living performers, who for the moment "make believe" or imagine themselves to be the old heroes.

To illustrate the matter simply, there was a great life lived by him who was called the Christ. Inevitably the life found its way into literature, and we have the Gospels. Around the life and literature sprang up a great religion. Its worship was at first simple,--the common prayer, the evening meal together, the remembered words of the Master, and the closing hymn.

Gradually a ritual was established, which grew more elaborate and impressive as the centuries went by. Scenes from the Master's life began to be represented in the churches, especially at Christmas time, when the story of Christ's birth was made more effective, to the eyes of a people who could not read, by a babe in a manger surrounded by magi and shepherds, with a choir of angels chanting the Gloria in Excelsis. Other impressive scenes from the Gospel followed; then the Old Testament was called upon, until a complete cycle of plays from the Creation to the Final Judgment was established, and we have the Mysteries and Miracle plays of the Middle Ages. Out of these came directly the drama of the Elizabethan Age.

PERIODS IN THE DEVELOPMENT OF THE DRAMA

THE RELIGIOUS PERIOD. In Europe, as in Greece, the drama had a distinctly religious origin. The first characters were drawn from the New Testament, and the object of the first plays was to make the church service more impressive, or to emphasize moral lessons by showing the reward of the good and the punishment of the evil doer. In the latter days of the Roman Empire the Church found the stage possessed by frightful plays, which debased the morals of a people already fallen too low. Reform seemed impossible; the corrupt drama was driven from the stage, and plays of every kind were forbidden. But mankind loves a spectacle, and soon the Church itself provided a substitute for the forbidden plays in the famous Mysteries and Miracles.

MIRACLE AND MYSTERY PLAYS. In France the name miracle was given to any play representing the lives of the saints, while the mystere represented scenes from the life of Christ or stories from the Old Testament associated with the coming of Messiah. In England this distinction was almost unknown; the name Miracle was used indiscriminately for all plays having their origin in the Bible or in the lives of the saints; and the name Mystery, to distinguish a certain class of plays, was not used until long after the religious drama had passed away.

The earliest Miracle of which we have any record in England is the Ludus de Sancta Katharina, which was performed in Dunstable about the year 1110. It is not known who wrote the original play of St. Catherine, but our first version was prepared by Geoffrey of St. Albans, a French school-teacher of Dunstable. Whether or not the play was given in English is not known, but it was customary in the earliest plays for the chief actors to speak in Latin or French, to show their importance, while minor and comic parts of the same play were given in English.

For four centuries after this first recorded play the Miracles increased steadily in number and popularity in England. They were given first very simply and impressively in the churches; then, as the actors increased in number and the plays in liveliness, they overflowed to the churchyards; but when fun and hilarity began to predominate even in the most sacred representations, the scandalized priests forbade plays altogether on church grounds. By the year 1300 the Miracles were out of ecclesiastical hands and adopted eagerly by the town guilds; and in the following two centuries we find the Church preaching against the abuse of the religious drama which it had itself introduced, and which at first had served a purely religious purpose. But by this time the Miracles had taken strong hold upon the English people, and they continued to be immensely popular until, in the sixteenth century, they were replaced by the Elizabethan drama.

The early Miracle plays of England were divided into two classes: the first, given at Christmas, included all plays connected with the birth of Christ; the second, at Easter, included the plays relating to his death and triumph. By the beginning of the fourteenth century all these plays were, in various localities, united in single cycles beginning with the Creation and ending with the Final Judgment. The complete cycle was presented every spring, beginning on Corpus Christi day; and as the presentation of so many plays meant a continuous outdoor festival of a week or more, this day was looked forward to as the happiest of the whole year.

Probably every important town in England had its own cycle of plays for its own guilds to perform, but nearly all have been lost. At the present day only four cycles exist (except in the most fragmentary condition), and these, though they furnish an interesting commentary on the times, add very little to our literature. The four cycles are the Chester and York plays, so called from the towns in which they were given; the Towneley or Wakefield plays, named for the Towneley family, which for a long time owned the manuscript; and the Coventry plays, which on doubtful evidence have been associated with the Grey Friars (Franciscans) of Coventry. The Chester cycle has 25 plays, the Wakefield 30, the Coventry 42, and the York 48. It is impossible to fix either the date or the authorship of any of these plays; we only know certainly that they were in great favor from the twelfth to the sixteenth century. The York plays are generally considered to be the best; but those of Wakefield show more humor and variety, and better workmanship. The former cycle especially shows a certain unity resulting from its aim to represent the whole of man's life from birth to death. The same thing is noticeable in Cursor Mundi, which, with the York and Wakefield cycles, belongs to the fourteenth century.

At first the actors as well as the authors of the Miracles were the priests a᾿nd their chosen assistants. Later, when The town guilds took up the plays and each guild became responsible for one or more of the series, the actors were carefully selected and trained. By four o'clock on the morning of Corpus Christi all the players had to be in their places in the movable theaters, which were scattered throughout the town in the squares and open places. Each of these theaters consisted of a two-story platform, set on wheels. The lower story was a dressing room for the actors; the upper story was the stage proper, and was reached by a trapdoor from below. When the play was over the platform was dragged away, and the next play in the cycle took its place. So in a single square several plays would be presented in rapid sequence to the same audience. Meanwhile the first play moved on to another square, where another audience was waiting to hear it.

Though the plays were distinctly religious in character, there is hardly one without its humorous element. In the play of Noah, for instance, Noah's shrewish wife makes fun for the audience by wrangling with her husband. In the Crucifixion play Herod is a prankish kind of tyrant who leaves the stage to rant among the audience; so that to "out-herod Herod" became a common proverb. In all the plays the devil is a favorite character and the butt of every joke. He also leaves the stage to play pranks or frighten the wondering children. On the side of the stage was often seen a huge dragon's head with gaping red jaws, belching forth fire and smoke, out of which poured a tumultuous troop of devils with clubs and pitchforks and gridirons to punish the wicked characters and to drag them away at last, howling and shrieking, into hell-mouth, as the dragon's head was called. So the fear of hell was ingrained into an ignorant people for four centuries. Alternating with these horrors were bits of rough horse-play and domestic scenes of peace and kindliness, representing the life of the English fields and homes. With these were songs and carols, like that of the Nativity, for instance:

As I out rode this enderes (last) night,
Of three jolly shepherds I saw a sight,
And all about their fold a star shone bright;
They sang terli terlow,
So merryly the shepherds their pipes can blow.
Down from heaven, from heaven so high,
Of angels there came a great companye

With mirth, and joy, and great solemnitye;

They sang terli terlow,

So merryly the shepherds their pipes can blow.

Such songs were taken home by the audience and sung for a season, as a popular tune is now caught from the stage and sung on the streets; and at times the whole audience would very likely join in the chorus.

After these plays were written according to the general outline of the Bible stories, no change was tolerated, the audience insisting, like children at "Punch and Judy," upon seeing the same things year after year. No originality in plot or treatment was possible, therefore; the only variety was in new songs and jokes, and in the pranks of the devil. Childish as such plays seem to us, they are part of the religious development of all uneducated people. Even now the Persian play of the "Martyrdom of Ali" is celebrated yearly, and the famous "Passion Play," a true Miracle, is given every ten years at Oberammergau.

THE MORAL PERIOD OF THE DRAMA. The second or moral period of the drama is shown by the increasing prevalence of the Morality plays. In these the characters were allegorical personages,--Life, Death, Repentance, Goodness, Love, Greed, and other virtues and vices. The Moralities may be regarded, therefore, as the dramatic counterpart of the once popular allegorical poetry exemplified by the Romance of the Rose. It did not occur to our first, unknown dramatists to portray men and women as they are until they had first made characters of abstract human qualities. Nevertheless, the Morality marks a distinct advance over the Miracle in that it gave free scope to the imagination for new plots and incidents. In Spain and Portugal these plays, under the name auto, were wonderfully developed by the genius of Calderon and Gil Vicente; but in England the Morality was a dreary kind of performance, like the allegorical poetry which preceded it. To enliven the audience the devil of the Miracle plays was introduced; and another lively personage called the Vice was the predecessor of our modern clown and jester. His business was to torment the "virtues" by mischievous pranks, and especially to make the devil's life a burden by beating him with a bladder or a wooden sword at every opportunity. The Morality generally ended in the triumph of virtue, the devil leaping into hell-mouth with Vice on his back.

The best known of the Moralities is "Everyman," which has recently been revived in England and America. The subject of the play is the summoning of every man by Death; and the moral is that nothing can take away the terror of the inevitable summons but an honest life and the comforts of religion. In its dramatic unity it suggests the pure Greek drama; there is no change of time or scene, and the stage is never empty from the beginning to the end of the performance. Other well-known Moralities are the "Pride of Life," "Hyckescorner," and "Castell of Perseverance." In the latter, man is represented as shut up in a castle garrisoned by the virtues and besieged by the vices.

Like the Miracle plays, most of the old Moralities are of unknown date and origin. Of the known authors of Moralities, two of the best are John Skelton, who wrote "Magnificence," and probably also "The Necromancer"; and Sir David Lindsay (1490-1555), "the poet of the Scotch Reformation," whose religious business it was to make rulers uncomfortable by telling them unpleasant truths in the form of poetry. With these men a new element enters into the Moralities. They satirize or denounce abuses of Church and State, and introduce living personages thinly disguised as allegories; so that the stage first becomes a power in shaping events and correcting abuses.

THE INTERLUDES. It is impossible to draw any accurate line of distinction between the Moralities and Interludes. In general we may think of the latter as dramatic scenes, sometimes given by themselves (usually with music and singing) at banquets and entertainments where a little fun was wanted; and again slipped into a Miracle play to enliven the audience after a solemn scene. Thus on the margin of a page of one of the old Chester plays we read, "The boye and pigge when the kinges are gone." Certainly this was no part of the original scene between Herod and the three kings. So also the quarrel between Noah and his wife is probably a late addition to an old play. The Interludes originated, undoubtedly, in a sense of humor; and to John Heywood (1497?-1580?), a favorite retainer and jester at the court of Mary, is due the credit for raising the Interlude to the distinct dramatic form known as comedy. Heywood's Interludes were written between 1520 and 1540. His most famous is "The Four P's," a contest of wit between a "Pardoner, a Palmer, a Pedlar and a Poticary." The characters here strongly suggest those of Chaucer. Another interesting Interlude is called "The Play of the Weather." In this Jupiter and the gods assemble to listen to complaints about the weather and to reform abuses. Naturally everybody wants his own kind of weather. The climax is reached by a boy who announces that a boy's pleasure consists in two things, catching birds and throwing snowballs, and begs for the weather to be such that he can always do both. Jupiter decides that he will do just as he pleases about the weather, and everybody goes home satisfied.

All these early plays were written, for the most part, in a mingling of prose and wretched doggerel, and add nothing to our literature. Their great work was to train actors, to keep alive the dramatic spirit, and to prepare the way for the true drama.

THE ARTISTIC PERIOD OF THE DRAMA. The artistic is the final stage in the development of the English drama. It differs radically from the other two in that its chief purpose is not to point a moral but to represent human life as it is. The artistic drama may have purpose, no less than the Miracle play, but the motive is always subordinate to the chief end of representing life itself.

The first true play in English, with a regular plot, divided into acts and scenes, is probably the comedy, "Ralph Royster Doyster." It was written by Nicholas Udall, master of Eton, and later of Westminster school, and was first acted by his schoolboys some time before 1556. The story is that of a conceited fop in love with a widow, who is already engaged to another man. The play is an adaptation of the Miles Gloriosus, a classic comedy by Plautus, and the English characters are more or less artificial; but as furnishing a model of a clear plot and natural dialogue, the influence of this first comedy, with its mixture of classic and English elements, can hardly be overestimated.

The next play, "Gammer Gurton's Needle" (cir. 1562), is a domestic comedy, a true bit of English realism, representing the life of the peasant class.

Gammer Gurton is patching the leather breeches of her man Hodge, when Gib, the cat, gets into the milk pan. While Gammer chases the cat the family needle is lost, a veritable calamity in those days. The whole household is turned upside down, and the neighbors are dragged into the affair. Various comical situations are brought about by Diccon, a thieving vagabond, who tells Gammer that her neighbor, Dame Chatte, has taken her needle, and who then hurries to tell Dame Chatte that she is accused by Gammer of stealing a favorite rooster. Naturally there is a terrible row when the two irate old women meet and misunderstand each other. Diccon also drags Doctor Rat, the curate, into the quarrel by telling him that, if he will but creep into Dame Chatte's cottage by a hidden way, he will find her using the stolen needle. Then Diccon secretly warns Dame Chatte that Gammer Gurton's man Hodge is coming to steal her chickens; and the old woman hides in the dark passage and cudgels the curate soundly with the door bar. All the parties are finally brought before the justice, when Hodge suddenly and painfully finds the lost needle--which is all the while stuck in his leather breeches--and the scene ends uproariously for both audience and actors.

This first wholly English comedy is full of fun and coarse humor, and is wonderfully true to the life it represents. It was long attributed to John Still, afterwards bishop of Bath; but the authorship is now definitely assigned to William Stevenson. Our earliest edition of the play was printed in 1575; but a similar play called "Dyccon of Bedlam" was licensed in 1552, twelve years before Shakespeare's birth.

To show the spirit and the metrical form of the play we give a fragment of the boy's description of the dullard Hodge trying to light a fire on the hearth from the cat's eyes, and another fragment of the old drinking song at the beginning of the second act.

At last in a dark corner two sparkes he thought he sees

Which were, indede, nought els but Gyb our cat's two eyes.

"Puffe!" quod Hodge, thinking therby to have fyre without doubt;

With that Gyb shut her two eyes, and so the fyre was out.

And by-and-by them opened, even as they were before;

With that the sparkes appeared, even as they had done of yore.

And, even as Hodge blew the fire, as he did thincke,

Gyb, as she felt the blast, strayght-way began to wyncke,

Tyll Hodge fell of swering, as came best to his turne,

The fier was sure bewicht, and therfore wold not burne.

At last Gyb up the stayers, among the old postes and pinnes,

And Hodge he hied him after till broke were both his shinnes,

Cursynge and swering othes, were never of his makyng,

That Gyb wold fyre the house if that shee were not taken.

Fyrste a Songe:

Backe and syde, go bare, go bare;
Booth foote and hande, go colde;
But, bellye, God sende thee good ale ynoughe,
Whether it be newe or olde!
I can not eate but lytle meate,
My stomacke is not good;
But sure I thinke that I can drycnke
With him that weares a hood.
Thoughe I go bare, take ye no care,
I am nothinge a-colde,
I stuffe my skyn so full within
Of ioly good ale and olde.
Backe and syde, go bare, etc.

Our first tragedy, "Gorboduc," was written by Thomas Sackville and Thomas Norton, and was acted in 1562, only two years before the birth of Shakespeare. It is remarkable not only as our first tragedy, but as the first play to be written in blank verse, the latter being most significant, since it started the drama into the style of verse best suited to the genius of English playwrights.

The story of "Gorboduc" is taken from the early annals of Britain and recalls the story used by Shakespeare in King Lear. Gorboduc, king of Britain, divides his kingdom between his sons Ferrex and Porrex. The sons quarrel, and Porrex, the younger, slays his brother, who is the queen's favorite. Videna, the queen, slays Porrex in revenge; the people rebel and slay Videna and Gorboduc; then the nobles kill the rebels, and in turn fall to fighting each other. The line of Brutus being extinct with the death of Gorboduc, the country falls into anarchy, with rebels, nobles, and a Scottish invader all fighting for the right of succession. The curtain falls upon a scene of bloodshed and utter confusion.

The artistic finish of this first tragedy is marred by the authors' evident purpose to persuade Elizabeth to marry. It aims to show the danger to which England is exposed by the uncertainty of succession. Otherwise the plan of the play follows the classical rule of Seneca.

There is very little action on the stage; bloodshed and battle are announced by a messenger; and the chorus, of four old men of Britain, sums up the situation with a few moral observations at the end of each of the first four acts.

CLASSICAL INFLUENCE UPON THE DRAMA. The revival of Latin literature had a decided influence upon the English drama as it developed from the Miracle plays. In the fifteenth century English teachers, in order to increase the interest in Latin, began to let their boys act the plays which they had read as literature, precisely as our colleges now present Greek or German plays at the yearly festivals. Seneca was the favorite Latin author, and all his tragedies were translated into English between 1559 and 1581. This was the exact period in which the first English playwrights were shaping their own ideas; but the severe simplicity of the classical drama seemed at first only to hamper the exuberant English spirit. To understand this, one has only to compare a tragedy of Seneca or of Euripides with one of Shakespeare, and see how widely the two masters differ in methods.

In the classic play the so-called dramatic unities of time, place, and action were strictly observed. Time and place must remain the same; the play could represent a period of only a few hours, and whatever action was introduced must take place at the spot where the play began. The characters, therefore, must remain unchanged throughout; there was no possibility of the child becoming a man, or of the man's growth with changing circumstances. As the play was within doors, all vigorous action was deemed out of place on the stage, and battles and important events were simply announced by a messenger. The classic drama also drew a sharp line between tragedy and comedy, all fun being rigorously excluded from serious representations.

The English drama, on the other hand, strove to represent the whole sweep of life in a single play. The scene changed rapidly; the same actors appeared now at home, now at court, now on the battlefield; and vigorous action filled the stage before the eyes of the spectators. The child of one act appeared as the man of the next, and the imagination of the spectator was called upon to bridge the gaps from place to place and from year to year. So the dramatist had free scope to present all life in a single place and a single hour. Moreover, since the world is always laughing and always crying at the same moment, tragedy and comedy were presented side by side, as they are in life itself. As Hamlet sings, after the play that amused the court but struck the king with deadly fear:

Why, let the stricken deer go weep,
The hart ungalled play;
For some must watch, while some must sleep:
So runs the world away.

Naturally, with these two ideals struggling to master the English drama, two schools of writers arose. The University Two Schools Wits, as men of learning were called, generally of Drama upheld the classical ideal, and ridiculed the crude-ness of the new English plays. Sackville and Norton were of this class, and "Gorboduc" was classic in its construction. In the "Defense of Poesie" Sidney upholds the classics and ridicules the too ambitious scope of the English drama. Against these were the popular playwrights, Lyly, Peele, Greene, Marlowe, and many others, who recognized the English love of action and disregarded the dramatic unities in their endeavor to present life as it is. In the end the native drama prevailed, aided by the popular taste which had been trained by four centuries of Miracles. Our first plays, especially of the romantic type, were extremely crude and often led to ridiculously extravagant scenes; and here is where the classic drama exercised an immense influence for good, by insisting upon beauty of form and definiteness of structure at a time when the tendency was to satisfy a taste for stage spectacles without regard to either.

In the year 1574 a royal permit to Lord Leicester's actors allowed them "to give plays anywhere throughout our realm of England," and this must be regarded as the beginning of the regular drama. Two years later the first playhouse, known as "The Theater," was built for these actors by James Burbage in Finsbury Fields, just north of London. It was in this theater that Shakespeare probably found employment when he first came to the city. The success of this venture was immediate, and the next thirty years saw a score of theatrical companies, at least seven regular theaters, and a dozen or more inn yards permanently fitted for the giving of plays,--all established in the city and its immediate suburbs. The growth seems all the more remarkable when we remember that the London of those days would now be considered a small city, having (in 1600) only about a hundred thousand inhabitants. A Dutch traveler, Johannes de Witt, who visited London in 1596, has given us the only contemporary drawing we possess of the interior of one of these theaters. They were built of stone and wood, round or octagonal in shape, and without a roof, being simply an inclosed courtyard. At one side was the stage, and before it on the bare ground, or pit, stood that large part of the audience who could afford to pay only an admission fee. The players and these groundlings were exposed to the weather; those that paid for seats were in galleries sheltered by a narrow porch-roof projecting inwards from the encircling walls; while the young nobles and gallants, who came to be seen and who could afford the extra fee, took seats on the stage itself, and smoked and chaffed the actors and threw nuts at the groundlings. The whole idea of these first theaters, according to De Witt, was like that of the Roman amphitheater; and the resemblance was heightened by the fact that, when no play was on the boards, the stage might be taken away and the pit given over to bull and bear baiting.

In all these theaters, probably, the stage consisted of a bare platform, with a curtain or "traverse" across the middle, separating the front from the rear stage. On the latter unexpected scenes or characters were "discovered" by simply drawing the curtain aside. At first little or no scenery was used, a gilded sign being the only announcement of a change of scene; and this very lack of scenery led to better acting, since the actors must be realistic enough to make the audience forget its shabby surroundings. By Shakespeare's day, however, painted scenery had appeared, first at university plays, and then in the regular theaters. In all our first plays female parts were taken by boy actors, who evidently were more distressing than the crude scenery, for contemporary literature has many satirical references to their acting, and even the tolerant Shakespeare writes:

Some squeaking Cleopatra boy my greatness.

However that may be, the stage was deemed unfit for women, and actresses were unknown in England until after the Restoration.

SHAKESPEARE'S PREDECESSORS IN THE DRAMA. The English drama as it developed from the Miracle plays has an interesting history. It began with schoolmasters, like Udall, who translated and adapted Latin plays for their boys to act, and who were naturally governed by classic ideals. It was continued by the choir masters of St. Paul and the Royal and the Queen's Chapel, whose companies of choirboy actors were famous in London and rivaled the players of the regular theaters. These choir masters were our first stage managers.

They began with masques and interludes and the dramatic presentation of classic myths modeled after the Italians; but some of them, like Richard Edwards (choir master of the Queen's Chapel in 1561), soon added farces from English country life and dramatized some of Chaucer's stories. Finally, the regular playwrights, Kyd, Nash, Lyly, Peele, Greene, and Marlowe, brought the English drama to the point where Shakespeare began to experiment upon it.

Each of these playwrights added or emphasized some essential element in the drama, which appeared later in the work of Shakespeare. Thus John Lyly (1554?-1606), who is now known chiefly as having developed the pernicious literary style called euphuism, is one of the most influential of the early dramatists. His court comedies are remarkable for their witty dialogue and for being our first plays to aim definitely at unity and artistic finish. Thomas Kyd's Spanish Tragedy (c. 1585) first gives us the drama, or rather the melodrama, of passion, copied by Marlowe and Shakespeare. This was the most popular of the early Elizabethan plays; it was revised again and again, and Ben Jonson is said to have written one version and to have acted the chief part of Hieronimo. And Robert Greene (1558?-1592) plays the chief part in the early development of romantic comedy, and gives us some excellent scenes of English country life in plays like Friar Bacon and Friar Bungay.

Even a brief glance at the life and work of these first playwrights shows three noteworthy things which have a bearing on Shakespeare's career: (1) These men were usually actors as well as dramatists. They knew the stage and the audience, and in writing their plays they remembered not only the actor's part but also the audience's love for stories and brave spectacles. "Will it act well, and will it please our audience," were the questions of chief concern to our early dramatists. (2) Their training began as actors; then they revised old plays, and finally became independent writers. In this their work shows an exact parallel with that of Shakespeare. (3) They often worked together, probably as Shakespeare worked with Marlowe and Fletcher, either in revising old plays or in creating new ones.

They had a common store of material from which they derived their stories and characters, hence their frequent repetition of names;

and they often produced two or more plays on the same subject. Much of Shakespeare's work depends, as we shall see, on previous plays; and even his Hamlet uses the material of an earlier play of the same name, probably by Kyd, which was well known to the London stage in 1589, some twelve years before Shakespeare's great work was written.

All these things are significant, if we are to understand the Elizabethan drama and the man who brought it to perfection. Shakespeare was not simply a great genius; he was also a great worker, and he developed in exactly the same way as did all his fellow craftsmen. And, contrary to the prevalent opinion, the Elizabethan drama is not a Minerva-like creation, springing full grown from the head of one man; it is rather an orderly though rapid development, in which many men bore a part. All our early dramatists are worthy of study for the part they played in the development of the drama; but we can here consider only one, the most typical of all, whose best work is often ranked with that of Shakespeare.

CHRISTOPHER MARLOWE (1564-1593)

Marlowe is one of the most suggestive figures of the English Renaissance, and the greatest of Shakespeare's predecessors. The glory of the Elizabethan drama dates from his Tamburlaine (1587), wherein the whole restless temper of the age finds expression:

Nature, that framed us of four elements

Warring within our breasts for regiment,

Doth teach us all to have aspiring minds:

Our souls--whose faculties can comprehend

The wondrous architecture of the world,

And measure every wandering planet's course,

Still climbing after knowledge infinite,

And always moving as the restless spheres--

Will us to wear ourselves and never rest.

Tamburlaine, Pt. I, II, vii.

Life. Marlowe was born in Canterbury, only a few months before Shakespeare. He was the son of a poor shoemaker, but through the kindness of a patron was educated at the town grammar school and then at Cambridge. When he came to London (c. 1584), his soul was surging with the ideals of the Renaissance, which later found expression in Faustus, the scholar longing for unlimited knowledge and for power to grasp the universe. Unfortunately, Marlowe had also the unbridled passions which mark the early, or Pagan Renaissance, as Taine calls it, and the conceit of a young man just entering the realms of knowledge. He became an actor and lived in a low-tavern atmosphere of excess and wretchedness. In 1587, when but twenty-three years old, he produced Tamburlaine, which brought him instant recognition. Thereafter, notwithstanding his wretched life, he holds steadily to a high literary purpose. Though all his plays abound in violence, no doubt reflecting many of the violent scenes in which he lived, he develops his "mighty line" and depicts great scenes in magnificent bursts of poetry, such as the stage had never heard before. In five years, while Shakespeare was serving his apprenticeship, Marlowe produced all his great work. Then he was stabbed in a drunken brawl and died wretchedly, as he had lived. The Epilogue of Faustus might be written across his tombstone:

Cut is the branch that might have grown full straight,
And burned is Apollo's laurel bough
That sometime grew within this learned man.

MARLOWE'S WORKS. In addition to the poem "Hero and Leander," to which we have referred, Marlowe is famous for four dramas, now known as the Marlowesque or one-man type of tragedy, each revolving about one central personality who is consumed by the lust of power. The first of these is Tamburlaine, the story of Timur the Tartar. Timur begins as a shepherd chief, who first rebels and then triumphs over the Persian king. Intoxicated by his success, Timur rushes like a tempest over the whole East. Seated on his chariot drawn by captive kings, with a caged emperor before him, he boasts of his power which overrides all things. Then, afflicted with disease, he raves against the gods and would overthrow them as he has overthrown earthly rulers. Tamburlaine is an epic rather than a drama; but one can understand its instant success with a people only half civilized, fond of military glory, and the instant adoption of its "mighty line" as the instrument of all dramatic expression.

Faustus, the second play, is one of the best of Marlowe's works. The story is that of a scholar who longs for infinite knowledge, and who turns from Theology, Philosophy, Medicine, and Law, the four sciences of the time, to the study of magic, much as a child might turn from jewels to tinsel and colored paper. In order to learn magic he sells himself to the devil, on condition that he shall have twenty-four years of absolute power and knowledge. The play is the story of those twenty-four years. Like Tamburlaine, it is lacking in dramatic construction, but has an unusual number of passages of rare poetic beauty. Milton's Satan suggests strongly that the author of Paradise Lost had access to Faustus and used it, as he may also have used Tamburlaine, for the magnificent panorama displayed by Satan in Paradise Regained. For instance, more than fifty years before Milton's hero says, "Which way I turn is hell, myself am hell," Marlowe had written:

Faust. How comes it then that thou art out of hell?

Mephisto. Why this is hell, nor am I out of it.

* * * * *

Hell hath no limits, nor is circumscribed
In one self place; for where we are is hell,
And where hell is there must we ever be.

Marlowe's third play is The Jew of Malta, a study of the lust for wealth, which centers about Barabas, a terrible old money lender, strongly suggestive of Shylock in The Merchant of Venice. The first part of the play is well constructed, showing a decided advance, but the last part is an accumulation of melodramatic horrors. Barabas is checked in his murderous career by falling into a boiling caldron which he had prepared for another, and dies blaspheming, his only regret being that he has not done more evil in his life. Marlowe's last play is Edward II, a tragic study of a king's weakness and misery. In point of style and dramatic construction, it is by far the best of Marlowe's plays, and is a worthy predecessor of Shakespeare's historical drama.

Marlowe is the only dramatist of the time who is ever compared with Shakespeare. When we remember that he died at twenty-nine, probably before Shakespeare had produced a single great play, we must wonder what he might have done had he outlived his wretched youth and become a man. Here and there his work is remarkable for its splendid imagination, for the stateliness of its verse, and for its rare bits of poetic beauty; but in dramatic instinct, in wide knowledge of human life, in humor, in delineation of woman's character, in the delicate fancy which presents an Ariel as perfectly as a Macbeth,--in a word, in all that makes a dramatic genius, Shakespeare stands alone. Marlowe simply prepared the way for the master who was to follow.

VARIETY OF THE EARLY DRAMA. The thirty years between our first regular English plays and Shakespeare's first comedy witnessed a development of the drama which astonishes us both by its rapidity and variety. We shall better appreciate Shakespeare's work if we glance for a moment at the plays that preceded him, and note how he covers the whole field and writes almost every form and variety of the drama known to his age.

First in importance, or at least in popular interest, are the new Chronicle plays, founded upon historical events and characters. They show the strong national spirit of the Elizabethan Age, and their popularity was due largely to the fact that audiences came to the theaters partly to gratify their awakened national spirit and to get their first knowledge of national history. Some of the Moralities, like Bayle's King Johan (1538), are crude Chronicle plays, and the early Robin Hood plays and the first tragedy, Gorboduc, show the same awakened popular interest in English history. During the reign of Elizabeth the popular Chronicle plays increased till we have the record of over two hundred and twenty, half of which are still extant, dealing with almost every important character, real or legendary, in English history. Of Shakespeare's thirty-seven dramas, ten are true Chronicle plays of English kings; three are from the legendary annals of Britain; and three more are from the history of other nations.

Other types of the early drama are less clearly defined, but we may sum them up under a few general heads: (1) The Domestic Drama began with crude home scenes introduced into the Miracles and developed in a score of different ways, from the coarse humor of Gammer Gurton's Needle to the Comedy of Manners of Jonson and the later dramatists. Shakespeare's Taming of the Shrew and Merry Wives of Windsor belong to this class. (2) The so-called Court Comedy is the opposite of the former in that it represented a different kind of life and was intended for a different audience. It was marked by elaborate dialogue, by jests, retorts, and endless plays on words, rather than by action.

It was made popular by Lyly's success, and was imitated in Shakespeare's first or "Lylian" comedies, such as Love's Labour's Lost, and the complicated Two Gentlemen of Verona. (3) Romantic Comedy and Romantic Tragedy suggest the most artistic and finished types of the drama, which were experimented upon by Peele, Greene, and Marlowe, and were brought to perfection in The Merchant of Venice, Romeo and Juliet, and The Tempest. (4) In addition to the above types were several others,--the Classical Plays, modeled upon Seneca and favored by cultivated audiences; the Melodrama, favorite of the groundlings, which depended not on plot or characters but upon a variety of striking scenes and incidents; and the Tragedy of Blood, always more or less melodramatic, like Kyd's Spanish Tragedy, which grew more blood-and-thundery in Marlowe and reached a climax of horrors in Shakespeare's Titus Andronicus. It is noteworthy that Hamlet, Lear, and Macbeth all belong to this class, but the developed genius of the author raised them to a height such as the Tragedy of Blood had never known before.

These varied types are quite enough to show with what doubtful and unguided experiments our first dramatists were engaged, like men first setting out in rafts and dugouts on an unknown sea. They are the more interesting when we remember that Shakespeare tried them all; that he is the only dramatist whose plays cover the whole range of the drama from its beginning to its decline. From the stage spectacle he developed the drama of human life; and instead of the doggerel and bombast of our first plays he gives us the poetry of Romeo and Juliet and Midsummer Night's Dream. In a word, Shakespeare brought order out of dramatic chaos. In a few short years he raised the drama from a blundering experiment to a perfection of form and expression which has never since been rivaled.

SHAKESPEARE

One who reads a few of Shakespeare's great plays and then the meager story of his life is generally filled with a vague wonder. Here is an unknown country boy, poor and poorly educated according to the standards of his age, who arrives at the great city of London and goes to work at odd jobs in a theater. In a year or two he is associated with scholars and dramatists, the masters of their age, writing plays of kings and clowns, of gentlemen and heroes and noble women, all of whose lives he seems to know by intimate association. In a few years more he leads all that brilliant group of poets and dramatists who have given undying glory to the Age of Elizabeth. Play after play runs from his pen, mighty dramas of human life and character following one another so rapidly that good work seems impossible; yet they stand the test of time, and their poetry is still unrivaled in any language. For all this great work the author apparently cares little, since he makes no attempt to collect or preserve his writings. A thousand scholars have ever since been busy collecting, identifying, classifying the works which this magnificent workman tossed aside so carelessly when he abandoned the drama and retired to his native village. He has a marvelously imaginative and creative mind; but he invents few, if any, new plots or stories. He simply takes an old play or an old poem, makes it over quickly, and lo! this old familiar material glows with the deepest thoughts and the tenderest feelings that ennoble our humanity; and each new generation of men finds it more wonderful than the last. How did he do it? That is still an unanswered question and the source of our wonder.

There are, in general, two theories to account for Shakespeare. The romantic school of writers have always held that in him "all came from within"; that his genius was his sufficient guide; and that to the overmastering power of his genius alone we owe all his great works. Practical, unimaginative men, on the other hand, assert that in Shakespeare "all came from without," and that we must study his environment rather than his genius, if we are to understand him. He lived in a play-loving age; he studied the crowds, gave them what they wanted, and simply reflected their own thoughts and feelings. In reflecting the English crowd about him he unconsciously reflected all crowds, which are alike in all ages; hence his continued popularity. And in being guided by public sentiment he was not singular, but followed the plain path that every good dramatist has always followed to success. Probably the truth of the matter is to be found somewhere between these two extremes. Of his great genius there can be no question; but there are other things to consider. As we have already noticed, Shakespeare was trained, like his fellow workmen, first as an actor, second as a reviser of old plays, and last as an independent dramatist. He worked with other playwrights and learned their secret. Like them, he studied and followed the public taste, and his work indicates at least three stages, from his first somewhat crude experiments to his finished masterpieces. So it would seem that in Shakespeare we have the result of hard work and of orderly human development, quite as much as of transcendent genius.

LIFE (1564-1616). Two outward influences were powerful in developing the genius of Shakespeare,--the little village of Stratford, center of the most beautiful and romantic district in rural England, and the great city of London, the center of the world's political activity. In one he learned to know the natural man in his natural environment; in the other, the social, the artificial man in the most unnatural of surroundings.

From the register of the little parish church at Stratford-on-Avon we learn that William Shakespeare was baptized there on the twenty-sixth of April, 1564 (old style). As it was customary to baptize children on the third day after birth, the twenty-third of April (May 3, according to our present calendar) is generally accepted as the poet's birthday.

His father, John Shakespeare, was a farmer's son from the neighboring village of Snitterfield, who came to Stratford about 1551, and began to prosper as a trader in corn, meat, leather, and other agricultural products. His mother, Mary Arden, was the daughter of a prosperous farmer, descended from an old Warwickshire family of mixed Anglo-Saxon and Norman blood. In 1559 this married couple sold a piece of land, and the document is signed, "The marke + of John Shacksper. The marke + of Mary Shacksper"; and from this it has been generally inferred that, like the vast majority of their countrymen, neither of the poet's parents could read or write. This was probably true of his mother; but the evidence from Stratford documents now indicates that his father could write, and that he also audited the town accounts; though in attesting documents he sometimes made a mark, leaving his name to be filled in by the one who drew up the document. Of Shakespeare's education we know little, except that for a few years he probably attended the endowed grammar school at Stratford, where he picked up the "small Latin and less Greek" to which his learned friend Ben Jonson refers. His real teachers, meanwhile, were the men and women and the natural influences which surrounded him. Stratford is a charming little village in beautiful Warwickshire, and near at hand were the Forest of Arden, the old castles of Warwick and Kenilworth, and the old Roman camps and military roads, to appeal powerfully to the boy's lively imagination. Every phase of the natural beauty of this exquisite region is reflected in Shakespeare's poetry; just as his characters reflect the nobility and the littleness, the gossip, vices, emotions, prejudices, and traditions of the people about him.

I saw a smith stand with his hammer, thus,
The whilst his iron did on the anvil cool,
With open mouth swallowing a tailor's news;
Who, with his shears and measure in his hand,
Standing on slippers, which his nimble haste
Had falsely thrust upon contrary feet,
Told of a many thousand warlike French
That were embattailed and ranked in Kent.

Such passages suggest not only genius but also a keen, sympathetic observer, whose eyes see every significant detail. So with the nurse in Romeo and Juliet, whose endless gossip and vulgarity cannot quite hide a kind heart. She is simply the reflection of some forgotten nurse with whom Shakespeare had talked by the wayside.

Not only the gossip but also the dreams, the unconscious poetry that sleeps in the heart of the common people, appeal tremendously to Shakespeare's imagination and are reflected in his greatest plays. Othello tries to tell a curt soldier's story of his love; but the account is like a bit of Mandeville's famous travels, teeming with the fancies that filled men's heads when the great round world was first brought to their attention by daring explorers. Here is a bit of folklore, touched by Shakespeare's exquisite fancy, which shows what one boy listened to before the fire at Halloween:

She comes
In shape no bigger than an agate-stone
On the fore-finger of an alderman,
Drawn with a team of little atomies
Athwart men's noses as they lie asleep;
Her waggon-spokes made of long spinners' legs,
The cover of the wings of grasshoppers,
The traces of the smallest spider's web,

The collars of the moonshine's watery beams,
Her whip of cricket's bone, the lash of film,
Her waggoner a small grey-coated gnat;
* * * * *
Her chariot is an empty hazel nut
Made by the joiner squirrel, or old grub,
Time out o' mind the fairies' coachmakers.
And in this state she gallops night by night
Through lovers' brains, and then they dream of love;
* * * * *
O'er lawyers' fingers, who straight dream on fees,
O'er ladies' lips, who straight on kisses dream.

So with Shakespeare's education at the hands of Nature, which came from keeping his heart as well as his eyes wide open to the beauty of the world. He speaks of a horse, and we know the fine points of a thoroughbred; he mentions the duke's hounds, and we hear them clamoring on a fox trail, their voices matched like bells in the frosty air; he stops for an instant in the sweep of a tragedy to note a flower, a star, a moonlit bank, a hilltop touched by the sunrise, and instantly we know what our own hearts felt but could not quite express when we saw the same thing. Because he notes and remembers every significant thing in the changing panorama of earth and sky, no other writer has ever approached him in the perfect natural setting of his characters.

When Shakespeare was about fourteen years old his father lost his little property and fell into debt, and the boy probably left school to help support the family of younger children. What occupation he followed for the next eight years is a matter of conjecture. From evidence found in his plays, it is alleged with some show of authority that he was a country schoolmaster and a lawyer's clerk, the character of Holofernes, in Love's Labour's Lost, being the warrant for one, and Shakespeare's knowledge of law terms for the other. But if we take such evidence, then Shakespeare must have been a botanist, because of his knowledge of wild flowers; a sailor, because he knows the ropes; a courtier, because of his extraordinary facility in quips and compliments and courtly language; a clown, because none other is so dull and foolish; a king, because Richard and Henry are true to life; a woman, because he has sounded the depths of a woman's feelings; and surely a Roman, because in Coriolanus and Julius Caesar he has shown us the Roman spirit better than have the Roman writers themselves. He was everything, in his imagination, and it is impossible from a study of his scenes and characters to form a definite opinion as to his early occupation.

In 1582 Shakespeare was married to Anne Hathaway, the daughter of a peasant family of Shottery, who was eight years older than her boy husband. From numerous sarcastic references to marriage made by the characters in his plays, and from the fact that he soon left his wife and family and went to London, it is generally alleged that the marriage was a hasty and unhappy one; but here again the evidence is entirely untrustworthy. In many Miracles as well as in later plays it was customary to depict the seamy side of domestic life for the amusement of the crowd; and Shakespeare may have followed the public taste in this as he did in other things. The references to love and home and quiet joys in Shakespeare's plays are enough, if we take such evidence, to establish firmly the opposite supposition, that his love was a very happy one. And the fact that, after his enormous success in London, he retired to Stratford to live quietly with his wife and daughters, tends to the same conclusion.

About the year 1587 Shakespeare left his family and went to London and joined himself to Burbage's company of players. A persistent tradition says that he had incurred the anger of Sir Thomas Lucy, first by poaching deer in that nobleman's park, and then, when haled before a magistrate, by writing a scurrilous ballad about Sir Thomas, which so aroused the old gentleman's ire that Shakespeare was obliged to flee the country. An old record says that the poet "was much given to all unluckiness in stealing venison and rabbits," the unluckiness probably consisting in getting caught himself, and not in any lack of luck in catching the rabbits. The ridicule heaped upon the Lucy family in Henry IV and the Merry Wives of Windsor gives some weight to this tradition. Nicholas Rowe, who published the first life of Shakespeare, is the authority for this story; but there is some reason to doubt whether, at the time when Shakespeare is said to have poached in the deer park of Sir Thomas Lucy at Charlescote, there were any deer or park at the place referred to. The subject is worthy of some scant attention, if only to show how worthless is the attempt to construct out of rumor the story of a great life which, fortunately perhaps, had no contemporary biographer.

Of his life in London from 1587 to 1611, the period of his greatest literary activity, we know nothing definitely. We can judge only from his plays, and from these it is evident that he entered into the stirring life of England's capital with the same perfect sympathy and understanding that marked him among the plain people of his native Warwickshire. The first authentic reference to him is in 1592, when Greene's bitter attack appeared, showing plainly that Shakespeare had in five years assumed an important position among playwrights. Then appeared the apology of the publishers of Greene's pamphlet, with their tribute to the poet's sterling character, and occasional literary references which show that he was known among his fellows as "the gentle Shakespeare." Ben Jonson says of him: "I loved the man and do honor his memory, on this side idolatry, as much as any. He was indeed honest, and of an open and free nature." To judge from only three of his earliest plays it would seem reasonably evident that in the first five years of his London life he had gained entrance to the society of gentlemen and scholars, had caught their characteristic mannerisms and expressions, and so was ready by knowledge and observation as well as by genius to weave into his dramas the whole stirring life of the English people. The plays themselves, with the testimony of contemporaries and his business success, are strong evidence against the tradition that his life in London was wild and dissolute, like that of the typical actor and playwright of his time.

Shakespeare's first work may well have been that of a general helper, an odd-job man, about the theater; but he soon became an actor, and the records of the old London theaters show that in the next ten years he gained a prominent place, though there is little reason to believe that he was counted among the "stars." Within two years he was at work on plays, and his course here was exactly like that of other playwrights of his time. He worked with other men, and he revised old plays before writing his own, and so gained a practical knowledge of his art. Henry VI (c. 1590-1591) is an example of this tinkering work, in which, however, his native power is unmistakably manifest. The three parts of Henry VI (and Richard III, which belongs with them) are a succession of scenes from English Chronicle history strung together very loosely;

and only in the last is there any definite attempt at unity. That he soon fell under Marlowe's influence is evident from the atrocities and bombast of Titus Andronicus and Richard III. The former may have been written by both playwrights in collaboration, or may be one of Marlowe's horrors left unfinished by his early death and brought to an end by Shakespeare. He soon broke away from this apprentice work, and then appeared in rapid succession Love's Labour's Lost, Comedy of Errors, Two Gentlemen of Verona, the first English Chronicle plays, A Midsummer Night's Dream, and Romeo and Juliet. This order is more or less conjectural; but the wide variety of these plays, as well as their unevenness and frequent crudities, marks the first or experimental stage of Shakespeare's work. It is as if the author were trying his power, or more likely trying the temper of his audience. For it must be remembered that to please his audience was probably the ruling motive of Shakespeare, as of the other early dramatists, during the most vigorous and prolific period of his career.

Shakespeare's poems, rather than his dramatic work, mark the beginning of his success. "Venus and Adonis" became immensely popular in London, and its dedication to the Earl of Southampton brought, according to tradition, a substantial money gift, which may have laid the foundation for Shakespeare's business success. He appears to have shrewdly invested his money, and soon became part owner of the Globe and Blackfriars theaters, in which his plays were presented by his own companies. His success and popularity grew amazingly. Within a decade of his unnoticed arrival in London he was one of the most famous actors and literary men in England. Following his experimental work there came a succession of wonderful plays,--Merchant of Venice, As You Like It, Twelfth Night, Julius Caesar, Hamlet, Macbeth, Othello, King Lear, Antony and Cleopatra. The great tragedies of this period are associated with a period of gloom and sorrow in the poet's life; but of its cause we have no knowledge. It may have been this unknown sorrow which turned his thoughts back to Stratford and caused, apparently, a dissatisfaction with his work and profession; but the latter is generally attributed to other causes. Actors and playwrights were in his day generally looked upon with suspicion or contempt; and Shakespeare, even in the midst of success, seems to have looked forward to the time when he could retire to Stratford to live the life of a farmer and country gentleman. His own and his father's families were first released from debt; then, in 1597, he bought New Place, the finest house in Stratford, and soon added a tract of farming land to complete his estate. His profession may have prevented his acquiring the title of "gentleman," or he may have only followed a custom of the time when he applied for and obtained a coat of arms for his father, and so indirectly secured the title by inheritance. His home visits grew more and more frequent till, about the year 1611, he left London and retired permanently to Stratford.

Though still in the prime of life, Shakespeare soon abandoned his dramatic work for the comfortable life of a country gentleman. Of his later plays, Coriolanus, Cymbeline, Winter's Tale, and Pericles show a decided falling off from his previous work, and indicate another period of experimentation; this time not to test his own powers but to catch the fickle humor of the public. As is usually the case with a theater-going people, they soon turned from serious drama to sentimental or more questionable spectacles; and with Fletcher, who worked with Shakespeare and succeeded him as the first playwright of London, the decline of the drama had already begun. In 1609, however, occurred an event which gave Shakespeare his chance for a farewell to the public. An English ship disappeared, and all on board were given up for lost. A year later the sailors returned home, and their arrival created intense excitement. They had been wrecked on the unknown Bermudas, and had lived there for ten months, terrified by mysterious noises which they thought came from spirits and devils. Five different accounts of this fascinating shipwreck were published, and the Bermudas became known as the "Ile of Divels." Shakespeare took this story--which caused as much popular interest as that later shipwreck which gave us Robinson Crusoe--and wove it into The Tempest. In the same year (1611) he probably sold his interest in the Globe and Blackfriars theaters, and his dramatic work was ended. A few plays were probably left unfinished and were turned over to Fletcher and other dramatists.

That Shakespeare thought little of his success and had no idea that his dramas were the greatest that the world ever produced seems evident from the fact that he made no attempt to collect or publish his works, or even to save his manuscripts, which were carelessly left to stage managers of the theaters, and so found their way ultimately to the ragman. After a few years of quiet life, of which we have less record than of hundreds of simple country gentlemen of the time, Shakespeare died on the probable anniversary of his birth, April 23, 1616. He was given a tomb in the chancel of the parish church, not because of his preeminence in literature, but because of his interest in the affairs of a country village. And in the sad irony of fate, the broad stone that covered his tomb--now an object of veneration to the thousands that yearly visit the little church--was inscribed as follows:

Good friend, for Jesus' sake forbeare
To dig the dust enclosed heare;
Bleste be the man that spares these stones,
And curst be he that moves my bones.

This wretched doggerel, over the world's greatest poet, was intended, no doubt, as a warning to some stupid sexton, lest he should empty the grave and give the honored place to some amiable gentleman who had given more tithes to the parish.

WORKS OF SHAKESPEARE. At the time of Shakespeare's death twenty-one plays existed in manuscripts in the various theaters. A few others had already been printed in quarto form, and the latter are the only publications that could possibly have met with the poet's own approval. More probably they were taken down in shorthand by some listener at the play and then "pirated" by some publisher for his own profit. The first printed collection of his plays, now called the First Folio (1623), was made by two actors, Heming and Condell, who asserted that they had access to the papers of the poet and had made a perfect edition, "in order to keep the memory of so worthy a friend and fellow alive." This contains thirty-six of the thirty-seven plays generally attributed to Shakespeare, Pericles being omitted. This celebrated First Folio was printed from playhouse manuscripts and from printed quartos containing many notes and changes by individual actors and stage managers. Moreover, it was full of typographical errors, though the editors alleged great care and accuracy; and so, though it is the only authoritative edition we have, it is of little value in determining the dates, or the classification of the plays as they existed in Shakespeare's mind.

Notwithstanding this uncertainty, a careful reading of the plays and poems leaves us with an impression of four different periods of work, probably corresponding with the growth and experience of the poet's life. These are: (1) a period of early experimentation. It is marked by youthfulness and exuberance of imagination, by extravagance of language, and by the frequent use of rimed couplets with his blank verse. The period dates from his arrival in London to 1595. Typical works of this first period are his early poems, Love's Labour's Lost, Two Gentlemen of Verona, and Richard III. (2) A period of rapid growth and development, from 1595 to 1600. Such plays as The Merchant of Venice, Midsummer Night's Dream, As You Like It, and Henry IV, all written in this period, show more careful and artistic work, better plots, and a marked increase in knowledge of human nature. (3) A period of gloom and depression, from 1600 to 1607, which marks the full maturity of his powers. What caused this evident sadness is unknown; but it is generally attributed to some personal experience, coupled with the political misfortunes of his friends, Essex and Southampton. The Sonnets with their note of personal disappointment, Twelfth Night, which is Shakespeare's "farewell to mirth," and his great tragedies, Hamlet, Lear, Macbeth, Othello, and Julius Caesar, belong to this period. (4) A period of restored serenity, of calm after storm, which marked the last years of the poet's literary work. The Winter's Tale and The Tempest are the best of his later plays; but they all show a falling off from his previous work, and indicate a second period of experimentation with the taste of a fickle public.

To read in succession four plays, taking a typical work from each of the above periods, is one of the very best ways of getting quickly at the real life and mind of Shakespeare. Following is a complete list with the approximate dates of his works, classified according to the above four periods.

First Period, Early Experiment. Venus and Adonis, Rape of Lucrece, 1594; Titus Andronicus, Henry VI (three parts), 1590-1591; Love's Labour's Lost, 1590; Comedy of Errors, Two Gentlemen of Verona, 1591-1592; Richard-III, 1593; Richard II, King John, 1594-1595.

Second Period, Development. Romeo and Juliet, Midsummer Night's Dream, 1595; Merchant of Venice, Henry IV (first part), 1596; Henry IV (second part), Merry Wives of Windsor, 1597; Much Ado About Nothing, 1598; As You Like It, Henry V, 1599.

Third Period, Maturity and Gloom. Sonnets (1600-?), Twelfth Night, 1600; Taming of the Shrew, Julius Caesar, Hamlet, Troilus and Cressida,

1601-1602; All's Well That Ends Well, Measure for Measure, 1603; Othello, 1604; King Lear, 1605; Macbeth, 1606; Antony and Cleopatra, Timon of Athens, 1607.

Fourth Period, Late Experiment. Coriolanus, Pericles, 1608; Cymbeline, 1609; Winter's Tale, 1610-1611; The Tempest, 1611; Henry VIII (unfinished).

CLASSIFICATION ACCORDING TO SOURCE. In history, legend, and story, Shakespeare found the material for nearly all his dramas; and so they are often divided into three classes, called historical plays, like Richard III and Henry V; legendary or partly historical plays, like Macbeth, King Lear, and Julius Caesar; and fictional plays, like Romeo and Juliet and The Merchant of Venice. Shakespeare invented few, if any, of the plots or stories upon which his dramas are founded, but borrowed them freely, after the custom of his age, wherever he found them. For his legendary and historical material he depended, largely on Holinshed's Chronicles of England, Scotland, and Ireland, and on North's translation of Plutarch's famous Lives.

A full half of his plays are fictional, and in these he used the most popular romances of the day, seeming to depend most on the Italian story-tellers. Only two or three of his plots, as in Love's Labour's Lost and Merry Wives of Windsor, are said to be original, and even these are doubtful. Occasionally Shakespeare made over an older play, as in Henry VI, Comedy of Errors, and Hamlet; and in one instance at least he seized upon an incident of shipwreck in which London was greatly interested, and made out of it the original and fascinating play of The Tempest, in much the same spirit which leads our modern playwrights when they dramatize a popular novel or a war story to catch the public fancy.

CLASSIFICATION ACCORDING TO DRAMATIC TYPE. Shakespeare's dramas are usually divided into three classes, called tragedies, comedies, and historical plays. Strictly speaking the drama has but two divisions, tragedy and comedy, in which are included the many subordinate forms of tragi-comedy, melodrama, lyric drama (opera), farce, etc. A tragedy is a drama in which the principal characters are involved in desperate circumstances or led by overwhelming passions. It is invariably serious and dignified.

The movement is always stately, but grows more and more rapid as it approaches the climax; and the end is always calamitous, resulting in death or dire misfortune to the principals. As Chaucer's monk says, before he begins to "biwayle in maner of tragedie":

Tragedie is to seyn a certeyn storie

Of him that stood in great prosperitee,

And is y-fallen out of heigh degree

Into miserie, and endeth wrecchedly.

A comedy, on the other hand, is a drama in which the characters are placed in more or less humorous situations. The movement is light and often mirthful, and the play ends in general good will and happiness. The historical drama aims to present some historical age or character, and may be either a comedy or a tragedy. The following list includes the best of Shakespeare's plays in each of the three classes; but the order indicates merely the author's personal opinion of the relative merits of the plays in each class. Thus Merchant of Venice would be the first of the comedies for the beginner to read, and Julius Caesar is an excellent introduction to the historical plays and the tragedies.

Comedies. Merchant of Venice, Midsummer Night's Dream, As You Like It, Winter's Tale, The Tempest, Twelfth Night. Tragedies. Romeo and Juliet, Macbeth, Hamlet, King Lear, Othello.

Historical Plays. Julius Caesar, Richard III, Henry IV, Henry V, Coriolanus, Antony and Cleopatra.

DOUBTFUL PLAYS. It is reasonably certain that some of the plays generally attributed to Shakespeare are partly the work of other dramatists. The first of these doubtful plays, often called the Pre-Shakespearian Group, are Titus Andronicus and the first part of Henry VI. Shakespeare probably worked with Marlowe in the two last parts of Henry VI and in Richard III. The three plays, Taming of the Shrew, Timon, and Pericles are only partly Shakespeare's work, but the other authors are unknown. Henry VIII is the work of Fletcher and Shakespeare, opinion being divided as to whether Shakespeare helped Fletcher, or whether it was an unfinished work of Shakespeare which was put into Fletcher's hands for completion. Two Noble Kinsmen is a play not ordinarily found in editions of Shakespeare, but it is often placed among his doubtful works. The greater part of the play is undoubtedly by Fletcher. Edward III is one of several crude plays published at first anonymously and later attributed to Shakespeare by publishers who desired to sell their wares. It contains a few passages that strongly suggest Shakespeare; but the external evidence is all against his authorship.

SHAKESPEARE'S POEMS. It is generally asserted that, if Shakespeare had written no plays, his poems alone would have given him a commanding place in the Elizabethan Age. Nevertheless, in the various histories of our literature there is apparent a desire to praise and pass over all but the Sonnets as rapidly as possible; and the reason may be stated frankly. His two long poems, "Venus and Adonis" and "The Rape of Lucrece," contain much poetic fancy; but it must be said of both that the subjects are unpleasant, and that they are dragged out to unnecessary length in order to show the play of youthful imagination. They were extremely popular in Shakespeare's day, but in comparison with his great dramatic works these poems are now of minor importance.

Shakespeare's Sonnets, one hundred and fifty-four in number, are the only direct expression of the poet's own feelings that we possess; for his plays are the most impersonal in all literature. They were published together in 1609; but if they had any unity in Shakespeare's mind, their plan and purpose are hard to discover. By some critics they are regarded as mere literary exercises; by others as the expression of some personal grief during the third period of the poet's literary career. Still others, taking a hint from the sonnet beginning "Two loves I have, of comfort and despair," divide them all into two classes, addressed to a man who was Shakespeare's friend, and to a woman who disdained his love. The reader may well avoid such classifications and read a few sonnets, like the twenty-ninth, for instance, and let them speak their own message. A few are trivial and artificial enough, suggesting the elaborate exercises of a piano player; but the majority are remarkable for their subtle thought and exquisite expression. Here and there is one, like that beginning

When to the sessions of sweet silent thought
I summon up remembrance of things past,

which will haunt the reader long afterwards, like the remembrance of an old German melody.

SHAKESPEARE'S PLACE AND INFLUENCE. Shakespeare holds, by general acclamation, the foremost place in the world's literature, and his overwhelming greatness renders it difficult to criticise or even to praise him. Two poets only, Homer and Dante, have been named with him; but each of these wrote within narrow limits, while Shakespeare's genius included all the world of nature and of men. In a word, he is the universal poet. To study nature in his works is like exploring a new and beautiful country; to study man in his works is like going into a great city, viewing the motley crowd as one views a great masquerade in which past and present mingle freely and familiarly, as if the dead were all living again. And the marvelous thing, in this masquerade of all sorts and conditions of men, is that Shakespeare lifts the mask from every face, lets us see the man as he is in his own soul, and shows us in each one some germ of good, some "soul of goodness" even in things evil. For Shakespeare strikes no uncertain note, and raises no doubts to add to the burden of your own. Good always overcomes evil in the long run; and love, faith, work, and duty are the four elements that in all ages make the world right. To criticise or praise the genius that creates these men and women is to criticise or praise humanity itself.

Of his influence in literature it is equally difficult to speak. Goethe expresses the common literary judgment when he says, "I do not remember that any book or person or event in my life ever made so great an impression upon me as the plays of Shakespeare." His influence upon our own language and thought is beyond calculation. Shakespeare and the King James Bible are the two great conservators of the English speech; and one who habitually reads them finds himself possessed of a style and vocabulary that are beyond criticism. Even those who read no Shakespeare are still unconsciously guided by him, for his thought and expression have so pervaded our life and literature that it is impossible, so long as one speaks the English language, to escape his influence.

His life was gentle, and the elements

So mixed in him, that Nature might stand up

And say to all the world, "This was a man!"

SHAKESPEARE'S CONTEMPORARIES AND SUCCESSORS IN THE DRAMA

DECLINE OF THE DRAMA. It was inevitable that the drama should decline after Shakespeare, for the simple reason that there was no other great enough to fill his place. Aside from this, other causes were at work, and the chief of these was at the very source of the Elizabethan dramas. It must be remembered that our first playwrights wrote to please their audiences; that the drama rose in England because of the desire of a patriotic people to see something of the stirring life of the times reflected on the stage.

For there were no papers or magazines in those days, and people came to the theaters not only to be amused but to be informed. Like children, they wanted to see a story acted; and like men, they wanted to know what it meant. Shakespeare fulfilled their desire. He gave them their story, and his genius was great enough to show in every play not only their own life and passions but something of the meaning of all life, and of that eternal justice which uses the war of human passions for its own great ends.

Thus good and evil mingle freely in his dramas; but the evil is never attractive, and the good triumphs as inevitably as fate. Though his language is sometimes coarse, we are to remember that it was the custom of his age to speak somewhat coarsely, and that in language, as in thought and feeling, Shakespeare is far above most of his contemporaries.

With his successors all this was changed. The audience itself had gradually changed, and in place of plain people eager for a story and for information, we see a larger and larger proportion of those who went to the play because they had nothing else to do. They wanted amusement only, and since they had blunted by idleness the desire for simple and wholesome amusement, they called for something more sensational. Shakespeare's successors catered to the depraved tastes of this new audience.

They lacked not only Shakespeare's genius, but his broad charity, his moral insight into life. With the exception of Ben Jonson, they neglected the simple fact that man in his deepest nature is a moral being, and that only a play which satisfies the whole nature of man by showing the triumph of the moral law can ever wholly satisfy an audience or a people. Beaumont and Fletcher, forgetting the deep meaning of life, strove for effect by increasing the sensationalism of their plays; Webster reveled in tragedies of blood and thunder; Massinger and Ford made another step downward, producing evil and licentious scenes for their own sake, making characters and situations more immoral till, notwithstanding these dramatists' ability, the stage had become insincere, frivolous, and bad. Ben Jonson's ode, "Come Leave the Loathed Stage," is the judgment of a large and honest nature grown weary of the plays and the players of the time. We read with a sense of relief that in 1642, only twenty-six years after Shakespeare's death, both houses of Parliament voted to close the theaters as breeders of lies and immorality.

BEN JONSON (1573?-1637)

Personally Jonson is the most commanding literary figure among the Elizabethans. For twenty-five years he was the literary dictator of London, the chief of all the wits that gathered nightly at the old Devil Tavern. With his great learning, his ability, and his commanding position as poet laureate, he set himself squarely against his contemporaries and the romantic tendency of the age. For two things he fought bravely,--to restore the classic form of the drama, and to keep the stage from its downward course. Apparently he failed; the romantic school fixed its hold more strongly than ever; the stage went swiftly to an end as sad as that of the early dramatists. Nevertheless his influence lived and grew more powerful till, aided largely by French influence, it resulted in the so-called classicism of the eighteenth century.

LIFE. Jonson was born at Westminster about the year 1573. His father, an educated gentleman, had his property confiscated and was himself thrown into prison by Queen Mary; so we infer the family was of some prominence. From his mother he received certain strong characteristics, and by a single short reference in Jonson's works we are led to see the kind of woman she was. It is while Jonson is telling Drummond of the occasion when he was thrown into prison, because some passages in the comedy of Eastward Ho! gave offense to King James, and he was in danger of a horrible death, after having his ears and nose cut off. He tells us how, after his pardon, he was banqueting with his friends, when his "old mother" came in and showed a paper full of "lusty strong poison," which she intended to mix with his drink just before the execution. And to show that she "was no churl," she intended first to drink of the poison herself. The incident is all the more suggestive from the fact that Chapman and Marston, one his friend and the other his enemy, were first cast into prison as the authors of Eastward Ho! and rough Ben Jonson at once declared that he too had had a small hand in the writing and went to join them in prison.

Jonson's father came out of prison, having given up his estate, and became a minister. He died just before the son's birth, and two years later the mother married a bricklayer of London. The boy was sent to a private school, and later made his own way to Westminster School, where the submaster, Camden, struck by the boy's ability, taught and largely supported him. For a short time he may have studied at the university in Cambridge; but his stepfather soon set him to learning the bricklayer's trade. He ran away from this, and went with the English army to fight Spaniards in the Low Countries. His best known exploit there was to fight a duel between the lines with one of the enemy's soldiers, while both armies looked on. Jonson killed his man, and took his arms, and made his way back to his own lines in a way to delight the old Norman troubadours. He soon returned to England, and married precipitately when only nineteen or twenty years old. Five years later we find him employed, like Shakespeare, as actor and reviser of old plays in the theater. Thereafter his life is a varied and stormy one. He killed an actor in a duel, and only escaped hanging by pleading "benefit of clergy"; but he lost all his poor goods and was branded for life on his left thumb. In his first great play, Every Man in His Humour (1598), Shakespeare acted one of the parts; and that may have been the beginning of their long friendship. Other plays followed rapidly. Upon the accession of James, Jonson's masques won him royal favor, and he was made poet laureate. He now became undoubted leader of the literary men of his time, though his rough honesty and his hatred of the literary tendencies of the age made him quarrel with nearly all of them.

In 1616, soon after Shakespeare's retirement, he stopped writing for the stage and gave himself up to study and serious work. In 1618 he traveled on foot to Scotland, where he visited Drummond, from whom we have the scant records of his varied life. His impressions of this journey, called Foot Pilgrimage, were lost in a fire before publication. Thereafter he produced less, and his work declined in vigor; but spite of growing poverty and infirmity we notice in his later work, especially in the unfinished Sad Shepherd, a certain mellowness and tender human sympathy which were lacking in his earlier productions. He died poverty stricken in 1637. Unlike Shakespeare's, his death was mourned as a national calamity, and he was buried with all honor in Westminster Abbey. On his grave was laid a marble slab, on which the words "O rare Ben Jonson" were his sufficient epitaph.

WORKS OF BEN JONSON. Jonson's work is in strong contrast with that of Shakespeare and of the later Elizabethan dramatists. Alone he fought against the romantic tendency of the age, and to restore the classic standards. Thus the whole action of his drama usually covers only a few hours, or a single day. He never takes liberties with historical facts, as Shakespeare does, but is accurate to the smallest detail. His dramas abound in classical learning, are carefully and logically constructed, and comedy and tragedy are kept apart, instead of crowding each other as they do in Shakespeare and in life. In one respect his comedies are worthy of careful reading,--they are intensely realistic, presenting men and women of the time exactly as they were. From a few of Jonson's scenes we can understand--better than from all the plays of Shakespeare--how men talked and acted during the Age of Elizabeth.

Jonson's first comedy, Every Man in His Humour, is a key to all his dramas. The word "humour" in his age stood for some characteristic whim or quality of society. Jonson gives to his leading character some prominent humor, exaggerates it, as the cartoonist enlarges the most characteristic feature of a face, and so holds it before our attention that all other qualities are lost sight of; which is the method that Dickens used later in many of his novels. Every Man in His Humour was the first of three satires. Its special aim was to ridicule the humors of the city. The second, Cynthia's Revels, satirizes the humors of the court; while the third, The Poetaster, the result of a quarrel with his contemporaries, was leveled at the false standards of the poets of the age.

The three best known of Jonson's comedies are Volpone, or the Fox, The Alchemist, and Epicoene, or the Silent Woman. Volpone is a keen and merciless analysis of a man governed by an overwhelming love of money for its own sake. The first words in the first scene are a key to the whole comedy:

(Volpone)

Good morning to the day; and next, my gold!

Open the shrine that I may see my saint.

(Mosca withdraws a curtain and discovers piles of

gold, plate, jewels, etc.)

Hail the world's soul, and mine!

Volpone's method of increasing his wealth is to play upon the avarice of men. He pretends to be at the point of death, and his "suitors," who know his love of gain and that he has no heirs, endeavor hypocritically to sweeten his last moments by giving him rich presents, so that he will leave them all his wealth. The intrigues of these suitors furnish the story of the play, and show to what infamous depths avarice will lead a man.

The Alchemist is a study of quackery on one side and of gullibility on the other, founded on the mediaeval idea of the philosopher's stone, and applies as well to the patent medicines and get-rich-quick schemes of our day as to the peculiar forms of quackery with which Jonson was more familiar. In plot and artistic construction The Alchemist is an almost perfect specimen of the best English drama. It has some remarkably good passages, and is the most readable of Jonson's plays.

Epicoene, or the Silent Woman, is a prose comedy exceedingly well constructed, full of life, abounding in fun and unexpected situations. Here is a brief outline from which the reader may sec of what materials Jonson made up his comedies.

The chief character is Morose, a rich old codger whose humor is a horror of noise. He lives in a street so narrow that it will admit no carriages; he pads the doors; plugs the keyhole; puts mattresses on the stairs. He dismisses a servant who wears squeaky boots; makes all the rest go about in thick stockings; and they must answer him by signs, since he cannot bear to hear anybody but himself talk. He disinherits his poor nephew Eugenie, and, to make sure that the latter will not get any money out of him, resolves to marry. His confidant in this delicate matter is Cutbeard the barber, who, unlike his kind, never speaks unless spoken to, and does not even knick his scissors as he works. Cutbeard (who is secretly in league with the nephew) tells him of Epicoene, a rare, silent woman, and Morose is so delighted with her silence that he resolves to marry her on the spot. Cutbeard produces a parson with a bad cold, who can speak only in a whisper, to marry them; and when the parson coughs after the ceremony Morose demands back five shillings of the fee. To save it the parson coughs more, and is hurriedly bundled out of the house.

The silent woman finds her voice immediately after the marriage, begins to talk loudly and to make reforms in the household, driving

Morose to distraction. A noisy dinner party from a neighboring house, with drums and trumpets and a quarreling man and wife, is skillfully guided in at this moment to celebrate the wedding. Morose flees for his life, and is found perched like a monkey on a crossbeam in the attic, with all his nightcaps tied over his ears. He seeks a divorce, but is driven frantic by the loud arguments of a lawyer and a divine, who are no other than Cutbeard and a sea captain disguised. When Morose is past all hope the nephew offers to release him from his wife and her noisy friends if he will allow him five hundred pounds a year. Morose offers him anything, everything, to escape his torment, and signs a deed to that effect. Then comes the surprise of the play when Eugenie whips the wig from Epicoene and shows a boy in disguise.

It will be seen that the Silent Woman, with its rapid action and its unexpected situations, offers an excellent opportunity for the actors; but the reading of the play, as of most of Jonson's comedies, is marred by low intrigues showing a sad state of morals among the upper classes.

Besides these, and many other less known comedies, Jonson wrote two great tragedies, Sejanus (1603) and Catiline (1611), upon severe classical lines. After ceasing his work for the stage, Jonson wrote many masques in honor of James I and of Queen Anne, to be played amid elaborate scenery by the gentlemen of the court. The best of these are "The Satyr," "The Penates," "Masque of Blackness," "Masque of Beauty," "Hue and Cry after Cupid," and "The Masque of Queens." In all his plays Jonson showed a strong lyric gift, and some of his little poems and songs, like "The Triumph of Charis," "Drink to Me Only with Thine Eyes," and "To the Memory of my Beloved Mother," are now better known than his great dramatic works. A single volume of prose, called Timber, or Discoveries made upon Men and Matter, is an interesting collection of short essays which are more like Bacon's than any other work of the age.

BEAUMONT AND FLETCHER. The work of these two men is so closely interwoven that, though Fletcher outlived Beaumont by nine years and the latter had no hand in some forty of the plays that bear their joint names, we still class them together, and only scholars attempt to separate their works so as to give each writer his due share. Unlike most of the Elizabethan dramatists, they both came from noble and cultured families and were university trained. Their work, in strong contrast with Jonson's, is intensely romantic, and in it all, however coarse or brutal the scene, there is still, as Emerson pointed out, the subtle "recognition of gentility."

Beaumont (1584-1616) was the brother of Sir John Beaumont of Leicestershire. From Oxford he came to London to study law, but soon gave it up to write for the stage. Fletcher (1579-1625) was the son of the bishop of London, and shows in all his work the influence of his high social position and of his Cambridge education. The two dramatists met at the Mermaid tavern under Ben Jonson's leadership and soon became inseparable friends, living and working together. Tradition has it that Beaumont supplied the judgment and the solid work of the play, while Fletcher furnished the high-colored sentiment and the lyric poetry, without which an Elizabethan play would have been incomplete. Of their joint plays, the two best known are Philaster, whose old theme, like that of Cymbeline and Griselda, is the jealousy of a lover and the faithfulness of a girl, and The Maid's Tragedy. Concerning Fletcher's work the most interesting literary question is how much did he write of Shakespeare's Henry VIII, and how much did Shakespeare help him in The Two Noble Kinsmen.

JOHN WEBSTER. Of Webster's personal history we know nothing except that he was well known as a dramatist under James I. His extraordinary powers of expression rank him with Shakespeare; but his talent seems to have been largely devoted to the blood-and-thunder play begun by Marlowe. His two best known plays are The White Devil (pub. 1612) and The Duchess of Malfi (pub. 1623). The latter, spite of its horrors, ranks him as one of the greatest masters of English tragedy. It must be remembered that he sought in this play to reproduce the Italian life of the sixteenth century, and for this no imaginary horrors are needed. The history of any Italian court or city in this period furnishes more vice and violence and dishonor than even the gloomy imagination of Webster could conceive. All the so-called blood tragedies of the Elizabethan period, from Thomas Kyd's Spanish Tragedy down, however much they may condemn the brutal taste of the English audiences, are still only so many search lights thrown upon a history of horrible darkness.

THOMAS MIDDLETON (1570?-1627). Middleton is best known by two great plays, The Changeling and Women Beware Women. In poetry and diction they are almost worthy at times to rank with

Shakespeare's plays; otherwise, in their sensationalism and unnaturalness they do violence to the moral sense and are repulsive to the modern reader. Two earlier plays, A Trick to catch the Old One, his best comedy, and A Fair Quarrel, his earliest tragedy, are less mature in thought and expression, but more readable, because they seem to express Middleton's own idea of the drama rather than that of the corrupt court and playwrights of his later age.

THOMAS HEYWOOD (1580?-1650?). Heywood's life, of which we know little in detail, covers the whole period of the Elizabethan drama. To the glory of that drama he contributed, according to his own statement, the greater part, at least, of nearly two hundred and twenty plays. It was an enormous amount of work; but he seems to have been animated by the modern literary spirit of following the best market and striking while the financial iron is hot. Naturally good work was impossible, even to genius, under such circumstances, and few of his plays are now known. The two best, if the reader would obtain his own idea of Heywood's undoubted ability, are A Woman killed with Kindness, a pathetic story of domestic life, and The Fair Maid of the West, a melodrama with plenty of fighting of the popular kind.

THOMAS DEKKER (1570-?). Dekker is in pleasing contrast with most of the dramatists of the time. All we know of him must be inferred from his works, which show a happy and sunny nature, pleasant and good to meet. The reader will find the best expression of Dekker's personality and erratic genius in The Shoemakers' Holiday, a humorous study of plain working people, and Old Fortunatus, a fairy drama of the wishing hat and no end of money. Whether intended for children or not, it had the effect of charming the elders far more than the young people, and the play became immensely popular.

MASSINGER, FORD, SHIRLEY. These three men mark the end of the Elizabethan drama. Their work, done largely while the struggle was on between the actors and the corrupt court, on one side, and the Puritans on the other, shows a deliberate turning away not only from Puritan standards but from the high ideals of their own art to pander to the corrupt taste of the upper classes.

Philip Massinger (1584-1640) was a dramatic poet of great natural ability; but his plots and situations are usually so strained and artificial that the modern reader finds no interest in them. In his best comedy,

A New Way to Pay Old Debts, he achieved great popularity and gave us one figure, Sir Giles Overreach, which is one of the typical characters of the English stage. His best plays are The Great Duke of Florence, The Virgin Martyr, and The Maid of Honour.

John Ford (1586-1642?) and James Shirley (1596-1666) have left us little of permanent literary value, and their works are read only by those who wish to understand the whole rise and fall of the drama. An occasional scene in Ford's plays is as strong as anything that the Elizabethan Age produced; but as a whole the plays are unnatural and tiresome. Probably his best play is The Broken Heart (1633). Shirley was given to imitation of his predecessors, and his very imitation is characteristic of an age which had lost its inspiration. A single play, Hyde Park, with its frivolous, realistic dialogue, is sometimes read for its reflection of the fashionable gossipy talk of the day. Long before Shirley's death the actors said, "Farewell! Othello's occupation's gone." Parliament voted to close the theaters, thereby saving the drama from a more inglorious death by dissipation.

THE PROSE WRITERS

FRANCIS BACON (1561-1626)

In Bacon we see one of those complex and contradictory natures which are the despair of the biographer. If the writer be an admirer of Bacon, he finds too much that he must excuse or pass over in silence; and if he takes his stand on the law to condemn the avarice and dishonesty of his subject, he finds enough moral courage and nobility to make him question the justice of his own judgment. On the one hand is rugged Ben Jonson's tribute to his power and ability, and on the other Hallam's summary that he was "a man who, being intrusted with the highest gifts of Heaven, habitually abused them for the poorest purposes of earth--hired them out for guineas, places, and titles in the service of injustice, covetousness, and oppression."

Laying aside the opinions of others, and relying only upon the facts of Bacon's life, we find on the one side the politician, cold, calculating, selfish, and on the other the literary and scientific man with an impressive devotion to truth for its own great sake; here a man using questionable means to advance his own interests, and there a man seeking with zeal and endless labor to penetrate the secret ways of Nature, with no other object than to advance the interests of his fellow-men. So, in our ignorance of the secret motives and springs of the man's life, judgment is necessarily suspended. Bacon was apparently one of those double natures that only God is competent to judge, because of the strange mixture of intellectual strength and moral weakness that is in them.

LIFE. Bacon was the son of Sir Nicholas Bacon, Lord Keeper of the Seal, and of the learned Ann Cook, sister-in-law to Lord Burleigh, greatest of the queen's statesmen. From these connections, as well as from native gifts, he was attracted to the court, and as a child was called by Elizabeth her "Little Lord Keeper." At twelve he went to Cambridge, but left the university after two years, declaring the whole plan of education to be radically wrong, and the system of Aristotle, which was the basis of all philosophy in those days, to be a childish delusion, since in the course of centuries it had "produced no fruit, but only a jungle of dry and useless branches." Strange, even for a sophomore of fourteen, thus to condemn the whole system of the universities; but such was the boy, and the system! Next year, in order to continue his education, he accompanied the English ambassador to France, where he is said to have busied himself chiefly with the practical studies of statistics and diplomacy.

Two years later he was recalled to London by the death of his father. Without money, and naturally with expensive tastes, he applied to his Uncle Burleigh for a lucrative position. It was in this application that he used the expression, so characteristic of the Elizabethan Age, that he "had taken all knowledge for his province." Burleigh, who misjudged him as a dreamer and self-seeker, not only refused to help him at the court but successfully opposed his advancement by Elizabeth. Bacon then took up the study of law, and was admitted to the bar in 1582. That he had not lost his philosophy in the mazes of the law is shown by his tract, written about this time, "On the Greatest Birth of Time," which was a plea for his inductive system of philosophy, reasoning from many facts to one law, rather than from an assumed law to particular facts, which was the deductive method that had been in use for centuries. In his famous plea for progress Bacon demanded three things: the free investigation of nature, the discovery of facts instead of theories, and the verification of results by experiment rather than by argument. In our day these are the A, B, C of science, but in Bacon's time they seemed revolutionary. As a lawyer he became immediately successful; his knowledge and power of pleading became widely known, and it was almost at the beginning of his career that Jonson wrote, "The fear of every one that heard him speak was that he should make an end." The publication of his Essays added greatly to his fame; but Bacon was not content. His head was buzzing with huge schemes,--the pacification of unhappy Ireland, the simplification of English law, the reform of the church, the study of nature, the establishment of a new philosophy. Meanwhile, sad to say, he played the game of politics for his personal advantage. He devoted himself to Essex, the young and dangerous favorite of the queen, won his friendship, and then used him skillfully to better his own position. When the earl was tried for treason it was partly, at least, through Bacon's efforts that he was convicted and beheaded; and though Bacon claims to have been actuated by a high sense of justice, we are not convinced that he understood either justice or friendship in appearing as queen's counsel against the man who had befriended him. His coldbloodedness and lack of moral sensitiveness appear even in his essays on "Love" and "Friendship." Indeed, we can understand his life only upon the theory that his intellectuality left him cold and dead to the higher sentiments of our humanity.

During Elizabeth's reign Bacon had sought repeatedly for high office, but had been blocked by Burleigh and perhaps also by the queen's own shrewdness in judging men. With the advent of James I (1603) Bacon devoted himself to the new ruler and rose rapidly in favor. He was knighted, and soon afterwards attained another object of his ambition in marrying a rich wife. The appearance of his great work, the Advancement of Learning, in 1605, was largely the result of the mental stimulus produced by his change in fortune. In 1613 he was made attorney-general, and speedily made enemies by using the office to increase his personal ends. He justified himself in his course by his devotion to the king's cause, and by the belief that the higher his position and the more ample his means the more he could do for science. It was in this year that Bacon wrote his series of State Papers, which show a marvelous grasp of the political tendencies of his age. Had his advice been followed, it would have certainly averted the struggle between king and parliament that followed speedily. In 1617 he was appointed to his father's office, Lord Keeper of the Seal, and the next year to the high office of Lord Chancellor. With this office he received the title of Baron Verulam, and later of Viscount St. Alban.

which he affixed with some vanity to his literary work. Two years later appeared his greatest work, the Novum Organum, called after Aristotle's famous Organon.

Bacon did not long enjoy his political honors. The storm which had been long gathering against James's government broke suddenly upon Bacon's head. When Parliament assembled in 1621 it vented its distrust of James and his favorite Villiers by striking unexpectedly at their chief adviser. Bacon was sternly accused of accepting bribes, and the evidence was so great that he confessed that there was much political corruption abroad in the land, that he was personally guilty of some of it, and he threw himself upon the mercy of his judges. Parliament at that time was in no mood for mercy. Bacon was deprived of his office and was sentenced to pay the enormous fine of 40,000 pounds, to be imprisoned during the king's pleasure, and thereafter to be banished forever from Parliament and court. Though the imprisonment lasted only a few days and the fine was largely remitted, Bacon's hopes and schemes for political honors were ended; and it is at this point of appalling adversity that the nobility in the man's nature asserts itself strongly. If the reader be interested to apply a great man's philosophy to his own life, he will find the essay, "Of Great Place," most interesting in this connection.

Bacon now withdrew permanently from public life, and devoted his splendid ability to literary and scientific work. He completed the Essays, experimented largely, wrote history, scientific articles, and one scientific novel, and made additions to his Instauratio Magna, the great philosophical work which was never finished. In the spring of 1626, while driving in a snowstorm, it occurred to him that snow might be used as a preservative instead of salt. True to his own method of arriving at truth, he stopped at the first house, bought a fowl, and proceeded to test his theory. The experiment chilled him, and he died soon after from the effects of his exposure. As Macaulay wrote, "the great apostle of experimental philosophy was destined to be its martyr."

WORKS OF BACON. Bacon's philosophic works, The Advancement of Learning and the Novum Organum, will be best understood in connection with the Instauratio Magna, or The Great Institution of True Philosophy, of which they were parts. The Instauratio was never completed, but the very idea of the work was magnificent,-

-to sweep away the involved philosophy of the schoolmen and the educational systems of the universities, and to substitute a single great work which should be a complete education, "a rich storehouse for the glory of the Creator and for the relief of man's estate." The object of this education was to bring practical results to all the people, instead of a little selfish culture and much useless speculation, which, he conceived, were the only products of the universities.

THE INSTAURATIO MAGNA. This was the most ambitious, though it is not the best known, of Bacon's works. For the insight it gives us into the author's mind, we note here a brief outline of his subject. It was divided into six parts, as follows:

1. Partitiones Scientiarum. This was to be a classification and summary of all human knowledge. Philosophy and all speculation must be cast out and the natural sciences established as the basis of all education. The only part completed was The Advancement of Learning, which served as an introduction.
2. Novum Organum, or the "new instrument," that is, the use of reason and experiment instead of the old Aristotelian logic. To find truth one must do two things: (a) get rid of all prejudices or idols, as Bacon called them. These "idols" are four: "idols of the tribe," that is, prejudices due to common methods of thought among all races; "idols of the cave or den," that is, personal peculiarities and prejudices; "idols of the market place," due to errors of language; and "idols of the theater," which are the unreliable traditions of men. (b) After discarding the above "idols" we must interrogate nature; must collect facts by means of numerous experiments, arrange them in order, and then determine the law that underlies them.

   It will be seen at a glance that the above is the most important of Bacon's works. The Organum was to be in several books, only two of which he completed, and these he wrote and rewrote twelve times until they satisfied him.
3. Historic Naturalis et Experimentalis, the study of all the phenomena of nature. Of four parts of this work which he completed, one of them at least, the Sylva Sylvarum, is decidedly

at variance with his own idea of fact and experiment. It abounds in fanciful explanations, more worthy of the poetic than of the scientific mind. Nature is seen to be full of desires and instincts; the air "thirsts" for light and fragrance; bodies rise or sink because they have an "appetite" for height or depth; the qualities of bodies are the result of an "essence," so that when we discover the essences of gold and silver and diamonds it will be a simple matter to create as much of them as we may need.

4. Scala Intellectus, or "Ladder of the Mind," is the rational application of the Organum to all problems. By it the mind should ascend step by step from particular facts and instances to general laws and abstract principles.
5. Prodromi, "Prophecies or Anticipations," is a list of discoveries that men shall make when they have applied Bacon's methods of study and experimentation.
6. Philosophia Secunda, which was to be a record of practical results of the new philosophy when the succeeding ages should have applied it faithfully.

It is impossible to regard even the outline of such a vast work without an involuntary thrill of admiration for the bold and original mind which conceived it. "We may," said Bacon, "make no despicable beginnings. The destinies of the human race must complete the work... for upon this will depend not only a speculative good but all the fortunes of mankind and all their power." There is the unconscious expression of one of the great minds of the world. Bacon was like one of the architects of the Middle Ages, who drew his plans for a mighty cathedral, perfect in every detail from the deep foundation stone to the cross on the highest spire, and who gave over his plans to the builders, knowing that, in his own lifetime, only one tiny chapel would be completed; but knowing also that the very beauty of his plans would appeal to others, and that succeeding ages would finish the work which he dared to begin.

THE ESSAYS. Bacon's famous Essays is the one work which will interest all students of our literature. His Instauratio was in Latin, written mostly by paid helpers from short English abstracts. He regarded

Latin as the only language worthy of a great work; but the world neglected his Latin to seize upon his English,--marvelous English, terse, pithy, packed with thought, in an age that used endless circumlocutions. The first ten essays, published in 1597, were brief notebook jottings of Bacon's observations. Their success astonished the author, but not till fifteen years later were they republished and enlarged. Their charm grew upon Bacon himself, and during his retirement he gave more thought to the wonderful language which he had at first despised as much as Aristotle's philosophy. In 1612 appeared a second edition containing thirty-eight essays, and in 1625, the year before his death, he republished the Essays in their present form, polishing and enlarging the original ten to fifty-eight, covering a wide variety of subjects suggested by the life of men around him.

Concerning the best of these essays there are as many opinions as there are readers, and what one gets out of them depends largely upon his own thought and intelligence. In this respect they are like that Nature to which Bacon directed men's thoughts. The whole volume may be read through in an evening; but after one has read them a dozen times he still finds as many places to pause and reflect as at the first reading. If one must choose out of such a storehouse, we would suggest "Studies," "Goodness," "Riches," "Atheism," "Unity in Religion," "Adversity," "Friendship," and "Great Place" as an introduction to Bacon's worldly-wise philosophy.

MISCELLANEOUS WORKS. Other works of Bacon are interesting as a revelation of the Elizabethan mind, rather than because of any literary value. The New Atlantis is a kind of scientific novel describing another Utopia as seen by Bacon. The inhabitants of Atlantis have banished Philosophy and applied Bacon's method of investigating Nature, using the results to better their own condition. They have a wonderful civilization, in which many of our later discoveries--academies of the sciences, observatories, balloons, submarines, the modification of species, and several others--were foreshadowed with a strange mixture of cold reason and poetic intuition. De Sapientia Veterum is a fanciful attempt to show the deep meaning underlying ancient myths,--a meaning which would have astonished the myth makers themselves. The History of Henry VII is a calm, dispassionate, and remarkably accurate history, which makes us regret that Bacon did not do more historical work. Besides these are metrical versions of certain Psalms--which are valuable, in view of the controversy anent Shakespeare's plays, for showing Bacon's utter inability to write poetry--and a large number of letters and state papers showing the range and power of his intellect.

BACON'S PLACE AND WORK. Although Bacon was for the greater part of his life a busy man of affairs, one cannot read his work without becoming conscious of two things,--a perennial freshness, which the world insists upon in all literature that is to endure, and an intellectual power which marks him as one of the great minds of the world.

Of late the general tendency is to give less and less prominence to his work in science and philosophy; but criticism of his Instauratio, in view of his lofty aim, is of small consequence. It is true that his "science" to-day seems woefully inadequate; true also that, though he sought to discover truth, he thought perhaps to monopolize it, and so looked with the same suspicion upon Copernicus as upon the philosophers. The practical man who despises philosophy has simply misunderstood the thing he despises. In being practical and experimental in a romantic age he was not unique, as is often alleged, but only expressed the tendency of the English mind in all ages. Three centuries earlier the monk Roger Bacon did more practical experimenting than the Elizabethan sage; and the latter's famous "idols" are strongly suggestive of the former's "Four Sources of Human Ignorance." Although Bacon did not make any of the scientific discoveries at which he aimed, yet the whole spirit of his work, especially of the Organum, has strongly influenced science in the direction of accurate observation and of carefully testing every theory by practical experiment.

"He that regardeth the clouds shall not sow," said a wise writer of old; and Bacon turned men's thoughts from the heavens above, with which they had been too busy, to the earth beneath, which they had too much neglected. In an age when men were busy with romance and philosophy, he insisted that the first object of education is to make a man familiar with his natural environment; from books he turned to men, from theory to fact, from philosophy to nature,--and that is perhaps his greatest contribution to life and literature. Like Moses upon

Pisgah, he stood high enough above his fellows to look out over a promised land, which his people would inherit, but into which he himself might never enter.

RICHARD HOOKER (1554?-1600). In strong contrast with Bacon is Richard Hooker, one of the greatest prose writers of the Elizabethan Age. One must read the story of his life, an obscure and lowly life animated by a great spirit, as told by Izaak Walton, to appreciate the full force of this contrast. Bacon took all knowledge for his province, but mastered no single part of it.

Hooker, taking a single theme, the law and practice of the English Church, so handled it that no scholar even of the present day would dream of superseding it or of building upon any other foundation than that which Hooker laid down. His one great work is The Laws of Ecclesiastical Polity, a theological and argumentative book; but, entirely apart from its subject, it will be read wherever men desire to hear the power and stateliness of the English language. Here is a single sentence, remarkable not only for its perfect form but also for its expression of the reverence for law which lies at the heart of Anglo-Saxon civilization:

Of law there can be no less acknowledged than that her seat is the bosom of God, her voice the harmony of the world; all things in heaven and earth do her homage; the very least as feeling her care, and the greatest as not exempted from her power; both angels and men, and creatures of what condition soever, though each in different sort and manner, yet all with uniform consent admiring her as the mother of their peace and joy.

SIDNEY AND RALEIGH. Among the prose writers of this wonderful literary age there are many others that deserve passing notice, though they fall far below the standard of Bacon and Hooker. Sir Philip Sidney (1554-1586), who has already been considered as a poet, is quite as well known by his prose works, Arcadia, a pastoral romance, and the Defense of Poesie, one of our earliest literary essays. Sidney, whom the poet Shelley has eulogized, represents the whole romantic tendency of his age; while Sir Walter Raleigh (1552?-1618) represents its adventurous spirit and activity. The life of Raleigh is an almost incomprehensible mixture of the poet, scholar, and adventurer; now helping the Huguenots or the struggling Dutch in Europe, and now leading an expedition into the unmapped wilds of the New World; busy here with court intrigues, and there with piratical attempts to capture the gold-laden Spanish galleons; one moment sailing the high seas in utter freedom, and the next writing history and poetry to solace his imprisonment. Such a life in itself is a volume far more interesting than anything that he wrote. He is the restless spirit of the Elizabethan Age personified.

Raleigh's chief prose works are the Discoverie of Guiana, a work which would certainly have been interesting enough had he told simply what he saw, but which was filled with colonization schemes and visions of an El Dorado to fill the eyes and ears of the credulous; and the History of the World, written to occupy his prison hours. The history is a wholly untrustworthy account of events from creation to the downfall of the Macedonian Empire. It is interesting chiefly for its style, which is simple and dignified, and for the flashes of wit and poetry that break into the fantastic combination of miracles, traditions, hearsay, and state records which he called history. In the conclusion is the famous apostrophe to Death, which suggests what Raleigh might have done had he lived less strenuously and written more carefully.

O eloquent, just, and mighty Death! whom none could advise thou hast persuaded; what none hath dared thou hast done; and whom all the world hath flattered thou only hast cast out of the world and despised; thou hast drawn together all the star-stretched greatness, all the pride, cruelty, and ambition of man, and covered it all over with these two narrow words, Hic jacet!

JOHN FOXE (1516-1587). Foxe will be remembered always for his famous Book of Martyrs, a book that our elders gave to us on Sundays when we were young, thinking it good discipline for us to afflict our souls when we wanted to be roaming the sunlit fields, or when in our enforced idleness we would, if our own taste in the matter had been consulted, have made good shift to be quiet and happy with Robinson Crusoe. So we have a gloomy memory of Foxe, and something of a grievance, which prevent a just appreciation of his worth.

Foxe had been driven out of England by the Marian persecutions, and in a wandering but diligent life on the Continent he conceived the idea of writing a history of the persecutions of the church from the earliest days to his own.

The part relating to England and Scotland was published, in Latin, in 1559 under a title as sonorous and impressive as the Roman office for the dead,--Rerum in Ecclesia Gestarum Maximarumque per Europam Persecutionum Commentarii. On his return to England Foxe translated this work, calling it the Acts and Monuments; but it soon became known as the Book of Martyrs, and so it will always be called.

Foxe's own bitter experience causes him to write with more heat and indignation than his saintly theme would warrant, and the "holy tone" sometimes spoils a narrative that would be impressive in its bare simplicity. Nevertheless the book has made for itself a secure place in our literature. It is strongest in its record of humble men, like Rowland Taylor and Thomas Hawkes, whose sublime heroism, but for this narrative, would have been lost amid the great names and the great events that fill the Elizabethan Age.

CAMDEN AND KNOX. Two historians, William Camden and John Knox, stand out prominently among the numerous historical writers of the age. Camden's Britannia (1586) is a monumental work, which marks the beginning of true antiquarian research in the field of history; and his Annals of Queen Elizabeth is worthy of a far higher place than has thus far been given it.

John Knox, the reformer, in his History of the Reformation in Scotland, has some very vivid portraits of his helpers and enemies. The personal and aggressive elements enter too strongly for a work of history; but the autobiographical parts show rare literary power. His account of his famous interview with Mary Queen of Scots is clear-cut as a cameo, and shows the man's extraordinary power better than a whole volume of biography. Such scenes make one wish that more of his time had been given to literary work, rather than to the disputes and troubles of his own Scotch kirk.

HAKLUYT AND PURCHAS. Two editors of this age have made for themselves an enviable place in our literature. They are Richard Hakluyt (1552?-1616) and Samuel Purchas (1575?-1626). Hakluyt was a clergyman who in the midst of his little parish set himself to achieve two great patriotic ends,--to promote the wealth and commerce of his country, and to preserve the memory of all his countrymen who added to the glory of the realm by their travels and explorations.

To further the first object he concerned himself deeply with the commercial interests of the East India Company, with Raleigh's colonizing plans in Virginia, and with a translation of De Soto's travels in America. To further the second he made himself familiar with books of voyages in all foreign languages and with the brief reports of explorations of his own countrymen. His Principal Navigations, Voyages, and Discoveries of the English Nation, in three volumes, appeared first in 1589, and a second edition followed in 1598-1600.

The first volume tells of voyages to the north; the second to India and the East; the third, which is as large as the other two, to the New World. With the exception of the very first voyage, that of King Arthur to Iceland in 517, which is founded on a myth, all the voyages are authentic accounts of the explorers themselves, and are immensely interesting reading even at the present day. No other book of travels has so well expressed the spirit and energy of the English race, or better deserves a place in our literature.

Samuel Purchas, who was also a clergyman, continued the work of Hakluyt, using many of the latter's unpublished manuscripts and condensing the records of numerous other voyages. His first famous book, Purchas, His Pilgrimage, appeared in 1613, and was followed by Hakluytus Posthumus, or Purchas His Pilgrimes, in 1625.

The very name inclines one to open the book with pleasure, and when one follows his inclination--which is, after all, one of the best guides in literature--he is rarely disappointed. Though it falls far below the standard of Hakluyt, both in accuracy and literary finish, there is still plenty to make one glad that the book was written and that he can now comfortably follow Purchas on his pilgrimage.

THOMAS NORTH. Among the translators of the Elizabethan Age Sir Thomas North (1535?-1601?) is most deserving of notice because of his version of Plutarch's Lives (1579) from which Shakespeare took the characters and many of the incidents for three great Roman plays. Thus in North we read:

Caesar also had Cassius in great jealousy and suspected him much: whereupon he said on a time to his friends: "What will Cassius do, think ye? I like not his pale looks." Another time when Caesar's friends warned him of Antonius and Dolabella, he answered them again, "I never reckon of them; but these pale-visaged and carrion lean people, I fear them most," meaning Brutus and Cassius.

Shakespeare merely touches such a scene with the magic of his genius, and his Caesar speaks:

Let me have men about me that are fat:

Sleek-headed men, and such as sleep o' nights.

Yond Cassius has a lean and hungry look:

He thinks too much: such men are dangerous.

A careful reading of North's Plutarch and then of the famous Roman plays shows to how great an extent Shakespeare was dependent upon his obscure contemporary.

North's translation, to which we owe so many heroic models in our literature, was probably made not from Plutarch but from Amyot's excellent French translation. Nevertheless he reproduces the spirit of the original, and notwithstanding our modern and more accurate translations, he remains the most inspiring interpreter of the great biographer whom Emerson calls "the historian of heroism."

SUMMARY OF THE AGE OF ELIZABETH. This period is generally regarded as the greatest in the history of our literature. Historically, we note in this age the tremendous impetus received from the Renaissance, from the Reformation, and from the exploration of the New World. It was marked by a strong national spirit, by patriotism, by religious tolerance, by social content, by intellectual progress, and by unbounded enthusiasm.

Such an age, of thought, feeling, and vigorous action, finds its best expression in the drama; and the wonderful development of the drama, culminating in Shakespeare, is the most significant characteristic of the Elizabethan period.

Though the age produced some excellent prose works, it is essentially an age of poetry; and the poetry is remarkable for its variety, its freshness, its youthful and romantic feeling. Both the poetry and the drama were permeated by Italian influence, which was dominant in English literature from Chaucer to the Restoration. The literature of this age is often called the literature of the Renaissance, though, as we have seen, the Renaissance itself began much earlier, and for a century and a half added very little to our literary possessions.

In our study of this great age we have noted (1) the Non-dramatic Poets, that is, poets who did not write for the stage. The center of this group is Edmund Spenser, whose Shepherd's Calendar (1579) marked the appearance of the first national poet since Chaucer's death in 1400. His most famous work is The Faery Queen. Associated with Spenser are the minor poets, Thomas Sackville, Michael Drayton, George Chapman, and Philip Sidney. Chapman is noted for his completion of Marlowe's poem, Hero and Leander, and for his translation of Homer's Iliad and Odyssey. Sidney, besides his poetry, wrote his prose romance Arcadia, and The Defense of Poesie, one of our earliest critical essays. The Rise of the Drama in England; the Miracle plays, Moralities, and Interludes; our first play, "Ralph Royster Doyster"; the first true English comedy, "Gammer Gurton's Needle," and the first tragedy, "Gorboduc"; the conflict between classic and native ideals in the English drama.

Shakespeare's Predecessors, Lyly, Kyd, Nash, Peele, Greene, Marlowe; the types of drama with which they experimented,--the Marlowesque, one-man type, or tragedy of passion, the popular Chronicle plays, the Domestic drama, the Court or Lylian comedy, Romantic comedy and tragedy, Classical plays, and the Melodrama. Marlowe is the greatest of Shakespeare's predecessors. His four plays are "Tamburlaine," "Faustus," "The Jew of Malta," and "Edward II."

Shakespeare, his life, work, and influence.

Shakespeare's Successors, Ben Jonson, Beaumont and Fletcher, Webster, Middleton, Heywood, Dekker; and the rapid decline of the drama. Ben Jonson is the greatest of this group. His chief comedies are "Every Man in His Humour," "The Silent Woman," and "The Alchemist"; his two extant tragedies are "Sejanus" and "Catiline."

The Prose Writers, of whom Bacon is the most notable. His chief philosophical work is the Instauratio Magna (incomplete), which includes "The Advancement of Learning" and the "Novum Organum"; but he is known to literary readers by his famous Essays. Minor prose writers are Richard Hooker, John Foxe, the historians Camden and Knox, the editors Hakluyt and Purchas, who gave us the stirring records of exploration, and Thomas North, the translator of Plutarch's Lives.

7

The Restoration Period of Literature

It seems a curious contradiction, at first glance, to place the return of Charles II at the beginning of modern England, as our historians are wont to do; for there was never a time when the progress of liberty, which history records, was more plainly turned backwards. The Puritan regime had been too severe; it had repressed too many natural pleasures. Now, released from restraint, society abandoned the decencies of life and the reverence for law itself, and plunged into excesses more unnatural than had been the restraints of Puritanism.

The inevitable effect of excess is disease, and for almost an entire generation following the Restoration, in 1660, England lay sick of a fever. Socially, politically, morally, London suggests an Italian city in the days of the Medici; and its literature, especially its drama, often seems more like the delirium of illness than the expression of a healthy mind. But even a fever has its advantages. Whatever impurity is in the blood "is burnt and purged away," and a man rises from fever with a new strength and a new idea of the value of life, like King Hezekiah, who after his sickness and fear of death resolved to "go softly" all his days.

The Restoration was the great crisis in English history; and that England lived through it was due solely to the strength and excellence of that Puritanism which she thought she had flung to the winds when she welcomed back a vicious monarch at Dover. The chief lesson of the Restoration was this,--that it showed by awful contrast the necessity of truth and honesty, and of a strong government of free men, for which the Puritan had stood like a rock in every hour of his rugged history. Through fever, England came slowly back to health; through gross corruption in society and in the state England learned that her people were at heart sober, sincere, religious folk, and that their character was naturally too strong to follow after pleasure and be satisfied. So Puritanism suddenly gained all that it had struggled for, and gained it even in the hour when all seemed lost, when Milton in his sorrow unconsciously portrayed the government of Charles and his Cabal in that tremendous scene of the council of the infernal peers in Pandemonium, plotting the ruin of the world.

Of the king and his followers it is difficult to write temperately. Most of the dramatic literature of the time is atrocious, and we can understand it only as we remember the character of the court and society for which it was written. Unspeakably vile in his private life, the king had no redeeming patriotism, no sense of responsibility to his country for even his public acts. He gave high offices to blackguards, stole from the exchequer like a common thief, played off Catholics and Protestants against each other, disregarding his pledges to both alike, broke his solemn treaty with the Dutch and with his own ministers, and betrayed his country for French money to spend on his own pleasures. It is useless to paint the dishonor of a court which followed gayly after such a leader. The first Parliament, while it contained some noble and patriotic members, was dominated by young men who remembered the excess of Puritan zeal, but forgot the despotism and injustice which had compelled Puritanism to stand up and assert the manhood of England. These young politicians vied with the king in passing laws for the subjugation of Church and State, and in their thirst for revenge upon all who had been connected with Cromwell's iron government. Once more a wretched formalism--that perpetual danger to the English Church--came to the front and exercised authority over the free churches. The House of Lords was largely increased by the creation of hereditary titles and estates for ignoble men and shameless women who had flattered the king's vanity. Even the Bench, that last strong refuge of English justice, was corrupted by the appointment of judges, like the brutal Jeffreys, whose aim, like that of their royal master, was to get money and to exercise power without personal responsibility. Amid all this dishonor the foreign influence and authority of Cromwell's strong government vanished like smoke. The valiant little Dutch navy swept the English fleet from the sea, and only the thunder of Dutch guns in the Thames, under the very windows of London, awoke the nation to the realization of how low it had fallen.

Two considerations must modify our judgment of this disheartening spectacle. First, the king and his court are not England. Though our histories are largely filled with the records of kings and soldiers, of intrigues and fighting, these no more express the real life of a people than fever and delirium express a normal manhood. Though king and court and high society arouse our disgust or pity, records are not wanting to show that private life in England remained honest and pure even in the worst days of the Restoration. While London society might be entertained by the degenerate poetry of Rochester and the dramas of Dryden and Wycherley, English scholars hailed Milton with delight; and the common people followed Bunyan and Baxter with their tremendous appeal to righteousness and liberty. Second, the king, with all his pretensions to divine right, remained only a figurehead; and the Anglo-Saxon people, when they tire of one figurehead, have always the will and the power to throw it overboard and choose a better one. The country was divided into two political parties: the Whigs, who sought to limit the royal power in the interests of Parliament and the people; and the Tories, who strove to check the growing power of the people in the interests of their hereditary rulers. Both parties, however, were largely devoted to the Anglican Church; and when James II, after four years of misrule, attempted to establish a national Catholicism by intrigues which aroused the protest of the Pope as well as of Parliament, then Whigs and Tories, Catholics and Protestants, united in England's last great revolution.

The complete and bloodless Revolution of 1688, which called William of Orange to the throne, was simply the indication of England's restored health and sanity. It proclaimed that she had not long forgotten, and could never again forget, the lesson taught her by Puritanism in its hundred years of struggle and sacrifice. Modern England was firmly established by the Revolution, which was brought about by the excesses of the Restoration.

LITERARY CHARACTERISTICS. In the literature of the Restoration we note a sudden breaking away from old standards, just as society broke away from the restraints of Puritanism. Many of the literary men had been driven out of England with Charles and his court, or else had followed their patrons into exile in the days of the Commonwealth. On their return they renounced old ideals and demanded that English poetry and drama should follow the style to which they had become accustomed in the gayety of Paris. We read with astonishment in Pepys's Diary (1660-1669) that he has been to see a play called Midsummer Night's Dream, but that he will never go again to hear Shakespeare, "for it is the most insipid, ridiculous play that ever I saw in my life." And again we read in the diary of Evelyn,--another writer who reflects with wonderful accuracy the life and spirit of the Restoration,--"I saw Hamlet played; but now the old plays begin to disgust this refined age, since his Majesty's being so long abroad." Since Shakespeare and the Elizabethans were no longer interesting, literary men began to imitate the French writers, with whose works they had just grown familiar; and here begins the so-called period of French influence, which shows itself in English literature for the next century, instead of the Italian influence which had been dominant since Spenser and the Elizabethans. One has only to consider for a moment the French writers of this period, Pascal, Bossuet, Fenelon, Malherbe, Corneille, Racine, Moliere,--all that brilliant company which makes the reign of Louis XIV the Elizabethan Age of French literature,--to see how far astray the early writers of the Restoration went in their wretched imitation. When a man takes another for his model, he should copy virtues not vices; but unfortunately many English writers reversed the rule, copying the vices of French comedy without any of its wit or delicacy or abundant ideas. The poems of Rochester, the plays of Dryden, Wycherley, Congreve, Vanbrugh, and Farquhar, all popular in their day, are mostly unreadable. Milton's "sons of Belial, flown with insolence and wine," is a good expression of the vile character of the court writers and of the London theaters for thirty years following the Restoration. Such work can never satisfy a people, and when Jeremy Collier, in 1698, published a vigorous attack upon the evil plays and the playwrights of the day, all London, tired of the coarseness and excesses of the Restoration, joined the literary revolution, and the corrupt drama was driven from the stage.

With the final rejection of the Restoration drama we reach a crisis in the history of our literature. The old Elizabethan spirit, with its patriotism, its creative vigor, its love of romance, and the Puritan spirit with its moral earnestness and individualism, were both things of the past; and at first there was nothing to take their places. Dryden, the greatest writer of the age, voiced a general complaint when he said that in his prose and poetry he was "drawing the outlines" of a new art, but had no teacher to instruct him. But literature is a progressive art, and soon the writers of the age developed two marked tendencies of their own,--the tendency to realism, and the tendency to that preciseness and elegance of expression which marks our literature for the next hundred years.

In realism--that is, the representation of men exactly as they are, the expression of the plain, unvarnished truth without regard to ideals or romance--the tendency was at first thoroughly bad. The early Restoration writers sought to paint realistic pictures of a corrupt court and society, and, as we have suggested, they emphasized vices rather than virtues, and gave us coarse, low plays without interest or moral significance. Like Hobbes, they saw only the externals of man, his body and appetites, not his soul and its ideals; and so, like most realists, they resemble a man lost in the woods, who wanders aimlessly around in circles, seeing the confusing trees but never the whole forest, and who seldom thinks of climbing the nearest high hill to get his bearings. Later, however, this tendency to realism became more wholesome. While it neglected romantic poetry, in which youth is eternally interested, it led to a keener study of the practical motives which govern human action.

The second tendency of the age was toward directness and simplicity of expression, and to this excellent tendency our literature is greatly indebted. In both the Elizabethan and the Puritan ages the general tendency of writers was towards extravagance of thought and language. Sentences were often involved, and loaded with Latin quotations and classical allusions. The Restoration writers opposed this vigorously. From France they brought back the tendency to regard established rules for writing, to emphasize close reasoning rather than romantic fancy, and to use short, clean-cut sentences without an unnecessary word. We see this French influence in the Royal Society, which had for one of its objects the reform of English prose by getting rid of its "swellings of style," and which bound all its members to use "a close, naked, natural way of speaking... as near to mathematical plainness as they can." Dryden accepted this excellent rule for his prose, and adopted the heroic couplet, as the next best thing, for the greater part of his poetry. As he tells us himself:

And this unpolished rugged verse I chose
As fittest for discourse, and nearest prose.

It is largely due to him that writers developed that formalism of style, that precise, almost mathematical elegance, miscalled classicism, which ruled English literature for the next century.

Another thing which the reader will note with interest in Restoration literature is the adoption of the heroic couplet; that is, two iambic pentameter lines which rime together, as the most suitable form of poetry. Waller, who began to use it in 1623, is generally regarded as the father of the couplet, for he is the first poet to use it consistently in the bulk of his poetry. Chaucer had used the rimed couplet wonderfully well in his Canterbury Tales, but in Chaucer it is the poetical thought more than the expression which delights us. With the Restoration writers, form counts for everything. Waller and Dryden made the couplet the prevailing literary fashion, and in their hands the couplet becomes "closed"; that is, each pair of lines must contain a complete thought, stated as precisely as possible. Thus Waller writes:

The soul's dark cottage, battered and decayed,
Lets in new light through chinks that time has made.

That is a kind of aphorism such as Pope made in large quantities in the following age. It contains a thought, is catchy, quotable, easy to remember; and the Restoration writers delighted in it. Soon this mechanical closed couplet, in which the second line was often made first, almost excluded all other forms of poetry. It was dominant in England for a full century, and we have grown familiar with it, and somewhat weary of its monotony, in such famous poems as Pope's "Essay on Man" and Goldsmith's "Deserted Village." These, however, are essays rather than poems. That even the couplet is capable of melody and variety is shown in Chaucer's Tales and in Keats's exquisite Endymion.

These four things, the tendency to vulgar realism in the drama, a general formalism which came from following set rules, the development of a simpler and more direct prose style, and the prevalence of the heroic couplet in poetry are the main characteristics of Restoration literature. They are all exemplified in the work of one man, John Dryden.

JOHN DRYDEN (1631-1700)

Dryden is the greatest literary figure of the Restoration, and in his work we have an excellent reflection of both the good and the evil tendencies of the age in which he lived. If we can think for a moment of literature as a canal of water, we may appreciate the figure that Dryden is the "lock by which the waters of English poetry were let down from the mountains of Shakespeare and Milton to the plain of Pope"; that is, he stands between two very different ages, and serves as a transition from one to the other.

LIFE. Dryden's life contains so many conflicting elements of greatness and littleness that the biographer is continually taken away from the facts, which are his chief concern, to judge motives, which are manifestly outside his knowledge and business. Judged by his own opinion of himself, as expressed in the numerous prefaces to his works, Dryden was the soul of candor, writing with no other master than literature, and with no other object than to advance the welfare of his age and nation. Judged by his acts, he was apparently a timeserver, catering to a depraved audience in his dramas, and dedicating his work with much flattery to those who were easily cajoled by their vanity into sharing their purse and patronage. In this, however, he only followed the general custom of the time, and is above many of his contemporaries.

Dryden was born in the village of Aldwinkle, Northamptonshire, in 1631. His family were prosperous people, who brought him up in the strict Puritan faith, and sent him first to the famous Westminster school and then to Cambridge. He made excellent use of his opportunities and studied eagerly, becoming one of the best educated men of his age, especially in the classics. Though of remarkable literary taste, he showed little evidence of literary ability up to the age of thirty. By his training and family connections he was allied to the Puritan party, and his only well-known work of this period, the "Heroic Stanzas," was written on the death of Cromwell:

His grandeur he derived from Heaven alone,
For he was great ere Fortune made him so;
And wars, like mists that rise against the sun,
Made him but greater seem, not greater grow.

In these four lines, taken almost at random from the "Heroic Stanzas," we have an epitome of the thought, the preciseness, and the polish that mark all his literary work.

This poem made Dryden well known, and he was in a fair way to become the new poet of Puritanism when the Restoration made a complete change in his methods. He had come to London for a literary life, and when the Royalists were again in power he placed himself promptly on the winning side. His "Astraea Redux," a poem of welcome to Charles II, and his "Panegyric to his Sacred Majesty," breathe more devotion to "the old goat," as the king was known to his courtiers, than had his earlier poems to Puritanism.

In 1667 he became more widely known and popular by his "Annus Mirabilis," a narrative poem describing the terrors of the great fire in London and some events of the disgraceful war with Holland; but with the theaters reopened and nightly filled, the drama offered the most attractive field to one who made his living by literature; so Dryden turned to the stage and agreed to furnish three plays yearly for the actors of the King's Theater. For nearly twenty years, the best of his life, Dryden gave himself up to this unfortunate work. Both by nature and habit he seems to have been clean in his personal life; but the stage demanded unclean plays, and Dryden followed his audience. That he deplored this is evident from some of his later work, and we have his statement that he wrote only one play, his best, to please himself. This was All for Love, which was written in blank verse, most of the others being in rimed couplets.

During this time Dryden had become the best known literary man of London, and was almost as much a dictator to the literary set which gathered in the taverns and coffeehouses as Ben Jonson had been before him. His work, meanwhile, was rewarded by large financial returns, and by his being appointed poet laureate and collector of the port of London. The latter office, it may be remembered, had once been held by Chaucer.

At fifty years of age, and before Jeremy Collier had driven his dramas from the stage, Dryden turned from dramatic work to throw himself into the strife of religion and politics, writing at this period his numerous prose and poetical treatises. In 1682 appeared his Religio Laici (Religion of a Layman), defending the Anglican Church against all other sects, especially the Catholics and Presbyterians; but three years later, when James II came to the throne with schemes to establish the Roman faith, Dryden turned Catholic and wrote his most famous religious poem, "The Hind and the Panther," beginning:

A milk-white Hind, immortal and unchanged,

Fed on the lawns and in the forest ranged;

Without unspotted, innocent within,

She feared no danger, for she knew no sin.

This hind is a symbol for the Roman Church; and the Anglicans, as a panther, are represented as persecuting the faithful. Numerous other sects--Calvinists, Anabaptists, Quakers--were represented by the wolf, boar, hare, and other animals, which gave the poet an excellent chance for exercising his satire. Dryden's enemies made the accusation, often since repeated, of hypocrisy in thus changing his church; but that he was sincere in the matter can now hardly be questioned, for he knew how to "suffer for the faith" and to be true to his religion, even when it meant misjudgment and loss of fortune. At the Revolution of 1688 he refused allegiance to William of Orange; he was deprived of all his offices and pensions, and as an old man was again thrown back on literature as his only means of livelihood. He went to work with extraordinary courage and energy, writing plays, poems, prefaces for other men, eulogies for funeral occasions,--every kind of literary work that men would pay for. His most successful work at this time was his translations, which resulted in the complete Aeneid and many selections from Homer, Ovid, and Juvenal, appearing in English rimed couplets. His most enduring poem, the splendid ode called "Alexander's Feast," was written in 1697. Three years later he published his last work, Fables, containing poetical paraphrases of the tales of Boccaccio and Chaucer, and the miscellaneous poems of his last years. Long prefaces were the fashion in Dryden's day, and his best critical work is found in his introductions. The preface to the Fables is generally admired as an example of the new prose style developed by Dryden and his followers.

From the literary view point these last troubled years were the best of Dryden's life, though they were made bitter by obscurity and by the criticism of his numerous enemies. He died in 1700 and was buried near Chaucer in Westminster Abbey.

WORKS OF DRYDEN. The numerous dramatic works of Dryden are best left in that obscurity into which they have fallen. Now and then they contain a bit of excellent lyric poetry, and in All for Love, another version of Antony and Cleopatra, where he leaves his cherished heroic couplet for the blank verse of Marlowe and Shakespeare, he shows what he might have done had he not sold his talents to a depraved audience. On the whole, reading his plays is like nibbling at a rotting apple; even the good spots are affected by the decay, and one ends by throwing the whole thing into the garbage can, where most of the dramatic works of this period belong.

The controversial and satirical poems are on a higher plane; though, it must be confessed, Dryden's satire often strikes us as cutting and revengeful, rather than witty. The best known of these, and a masterpiece of its kind, is "Absalom and Achitophel," which is undoubtedly the most powerful political satire in our language. Taking the Bible story of David and Absalom, he uses it to ridicule the Whig party and also to revenge himself upon his enemies.

Charles II appeared as King David; his natural son, the Duke of Monmouth, who was mixed up in the Rye House Plot, paraded as Absalom; Shaftesbury was Achitophel, the evil Counselor; and the Duke of Buckingham was satirized as Zimri. The poem had enormous political influence, and raised Dryden, in the opinion of his contemporaries, to the front rank of English poets. Two extracts from the powerful characterizations of Achitophel and Zimri are given here to show the style and spirit of the whole work.

(SHAFTESBURY)

Of these the false Àchitophel was first;
A name to all succeeding ages cursed:
For close designs and crooked counsels fit;
Sagacious, bold, and turbulent of wit;
Restless, unfixed in principles and place;
In power unpleased, impatient of disgrace:
A fiery soul, which, working out its way,
Fretted the pygmy body to decay....
A daring pilot in extremity,

Pleased with the danger, when the waves went high
He sought the storms: but for a calm unfit,
Would steer too nigh the sands to boast his wit.
Great wits are sure to madness near allied,
And thin partitions do their bounds divide;
Else why should he, with wealth and honor blest,
Refuse his age the needful hours of rest?
Punish a body which he could not please;
Bankrupt of life, yet prodigal of ease?
And all to leave what with his toil he won,
To that unfeathered two-legged thing, a son....
In friendship false, implacable in hate;
Resolved to ruin or to rule the state;...
Then seized with fear, yet still affecting fame,
Usurped a patriot's all-atoning name.
So easy still it proves in factious times
With public zeal to cancel private crimes.

(THE DUKE OF BUCKINGHAM)

Some of their chiefs were princes of the land;
In the first rank of these did Zimri stand,
A man so various, that he seemed to be
Not one, but all mankind's epitome:
Stiff in opinions, always in the wrong,
Was everything by starts and nothing long;
But, in the course of one revolving moon,
Was chymist, fiddler, statesman, and buffoon;
Then all for women, painting, rhyming, drinking,
Besides ten thousand freaks that died in thinking.
Blest madman, who could every hour employ
With something new to wish or to enjoy!

Railing and praising were his usual themes,
And both, to show his judgment, in extremes:
So over-violent, or over-civil,
That every man with him was God or devil.

Of the many miscellaneous poems of Dryden, the curious reader will get an idea of his sustained narrative power from the Annus Mirabilis. The best expression of Dryden's literary genius, however, is found in "Alexander's Feast," which is his most enduring ode, and one of the best in our language.

As a prose writer Dryden had a very marked influence on our literature in shortening his sentences, and especially in writing naturally, without depending on literary ornamentation to give effect to what he is saying. If we compare his prose with that of Milton, or Browne, or Jeremy Taylor, we note that Dryden cares less for style than any of the others, but takes more pains to state his thought clearly and concisely, as men speak when they wish to be understood. The classical school, which followed the Restoration, looked to Dryden as a leader, and to him we owe largely that tendency to exactness of expression which marks our subsequent prose writing. With his prose, Dryden rapidly developed his critical ability, and became the foremost critic of his age. His criticisms, instead of being published as independent works, were generally used as prefaces or introductions to his poetry. The best known of these criticisms are the preface to the Fables, "Of Heroic Plays," "Discourse on Satire," and especially the "Essay of Dramatic Poesy" (1668), which attempts to lay a foundation for all literary criticism.

DRYDEN'S INFLUENCE ON LITERATURE. Dryden's place among authors is due partly to his great influence on the succeeding age of classicism. Briefly, this influence may be summed up by noting the three new elements which he brought into our literature. These are: (1) the establishment of the heroic couplet as the fashion for satiric, didactic, and descriptive poetry; (2) his development of a direct, serviceable prose style such as we still cultivate; and (3) his development of the art of literary criticism in his essays and in the numerous prefaces to his poems. This is certainly a large work for one man to accomplish, and Dryden is worthy of honor, though comparatively little of what he wrote is now found on our bookshelves.

SAMUEL BUTLER (1612-1680). In marked contrast with Dryden, who devoted his life to literature and won his success by hard work, is Samuel Butler, who jumped into fame by a single, careless work, which represents not any serious intent or effort, but the pastime of an idle hour. We are to remember that, though the Royalists had triumphed in the Restoration, the Puritan spirit was not dead, nor even sleeping, and that the Puritan held steadfastly to his own principles. Against these principles of justice, truth, and liberty there was no argument, since they expressed the manhood of England; but many of the Puritan practices were open to ridicule, and the Royalists, in revenge for their defeat, began to use ridicule without mercy. During the early years of the Restoration doggerel verses ridiculing Puritanism, and burlesque,--that is, a ridiculous representation of serious subjects, or a serious representation of ridiculous subjects,--were the most popular form of literature with London society. Of all this burlesque and doggerel the most famous is Butler's Hudibras, a work to which we can trace many of the prejudices that still prevail against Puritanism.

Of Butler himself we know little; he is one of the most obscure figures in our literature. During the days of Cromwell's Protectorate he was in the employ of Sir Samuel Luke, a crabbed and extreme type of Puritan nobleman, and here he collected his material and probably wrote the first part of his burlesque, which, of course, he did not dare to publish until after the Restoration.

Hudibras is plainly modeled upon the Don Quixote of Cervantes. It describes the adventures of a fanatical justice of the peace, Sir Hudibras, and of his squire, Ralpho, in their endeavor to put down all innocent pleasures. In Hudibras and Ralpho the two extreme types of the Puritan party, Presbyterians and Independents, are mercilessly ridiculed. When the poem first appeared in public, in 1663, after circulating secretly for years in manuscript, it became at once enormously popular.

The king carried a copy in his pocket, and courtiers vied with each other in quoting its most scurrilous passages. A second and a third part, continuing the adventures of Hudibras, were published in 1664 and 1668. At best the work is a wretched doggerel, but it was clever enough and strikingly original; and since it expressed the Royalist spirit towards the Puritans, it speedily found its place in a literature which reflects every phase of human life. A few odd lines are given here to show the character of the work, and to introduce the reader to the best known burlesque in our language:

He was in logic a great critic,
Profoundly skilled in analytic;
He could distinguish, and divide
A hair 'twixt south and southwest side;
On either which he would dispute,
Confute, change hands, and still confute;
He'd undertake to prove, by force
Of argument, a man's no horse;
He'd run in debt by disputation,
And pay with ratiocination.
For he was of that stubborn crew
Of errant saints, whom all men grant
To be the true Church Militant;
Such as do build their faith upon
The holy text of pike and gun;
Decide all controversies by
Infallible artillery;
And prove their doctrine orthodox
By apostolic blows and knocks;
Compound for sins they are inclined to,
By damning those they have no mind to.

HOBBES AND LOCKE. Thomas Hobbes (1588-1679) is one of the writers that puzzle the historian with a doubt as to whether or not he should be included in the story of literature. The one book for which he is famous is called Leviathan, or the Matter, Form, and Power of a Commonwealth (1651). It is partly political, partly a philosophical book, combining two central ideas which challenge and startle the attention, namely, that self-interest is the only guiding power of humanity, and that blind submission to rulers is the only true basis of government. In a word, Hobbes reduced human nature to its purely animal aspects, and then asserted confidently that there was nothing more to study. Certainly, therefore, as a reflection of the underlying spirit of Charles and his followers it has no equal in any purely literary work of the time. John Locke (1632-1704) is famous as the author of a single great philosophical work, the Essay concerning Human Understanding (1690). This is a study of the nature of the human mind and of the origin of ideas, which, far more than the work of Bacon and Hobbes, is the basis upon which English philosophy has since been built. Aside from their subjects, both works are models of the new prose, direct, simple, convincing, for which Dryden and the Royal Society labored. They are known to every student of philosophy, but are seldom included in a work of literature.

EVELYN AND PEPYS. These two men, John Evelyn (1620-1706) and Samuel Pepys (1633-1703), are famous as the writers of diaries, in which they jotted down the daily occurrences of their own lives, without any thought that the world would ever see or be interested in what they had written. Evelyn was the author of Sylva, the first book on trees and forestry in English, and Terra, which is the first attempt at a scientific study of agriculture; but the world has lost sight of these two good books, while it cherishes his diary, which extends over the greater part of his life and gives us vivid pictures of society in his time, and especially of the frightful corruption of the royal court.

Pepys began life in a small way as a clerk in a government office, but soon rose by his diligence and industry to be Secretary of the Admiralty. Here he was brought into contact with every grade of society, from the king's ministers to the poor sailors of the fleet. Being inquisitive as a blue jay, he investigated the rumors and gossip of the court, as well as the small affairs of his neighbors, and wrote them all down in his diary with evident interest. But because he chattered most freely, and told his little book a great many secrets which it were not well for the world to know, he concealed everything in shorthand,--and here again he was like the blue jay, which carries off and hides every bright trinket it discovers. The Diary covers the years from 1660 to 1669, and gossips about everything, from his own position and duties at the office, his dress and kitchen and cook and children, to the great political intrigues of office and the scandals of high society. No other such minute-picture of the daily life of an age has been written. Yet for a century and a half it remained entirely unknown, and not until 1825 was Pepys's shorthand deciphered and published. Since then it has been widely read, and is still one of the most interesting examples of diary writing that we possess. Following are a few extracts, covering only a few days in April, 1663, from which one may infer the minute and interesting character of the work that this clerk, politician, president of the Royal Society, and general busybody wrote to please himself:

April 1st. I went to the Temple to my Cozen Roger Pepys, to see and talk with him a little: who tells me that, with much ado, the Parliament do agree to throw down Popery; but he says it is with so much spite and passion, and an endeavor of bringing all Nonconformists into the same condition, that he is afeard matters will not go so well as he could wish.... To my office all the afternoon; Lord! how Sir J. Minnes, like a mad coxcomb, did swear and stamp, swearing that Commissioner Pett hath still the old heart against the King that ever he had,... and all the damnable reproaches in the world, at which I was ashamed, but said little; but, upon the whole, I find him still a foole, led by the nose with stories told by Sir W. Batten, whether with or without reason. So, vexed in my mind to see things ordered so unlike gentlemen, or men of reason, I went home and to bed.

3d. To White Hall and to Chappell, which being most monstrous full, I could not go into my pew, but sat among the quire. Dr. Creeton, the Scotchman, preached a most admirable, good, learned, honest, and most severe sermon, yet comicall.... He railed bitterly ever and anon against John Calvin and his brood, the Presbyterians, and against the present terme, now in use, of "tender consciences."

He ripped up Hugh Peters (calling him the execrable skellum), his preaching and stirring up the mayds of the city to bring in their bodkins and thimbles. Thence going out of White Hall, I met Captain Grove, who did give me a letter directed to myself from himself. I discerned money to be in it, and took it, knowing, as I found it to be, the proceed of the place I have got him, the taking up of vessels for Tangier. But I did not open it till I came home to my office, and there I broke it open, not looking into it till all the money was out, that I might say I saw no money in the paper, if ever I should be questioned about it. There was a piece of gold and 4L in silver.

4th. To my office. Home to dinner, whither by and by comes Roger Pepys, etc. Very merry at, before, and after dinner, and the more for that my dinner was great, and most neatly dressed by our owne only mayde. We had a fricasee of rabbits and chickens, a leg of mutton boiled, three carps in a dish, a great dish of a side of lambe, a dish of roasted pigeons, a dish of four lobsters, three tarts, a lamprey pie (a most rare pie), a dish of anchovies, good wine of several sorts, and all things mighty noble and to my great content.

5th (Lord's day). Up and spent the morning, till the Barber came, in reading in my chamber part of Osborne's Advice to his Son, which I shall not never enough admire for sense and language, and being by and by trimmed, to Church, myself, wife, Ashwell, etc. Home and, while dinner was prepared, to my office to read over my vows with great affection and to very good purpose. Then to church again, where a simple bawling young Scot preached.

19th (Easter day). Up and this day put on my close-kneed coloured suit, which, with new stockings of the colour, with belt and new gilt-handled sword, is very handsome. To church alone, and after dinner to church again, where the young Scotchman preaching, I slept all the while. After supper, fell in discourse of dancing, and I find that Ashwell hath a very fine carriage, which makes my wife almost ashamed of herself to see herself so outdone, but to-morrow she begins to learn to dance for a month or two. So to prayers and to bed. Will being gone, with my leave, to his father's this day for a day or two, to take physique these holydays.

23d. St. George's day and Coronacion, the King and Court being at Windsor, at the installing of the King of Denmarke by proxy and the Duke of Monmouth.... Spent the evening with my father. At cards till late, and being at supper, my boy being sent for some mustard to a neat's tongue, the rogue staid half an houre in the streets, it seems at a bonfire, at which I was very angry, and resolve to beat him to-morrow.

24th. Up betimes, and with my salt eele went down into the parler and there got my boy and did beat him till I was fain to take breath two or three times, yet for all I am afeard it will make the boy never the better, he is grown so hardened in his tricks, which I am sorry for, he being capable of making a brave man, and is a boy that I and my wife love very well.

SUMMARY OF THE RESTORATION PERIOD. The chief thing to note in England during the Restoration is the tremendous social reaction from the restraints of Puritanism, which suggests the wide swing of a pendulum from one extreme to the other. For a generation many natural pleasures had been suppressed; now the theaters were reopened, bull and bear baiting revived, and sports, music, dancing,--a wild delight in the pleasures and vanities of this world replaced that absorption in "other-worldliness" which characterized the extreme of Puritanism. In literature the change is no less marked. From the Elizabethan drama playwrights turned to coarse, evil scenes, which presently disgusted the people and were driven from the stage. From romance, writers turned to realism; from Italian influence with its exuberance of imagination they turned to France, and learned to repress the emotions, to follow the head rather than the heart, and to write in a clear, concise, formal style, according to set rules. Poets turned from the noble blank verse of Shakespeare and Milton, from the variety and melody which had characterized English poetry since Chaucer's day, to the monotonous heroic couplet with its mechanical perfection.

The greatest writer of the age is John Dryden, who established the heroic couplet as the prevailing verse form in English poetry, and who developed a new and serviceable prose style suited to the practical needs of the age. The popular ridicule of Puritanism in burlesque and doggerel is best exemplified in Butler's Hudibras. The realistic tendency, the study of facts and of men as they are, is shown in the work of the Royal Society, in the philosophy of Hobbes and Locke, and in the diaries of Evelyn and Pepys, with their minute pictures of social life. The age was one of transition from the exuberance and vigor of Renaissance literature to the formality and polish of the Augustan Age. In strong contrast with the preceding ages, comparatively little of Restoration literature is familiar to modern readers.

8

English Literature in Eighteenth Century

The Revolution of 1688, which banished the last of the Stuart kings and called William of Orange to the throne, marks the end of the long struggle for political freedom in England. Thereafter the Englishman spent his tremendous energy, which his forbears had largely spent in fighting for freedom, in endless political discussions and in efforts to improve his government. In order to bring about reforms, votes were now necessary; and to get votes the people of England must be approached with ideas, facts, arguments, information. So the newspaper was born, and literature in its widest sense, including the book, the newspaper, and the magazine, became the chief instrument of a nation's progress.

The first half of the eighteenth century is remarkable for the rapid social development in England. Hitherto men had been more or less governed by the narrow, isolated standards of the Middle Ages, and when they differed they fell speedily to blows. Now for the first time they set themselves to the task of learning the art of living together, while still holding different opinions. In a single generation nearly two thousand public coffeehouses, each a center of sociability, sprang up in London alone, and the number of private clubs is quite as astonishing. This new social life had a marked effect in polishing men's words and manners. The typical Londoner of Queen Anne's day was still rude, and a little vulgar in his tastes; the city was still very filthy, the streets unlighted and infested at night by bands of rowdies and "Mohawks"; but outwardly men sought to refine their manners according to prevailing standards; and to be elegant, to have "good form," was a man's first duty, whether he entered society or wrote literature. One can hardly read a book or poem of the age without feeling this superficial elegance. Government still had its opposing Tory and Whig parties, and the Church was divided into Catholics, Anglicans, and Dissenters; but the growing social life offset many antagonisms, producing at least the outward impression of peace and unity. Nearly every writer of the age busied himself with religion as well as with party politics, the scientist Newton as sincerely as the churchman Barrow, the philosophical Locke no less earnestly than the evangelical Wesley; but nearly all tempered their zeal with moderation, and argued from reason and Scripture, or used delicate satire upon their opponents, instead of denouncing them as followers of Satan. There were exceptions, of course; but the general tendency of the age was toward toleration. Man had found himself in the long struggle for personal liberty; now he turned to the task of discovering his neighbor, of finding in Whig and Tory, in Catholic and Protestant, in Anglican and Dissenter, the same general human characteristics that he found in himself. This good work was helped, moreover, by the spread of education and by the growth of the national spfrit, following the victories of Marlborough on the Continent. In the midst of heated argument it needed only a word--Gibraltar, Blenheim, Ramillies, Malplaquet--or a poem of victory written in a garret to tell a patriotic people that under their many differences they were all alike Englishmen.

In the latter half of the century the political and social progress is almost bewildering. The modern form of cabinet government responsible to Parliament and the people had been established under George I; and in 1757 the cynical and corrupt practices of Walpole, premier of the first Tory cabinet, were replaced by the more enlightened policies of Pitt. Schools were established; clubs and coffeehouses increased; books and magazines multiplied until the press was the greatest visible power in England; the modern great dailies, the Chronicle, Post, and Times, began their career of public education. Religiously, all the churches of England felt the quickening power of that tremendous spiritual revival known as Methodism, under the preaching of Wesley and Whitefield. Outside her own borders three great men--Clive in India, Wolfe on the Plains of Abraham, Cook in Australia and the islands of the Pacific--were unfurling the banner of St. George over the untold wealth of new lands, and spreading the world-wide empire of the Anglo-Saxons.

LITERARY CHARACTERISTICS. In every preceding age we have noted especially the poetical works, which constitute, according to Matthew Arnold, the glory of English literature. Now for the first time we must chronicle the triumph of English prose. A multitude of practical interests arising from the new social and political conditions demanded expression, not simply in books, but more especially in pamphlets, magazines, and newspapers. Poetry was inadequate for such a task; hence the development of prose, of the "unfettered word," as Dante calls it,--a development which astonishes us by its rapidity and excellence. The graceful elegance of Addison's essays, the terse vigor of Swift's satires, the artistic finish of Fielding's novels, the sonorous eloquence of Gibbon's history and of Burke's orations,--these have no parallel in the poetry of the age. Indeed, poetry itself became prosaic in this respect, that it was used not for creative works of imagination, but for essays, for satire, for criticism,--for exactly the same practical ends as was prose. The poetry of the first half of the century, as typified in the work of Pope, is polished and witty enough, but artificial; it lacks fire, fine feeling, enthusiasm, the glow of the Elizabethan Age and the moral earnestness of Puritanism. In a word, it interests us as a study of life, rather than delights or inspires us by its appeal to the imagination. The variety and excellence of prose works, and the development of a serviceable prose style, which had been begun by Dryden, until it served to express clearly every human interest and emotion,--these are the chief literary glories of the eighteenth century.

In the literature of the preceding age we noted two marked tendencies,--the tendency to realism in subject-matter, and the tendency to polish and refinement of expression. Both these tendencies were continued in the Augustan Age, and are seen clearly in the poetry of Pope, who brought the couplet to perfection, and in the prose of Addison. A third tendency is shown in the prevalence of satire, resulting from the unfortunate union of politics with literature. We have already noted the power of the press in this age, and the perpetual strife of political parties. Nearly every writer of the first half of the century was used and rewarded by Whigs or Tories for satirizing their enemies and for advancing their special political interests. Pope was a marked exception, but he nevertheless followed the prose writers in using satire too largely in his poetry. Now satire--that is, a literary work which searches out the faults of men or institutions in order to hold them up to ridicule--is at best a destructive kind of criticism. A satirist is like a laborer who clears away the ruins and rubbish of an old house before the architect and builders begin on a new and beautiful structure. The work may sometimes be necessary, but it rarely arouses our enthusiasm. While the satires of Pope, Swift, and Addison are doubtless the best in our language, we hardly place them with our great literature, which is always constructive in spirit; and we have the feeling that all these men were capable of better things than they ever wrote.

THE CLASSIC AGE. The period we are studying is known to us by various names. It is often called the Age of Queen Anne; but, unlike Elizabeth, this "meekly stupid" queen had practically no influence upon our literature. The name Classic Age is more often heard; but in using it we should remember clearly these three different ways in which the word "classic" is applied to literature: (1) the term "classic" refers, in general, to writers of the highest rank in any nation. As used in our literature, it was first applied to the works of the great Greek and Roman writers, like Homer and Virgil; and any English book which followed the simple and noble method of these writers was said to have a classic style. Later the term was enlarged to cover the great literary works of other ancient nations; so that the Bible and the Avestas, as well as the Iliad and the Aeneid, are called classics. (2) Every national literature has at least one period in which an unusual number of great writers are producing books, and this is called the classic period of a nation's literature. Thus the reign of Augustus is the classic or golden age of Rome; the generation of Dante is the classic age of Italian literature; the age of Louis XIV is the French classic age; and the age of Queen Anne is often called the classic age of England. (3) The word "classic" acquired an entirely different meaning in the period we are studying; and we shall better understand this by reference to the preceding ages. The Elizabethan writers were led by patriotism, by enthusiasm, and, in general, by romantic emotions.

They wrote in a natural style, without regard to rules; and though they exaggerated and used too many words, their works are delightful because of their vigor and freshness and fine feeling. In the following age patriotism had largely disappeared from politics and enthusiasm from literature. Poets no longer wrote naturally, but artificially, with strange and fantastic verse forms to give effect, since fine feeling was wanting. And this is the general character of the poetry of the Puritan Age. Gradually our writers rebelled against the exaggerations of both the natural and the fantastic style. They demanded that poetry should follow exact rules; and in this they were influenced by French writers, especially by Boileau and Rapin, who insisted on precise methods of writing poetry, and who professed to have discovered their rules in the classics of Horace and Aristotle.

In our study of the Elizabethan drama we noted the good influence of the classic movement in insisting upon that beauty of form and definiteness of expression which characterize the dramas of Greece and Rome; and in the work of Dryden and his followers we see a revival of classicism in the effort to make English literature conform to rules established by the great writers of other nations. At first the results were excellent, especially in prose; but as the creative vigor of the Elizabethans was lacking in this age, writing by rule soon developed a kind of elegant formalism, which suggests the elaborate social code of the time.

Just as a gentleman might not act naturally, but must follow exact rules in doffing his hat, or addressing a lady, or entering a room, or wearing a wig, or offering his snuffbox to a friend, so our writers lost individuality and became formal and artificial.

The general tendency of literature was to look at life critically, to emphasize intellect rather than imagination, the form rather than the content of a sentence. Writers strove to repress all emotion and enthusiasm, and to use only precise and elegant methods of expression.

This is what is often meant by the "classicism" of the ages of Pope and Johnson. It refers to the critical, intellectual spirit of many writers, to the fine polish of their heroic couplets or the elegance of their prose, and not to any resemblance which their work bears to true classic literature. In a word, the classic movement had become pseudo-classic, i.e. a false or sham classicism; and the latter term is now often used to designate a considerable part of eighteenth-century literature. To avoid this critical difficulty we have adopted the term Augustan Age, a name chosen by the writers themselves, who saw in Pope, Addison, Swift, Johnson, and Burke the modern parallels to Horace, Virgil, Cicero, and all that brilliant company who made Roman literature famous in the days of Augustus.

ALEXANDER POPE (1688-1744)

Pope is in many respects a unique figure. In the first place, he was for a generation "the poet" of a great nation. To be sure, poetry was limited in the early eighteenth century; there were few lyrics, little or no love poetry, no epics, no dramas or songs of nature worth considering; but in the narrow field of satiric and didactic verse Pope was the undisputed master. His influence completely dominated the poetry of his age, and many foreign writers, as well as the majority of English poets, looked to him as their model. Second, he was a remarkably clear and adequate reflection of the spirit of the age in which he lived. There is hardly an ideal, a belief, a doubt, a fashion, a whim of Queen Anne's time, that is not neatly expressed in his poetry. Third, he was the only important writer of that age who gave his whole life to letters. Swift was a clergyman and politician; Addison was secretary of state; other writers depended on patrons or politics or pensions for fame and a livelihood; but Pope was independent, and had no profession but literature. And fourth, by the sheer force of his ambition he won his place, and held it, in spite of religious prejudice, and in the face of physical and temperamental obstacles that would have discouraged a stronger man. For Pope was deformed and sickly, dwarfish in soul and body. He knew little of the world of nature or of the world of the human heart. He was lacking, apparently, in noble feeling, and instinctively chose a lie when the truth had manifestly more advantages. Yet this jealous, peevish, waspish little man became the most famous poet of his age and the acknowledged leader of English literature. We record the fact with wonder and admiration; but we do not attempt to explain it.

LIFE. Pope was born in London in 1688, the year of the Revolution. His parents were both Catholics, who presently removed from London and settled in Binfield, near Windsor, where the poet's childhood was passed. Partly because of an unfortunate prejudice against Catholics in the public schools, partly because of his own weakness and deformity, Pope received very little school education, but browsed for himself among English books and picked up a smattering of the classics. Very early he began to write poetry, and records the fact with his usual vanity:

As yet a child, nor yet a fool to fame,
I lisped in numbers, for the numbers came.

Being debarred by his religion from many desirable employments, he resolved to make literature his life work; and in this he resembled Dryden, who, he tells us, was his only master, though much of his work seems to depend on Boileau, the French poet and critic. When only sixteen years old he had written his "Pastorals"; a few years later appeared his "Essay on Criticism," which made him famous. With the publication of the Rape of the Lock, in 1712, Pope's name was known and honored all over England, and this dwarf of twenty-four years, by the sheer force of his own ambition, had jumped to the foremost place in English letters. It was soon after this that Voltaire called him "the best poet of England and, at present, of all the world,"--which is about as near the truth as Voltaire generally gets in his numerous universal judgments. For the next twelve years Pope was busy with poetry, especially with his translations of Homer; and his work was so successful financially that he bought a villa at Twickenham, on the Thames, and remained happily independent of wealthy patrons for a livelihood.

Led by his success, Pope returned to London and for a time endeavored to live the gay and dissolute life which was supposed to be suitable for a literary genius; but he was utterly unfitted for it, mentally and physically, and soon retired to Twickenham. There he gave himself up to poetry, manufactured a little garden more artificial than his verses, and cultivated his friendship with Martha Blount, with whom for many years he spent a good part of each day, and who remained faithful to him to the end of his life. At Twickenham he wrote his Moral Epistles (poetical satires modeled after Horace) and revenged himself upon all his critics in the bitter abuse of the Dunciad. He died in 1744 and was buried at Twickenham, his religion preventing him from the honor, which was certainly his due, of a resting place in Westminster Abbey.

WORKS OF POPE. For convenience we may separate Pope's work into three groups, corresponding to the early, middle, and later period of his life. In the first he wrote his "Pastorals," "Windsor Forest," "Messiah," "Essay on Criticism," "Eloise to Abelard," and the Rape of the Lock; in the second, his translations of Homer; in the third the Dunciad and the Epistles, the latter containing the famous "Essay on Man" and the "Epistle to Dr. Arbuthnot," which is in truth his "Apologia," and in which alone we see Pope's life from his own view point. The "Essay on Criticism" sums up the art of poetry as taught first by Horace, then by Boileau and the eighteenth-century classicists. Though written in heroic couplets, we hardly consider this as a poem but rather as a storehouse of critical maxims. "For fools rush in where angels fear to tread"; "To err is human, to forgive divine"; "A little learning is a dangerous thing,"--these lines, and many more like them from the same source, have found their way into our common speech, and are used, without thinking of the author, whenever we need an apt quotation.

The Rape of the Lock is a masterpiece of its kind, and comes nearer to being a "creation" than anything else that Pope has written. The occasion of the famous poem was trivial enough. A fop at the court of Queen Anne, one Lord Petre, snipped a lock of hair from the abundant curls of a pretty maid of honor named Arabella Fermor. The young lady resented it, and the two families were plunged into a quarrel which was the talk of London. Pope, being appealed to, seized the occasion to construct, not a ballad, as the Cavaliers would have done, nor an epigram, as French poets love to do, but a long poem in which all the mannerisms of society are pictured in minutest detail and satirized with the most delicate wit. The first edition, consisting of two cantos, was published in 1712; and it is amazing now to read of the trivial character of London court life at the time when English soldiers were battling for a great continent in the French and Indian wars. Its instant success caused Pope to lengthen the poem by three more cantos; and in order to make a more perfect burlesque of an epic poem, he introduces gnomes, sprites, sylphs, and salamanders, instead of the gods of the great epics, with which his readers were familiar. The poem is modeled after two foreign satires: Boileau's Le Lutrin (reading desk), a satire on the French clergy, who raised a huge quarrel over the location of a lectern; and La Secchia Rapita (stolen bucket), a famous Italian satire on the petty causes of the endless Italian wars. Pope, however, went far ahead of his masters in style and in delicacy of handling a mock-heroic theme, and during his lifetime the Rape of the Lock was considered as the greatest poem of its kind in all literature. The poem is still well worth reading; for as an expression of the artificial life of the age--of its cards, parties, toilettes, lapdogs, tea-drinking, snuff-taking, and idle vanities--it is as perfect in its way as Tamburlaine, which reflects the boundless ambition of the Elizabethans. The fame of Pope's Iliad, which was financially the most successful of his books, was due to the fact that he interpreted Homer in the elegant, artificial language of his own age. Not only do his words follow literary fashions but even the Homeric characters lose their strength and become fashionable men of the court. So the criticism of the scholar Bentley was most appropriate when he said, "It is a pretty poem, Mr. Pope, but you must not call it Homer." Pope translated the entire Iliad and half of the Odyssey; and the latter work was finished by two Cambridge scholars, Elijah Fenton and William Broome, who imitated the mechanical couplets so perfectly that it is difficult to distinguish their work from that of the greatest poet of the age. A single selection is given to show how, in the nobler passages, even Pope may faintly suggest the elemental grandeur of Homer:

The troops exulting sat in order round,
And beaming fires illumined all the ground.
As when the moon, refulgent lamp of night,
O'er Heaven's clear azure spreads her sacred light,
When not a breath disturbs the deep serene,
And not a cloud o'ercasts the solemn scene;
Around her throne the vivid planets roll,
And stars unnumbered gild the glowing pole,
O'er the dark trees a yellower verdure shed,
And tip with silver every mountain's head.

The "Essay" is the best known and the most quoted of all Pope's works. Except in form it is not poetry, and when one considers it as an essay and reduces it to plain prose, it is found to consist of numerous literary ornaments without any very solid structure of thought to rest upon. The purpose of the essay is, in Pope's words, to "vindicate the ways of God to Man"; and as there are no unanswered problems in Pope's philosophy, the vindication is perfectly accomplished in four poetical epistles, concerning man's relations to the universe, to himself, to society, and tc happiness. The final result is summed up in a few well-known lines:

All nature is but art, unknown to thee;
All chance, direction which thou canst not see;
All discord, harmony not understood;

All partial evil, universal good:
And, spite of pride, in erring reason's spite,
One truth is clear, whatever is, is right.

Like the "Essay on Criticism," the poem abounds in quotable lines, such as the following, which make the entire work well worth reading:

Hope springs eternal in the human breast:
Man never is, but always to be blest.
Know then thyself, presume not God to scan;
The proper study of Mankind is Man.
The same ambition can destroy or save,
And makes a patriot as it makes a knave.
Honor and shame from no condition rise;
Act well your part, there all the honor lies.
Vice is a monster of so frightful mien,
As, to be hated, needs but to be seen;
Yet seen too oft, familiar with her face,
We first endure, then pity, then embrace.
Behold the child, by Nature's kindly law,
Pleased with a rattle, tickled with a straw:
Some livelier plaything gives his youth delight,
A little louder, but as empty quite:
Scarfs, garters, gold, amuse his riper stage,
And beads and prayer books are the toys of age:
Pleased with this bauble still, as that before;
Till tired he sleeps, and Life's poor play is o'er.

The Dunciad (i.e. the "Iliad of the Dunces") began originally as a controversy concerning Shakespeare, but turned out to be a coarse and revengeful satire upon all the literary men of the age who had aroused Pope's anger by their criticism or lack of appreciation of his genius. Though brilliantly written and immensely popular at one time, its present effect on the reader is to arouse a sense of pity that a man of such acknowledged power and position should abuse both by devoting his talents to personal spite and petty quarrels. Among the rest of his numerous works the reader will find Pope's estimate of himself best set forth in his "Epistle to Dr. Arbuthnot," and it will be well to close our study of this strange mixture of vanity and greatness with "The Universal Prayer," which shows at least that Pope had considered, and judged himself, and that all further judgment is consequently superfluous.

JONATHAN SWIFT (1667-1745)

In each of Marlowe's tragedies we have the picture of a man dominated by a single passion, the lust of power for its own sake. In each we see that a powerful man without self-control is like a dangerous instrument in the hands of a child; and the tragedy ends in the destruction of the man by the ungoverned power which he possesses. The life of Swift is just such a living tragedy. He had the power of gaining wealth, like the hero of the Jew of Malta; yet he used it scornfully, and in sad irony left what remained to him of a large property to found a hospital for lunatics. By hard work he won enormous literary power, and used it to satirize our common humanity. He wrested political power from the hands of the Tories, and used it to insult the very men who had helped him, and who held his fate in their hands. By his dominant personality he exercised a curious power over women, and used it brutally to make them feel their inferiority. Being loved supremely by two good women, he brought sorrow and death to both, and endless misery to himself. So his power brought always tragedy in its wake. It is only when we remember his life of struggle and disappointment and bitterness that we can appreciate the personal quality in his satire, and perhaps find some sympathy for this greatest genius of all the Augustan writers.

LIFE. Swift was born in Dublin, of English parents, in 1667. His father died before he was born; his mother was poor, and Swift, though proud as Lucifer, was compelled to accept aid from relatives, who gave it grudgingly. At the Kilkenny school, and especially at Dublin University, he detested the curriculum, reading only what appealed to his own nature; but, since a degree was necessary to his success, he was compelled to accept it as a favor from the examiners, whom he despised in his heart. After graduation the only position open to him was with a distant relative, Sir William Temple, who gave him the position of private secretary largely on account of the unwelcome relationship.

Temple was a statesman and an excellent diplomatist; but he thought himself to be a great writer as well, and he entered into a literary controversy concerning the relative merits of the classics and modern literature. Swift's first notable work, The Battle of the Books, written at this time but not published, is a keen satire upon both parties in the controversy.

The first touch of bitterness shows itself here; for Swift was in a galling position for a man of his pride, knowing his intellectual superiority to the man who employed him, and yet being looked upon as a servant and eating at the servants' table. Thus he spent ten of the best years of his life in the pretty Moor Park, Surrey, growing more bitter each year and steadily cursing his fate. Nevertheless he read and studied widely, and, after his position with Temple grew unbearable, quarreled with his patron, took orders, and entered the Church of England. Some years later we find him settled in the little church of Laracor, Ireland,--a country which he disliked intensely, but whither he went because no other "living" was open to him.

In Ireland, faithful to his church duties, Swift labored to better the condition of the unhappy people around him. Never before had the poor of his parishes been so well cared for; but Swift chafed under his yoke, growing more and more irritated as he saw small men advanced to large positions, while he remained unnoticed in a little country church,--largely because he was too proud and too blunt with those who might have advanced him. While at Laracor he finished his Tale of a Tub, a satire on the various churches of the day, which was published in London with the Battle of the Books in 1704. The work brought him into notice as the most powerful satirist of the age, and he soon gave up his church to enter the strife of party politics. The cheap pamphlet was then the most powerful political weapon known; and as Swift had no equal at pamphlet writing, he soon became a veritable dictator. For several years, especially from 1710 to 1713, Swift was one of the most important figures in London. The Whigs feared the lash of his satire; the Tories feared to lose his support. He was courted, flattered, cajoled on every side; but the use he made of his new power is sad to contemplate. An unbearable arrogance took possession of him. Lords, statesmen, even ladies were compelled to sue for his favor and to apologize for every fancied slight to his egoism. It is at this time that he writes in his Journal to Stella:

Mr. Secretary told me the Duke of Buckingham had been talking much about me and desired my acquaintance. I answered it could not be, for he had not yet made sufficient advances; then Shrewsbury said he thought the Duke was not used to make advances. I said I could not help that, for I always expected advances in proportion to men's quality, and more from a Duke than any other man.

Writing to the Duchess of Queensberry he says:

I am glad you know your duty; for it has been a known and established rule above twenty years in England that the first advances have been constantly made me by all ladies who aspire to my acquaintance, and the greater their quality the greater were their advances. When the Tories went out of power Swift's position became uncertain. He expected and had probably been promised a bishopric in England, with a seat among the peers of the realm; but the Tories offered him instead the place of dean of St. Patrick's Cathedral in Dublin. It was galling to a man of his proud spirit; but after his merciless satire on religion, in The Tale of a Tub, any ecclesiastical position in England was rendered impossible. Dublin was the best he could get, and he accepted it bitterly, once more cursing the fate which he had brought upon himself.

With his return to Ireland begins the last act in the tragedy of his life. His best known literary work, Gulliver's Travels, was done here; but the bitterness of life grew slowly to insanity, and a frightful personal sorrow, of which he never spoke, reached its climax in the death of Esther Johnson, a beautiful young woman, who had loved Swift ever since the two had met in Temple's household, and to whom he had written his Journal to Stella. During the last years of his life a brain disease, of which he had shown frequent symptoms, fastened its terrible hold upon Swift, and he became by turns an idiot and a madman. He died in 1745, and when his will was opened it was found that he had left all his property to found St. Patrick's Asylum for lunatics and incurables. It stands to-day as the most suggestive monument of his peculiar genius.

THE WORKS OF SWIFT. From Swift's life one can readily foresee the kind of literature he will produce. Taken together his works are a monstrous satire on humanity; and the spirit of that satire is shown clearly in a little incident of his first days in London. There was in the city at that time a certain astrologer named Partridge, who duped the public by calculating nativities from the stars, and by selling a yearly almanac predicting future events. Swift, who hated all shams, wrote, with a great show of learning, his famous Bickerstaff Almanac, containing "Predictions for the Year 1708, as Determined by the Unerring Stars." As Swift rarely signed his name to any literary work, letting it stand or fall on its own merits, his burlesque appeared over the pseudonym of Isaac Bickerstaff, a name afterwards made famous by Steele in The Tatler. Among the predictions was the following:

My first prediction is but a trifle; yet I will mention it to show how ignorant those sottish pretenders to astrology are in their own concerns: it relates to Partridge the almanack maker; I have consulted the star of his nativity by my own rules, and find he will infallibly die upon the 29th of March next, about eleven at night, of a raging fever; therefore I advise him to consider of it, and settle his affairs in time.

On March 30, the day after the prediction was to be fulfilled, there appeared in the newspapers a letter from a revenue officer giving the details of Partridge's death, with the doings of the bailiff and the coffin maker; and on the following morning appeared an elaborate "Elegy of Mr. Partridge." When poor Partridge, who suddenly found himself without customers, published a denial of the burial, Swift answered with an elaborate "Vindication of Isaac Bickerstaff," in which he proved by astrological rules that Partridge was dead, and that the man now in his place was an impostor trying to cheat the heirs out of their inheritance.

This ferocious joke is suggestive of all Swift's satires. Against any case of hypocrisy or injustice he sets up a remedy of precisely the same kind, only more atrocious, and defends his plan with such seriousness that the satire overwhelms the reader with a sense of monstrous falsity. Thus his solemn "Argument to prove that the Abolishing of Christianity may be attended with Some Inconveniences" is such a frightful satire upon the abuses of Christianity by its professed followers that it is impossible for us to say whether Swift intended to point out needed reforms, or to satisfy his conscience, or to perpetrate a joke on the Church, as he had done on poor Partridge. So also with his "Modest Proposal," concerning the children of Ireland, which sets up the proposition that poor Irish farmers ought to raise children as dainties, to be eaten, like roast pigs, on the tables of prosperous Englishmen.

In this most characteristic work it is impossible to find Swift or his motive. The injustice under which Ireland suffered, her perversity in raising large families to certain poverty, and the indifference of English politicians to her suffering and protests are all mercilessly portrayed; but why? That is still the unanswered problem of Swift's life and writings.

Swift's two greatest satires are his Tale of a Tub and Gulliver's Travels. The Tale began as a grim exposure of the alleged weaknesses of three principal forms of religious belief, Catholic, Lutheran, and Calvinist, as opposed to the Anglican; but it ended in a satire upon all science and philosophy.

Swift explains his whimsical title by the custom of mariners in throwing out a tub to a whale, in order to occupy the monster's attention and divert it from an attack upon the ship,--which only proves how little Swift knew of whales or sailors. But let that pass. His book is a tub thrown out to the enemies of Church and State to keep them occupied from further attacks or criticism; and the substance of the argument is that all churches, and indeed all religion and science and statesmanship, are arrant hypocrisy. The best known part of the book is the allegory of the old man who died and left a coat (which is Christian Truth) to each of his three sons, Peter, Martin, and Jack, with minute directions for its care and use. These three names stand for Catholics, Lutherans, and Calvinists; and the way in which the sons evade their father's will and change the fashion of their garment is part of the bitter satire upon all religious sects. Though it professes to defend the Anglican Church, that institution fares perhaps worse than the others; for nothing is left to her but a thin cloak of custom under which to hide her alleged hypocrisy.

In Gulliver's Travels the satire grows more unbearable. Strangely enough, this book, upon which Swift's literary fame generally rests, was not written from any literary motive, but rather as an outlet for the author's own bitterness against fate and human society. It is still read with pleasure, as Robinson Crusoe is read, for the interesting adventures of the hero; and fortunately those who read it generally overlook its degrading influence and motive.

Gulliver's Travels records the pretended four voyages of one Lemuel Gulliver, and his adventures in four astounding countries. The first book tells of his voyage and shipwreck in Lilliput, where the inhabitants are about as tall as one's thumb, and all their acts and motives are on the same dwarfish scale. In the petty quarrels of these dwarfs we are supposed to see the littleness of humanity. The statesmen who obtain place and favor by cutting monkey capers on the tight rope before their sovereign, and the two great parties, the Littleendians and Bigendians, who plunge the country into civil war over the momentous question of whether an egg should be broken on its big or on its little end, are satires on the politics of Swift's own day and generation. The style is simple and convincing; the surprising situations and adventures are as absorbing as those of Defoe's masterpiece; and altogether it is the most interesting of Swift's satires.

On the second voyage Gulliver is abandoned in Brobdingnag, where the inhabitants are giants, and everything is done upon an enormous scale. The meanness of humanity seems all the more detestable in view of the greatness of these superior beings. When Gulliver tells about his own people, their ambitions and wars and conquests, the giants can only wonder that such great venom could exist in such little insects.

In the third voyage Gulliver continues his adventures in Laputa, and this is a satire upon all the scientists and philosophers. Laputa is a flying island, held up in the air by a loadstone; and all the professors of the famous academy at Lagado are of the same airy constitution. The philosopher who worked eight years to extract sunshine from cucumbers is typical of Swift's satiric treatment of all scientific problems. It is in this voyage that we hear of the Struldbrugs, a ghastly race of men who are doomed to live upon earth after losing hope and the desire for life. The picture is all the more terrible in view of the last years of Swift's own life, in which he was compelled to live on, a burden to himself and his friends.

In these three voyages the evident purpose is to strip off the veil of habit and custom, with which men deceive themselves, and show the crude vices of humanity as Swift fancies he sees them. In the fourth voyage the merciless satire is carried out to its logical conclusion. This brings us to the land of the Houyhnhnms, in which horses, superior and intelligent creatures, are the ruling animals. All our interest, however, is centered on the Yahoos, a frightful race, having the form and appearance of men, but living in unspeakable degradation.

The Journal to Stella, written chiefly in the years 1710-1713 for the benefit of Esther Johnson, is interesting to us for two reasons. It is, first, an excellent commentary on contemporary characters and political events, by one of the most powerful and original minds of the age; and second, in its love passages and purely personal descriptions it gives us the best picture we possess of Swift himself at the summit of his power and influence. As we read now its words of tenderness for the woman who loved him, and who brought almost the only ray of sunlight into his life, we can only wonder and be silent. Entirely different are his Drapier's Letters, a model of political harangue and of popular argument, which roused an unthinking English public and did much benefit to Ireland by preventing the politicians' plan of debasing the Irish coinage. Swift's poems, though vigorous and original (like Defoe's, of the same period), are generally satirical, often coarse, and seldom rise above doggerel. Unlike his friend Addison, Swift saw, in the growing polish and decency of society, only a mask for hypocrisy; and he often used his verse to shock the new-born modesty by pointing out some native ugliness which his diseased mind discovered under every beautiful exterior.

That Swift is the most original writer of his time, and one of the greatest masters of English prose, is undeniable. Directness, vigor, simplicity, mark every page. Among writers of that age he stands almost alone in his disdain of literary effects. Keeping his object steadily before him, he drives straight on to the end, with a convincing power that has never been surpassed in our language. Even in his most grotesque creations, the reader never loses the sense of reality, of being present as an eyewitness of the most impossible events, so powerful and convincing is Swift's prose. Defoe had the same power; but in writing Robinson Crusoe, for instance, his task was comparatively easy, since his hero and his adventures were both natural; while Swift gives reality to pygmies, giants, and the most impossible situations, as easily as if he were writing of facts. Notwithstanding these excellent qualities, the ordinary reader will do well to confine himself to Gulliver's Travels and a book of well-chosen selections. For, it must be confessed, the bulk of Swift's work is not wholesome reading. It is too terribly satiric and destructive; it emphasizes the faults and failings of humanity; and so runs counter to the general course of our literature, which from Cynewulf to Tennyson follows the Ideal, as Merlin followed the Gleam, and is not satisfied till the hidden beauty of man's soul and the divine purpose of his struggle are manifest.

JOSEPH ADDISON (1672-1719)

In the pleasant art of living with one's fellows, Addison is easily a master. It is due to his perfect expression of that art, of that new social life which, as we have noted, was characteristic of the Age of Anne, that Addison occupies such a large place in the history of literature. Of less power and originality than Swift, he nevertheless wields, and deserves to wield, a more lasting influence. Swift is the storm, roaring against the ice and frost of the late spring of English life. Addison is the sunshine, which melts the ice and dries the mud and makes the earth thrill with light and hope. Like Swift, he despised shams, but unlike him, he never lost faith in humanity; and in all his satires there is a gentle kindliness which makes one think better of his fellow-men, even while he laughs at their little vanities.

Two things Addison did for our literature which are of inestimable value. First, he overcame a certain corrupt tendency bequeathed by Restoration literature. It was the apparent aim of the low drama, and even of much of the poetry of that age, to make virtue ridiculous and vice attractive. Addison set himself squarely against this unworthy tendency. To strip off the mask of vice, to show its ugliness and deformity, but to reveal virtue in its own native loveliness,--that was Addison's purpose; and he succeeded so well that never, since his day, has our English literature seriously followed after false gods. As Macaulay says, "So effectually did he retort on vice the mockery which had recently been directed against virtue, that since his time the open violation of decency has always been considered amongst us a sure mark of a fool." And second, prompted and aided by the more original genius of his friend Steele, Addison seized upon the new social life of the clubs and made it the subject of endless pleasant essays upon types of men and manners. The Tatler and The Spectator are the beginning of the modern essay; and their studies of human character, as exemplified in Sir Roger de Coverley, are a preparation for the modern novel.

LIFE. Addison's life, like his writings, is in marked contrast to that of Swift. He was born in Milston, Wiltshire, in 1672. His father was a scholarly English clergyman, and all his life Addison followed naturally the quiet and cultured ways to which he was early accustomed. At the famous Charterhouse School, in London, and in his university life at Oxford, he excelled in character and scholarship and became known as a writer of graceful verses.

He had some intention, at one time, of entering the Church, but was easily persuaded by his friends to take up the government service instead. Unlike Swift, who abused his political superiors, Addison took the more tactful way of winning the friendship of men in large places. His lines to Dryden won that literary leader's instant favor, and one of his Latin poems, "The Peace of Ryswick" (1697), with its kindly appreciation of King William's statesmen, brought him into favorable political notice. It brought him also a pension of three hundred pounds a year, with a suggestion that he travel abroad and cultivate the art of diplomacy; which he promptly did to his own great advantage.

From a literary view point the most interesting work of Addison's early life is his Account of the Greatest English Poets (1693), written while he was a fellow of Oxford University. One rubs his eyes to find Dryden lavishly praised, Spenser excused or patronized, while Shakespeare is not even mentioned. But Addison was writing under Boileau's "classic" rules; and the poet, like the age, was perhaps too artificial to appreciate natural genius.

While he was traveling abroad, the death of William and the loss of power by the Whigs suddenly stopped Addison's pension; necessity brought him home, and for a time he lived in poverty and obscurity. Then occurred the battle of Blenheim, and in the effort to find a poet to celebrate the event, Addison was brought to the Tories' attention. His poem, "The Campaign," celebrating the victory, took the country by storm. Instead of making the hero slay his thousands and ten thousands, like the old epic heroes, Addison had some sense of what is required in a modern general, and so made Marlborough direct the battle from the outside, comparing him to an angel riding on the whirlwind:

'T was then great Marlbro's mighty soul was proved,
That, in the shock of charging hosts unmoved,
Amidst confusion, horror, and despair,
Examined all the dreadful scenes of war;

In peaceful thought the field of death surveyed,
To fainting squadrons sent the timely aid,
Inspired repulsed battalions to engage,
And taught the doubtful battle where to rage.
So when an angel by divine command
With rising tempests shakes a guilty land,
(Such as of late o'er pale Britannia past,)
Calm and serene he drives the furious blast;
And, pleased th' Almighty's orders to perform,
Rides in the whirlwind, and directs the storm.

That one doubtful simile made Addison's fortune. Never before or since was a poet's mechanical work so well rewarded. It was called the finest thing ever written, and from that day Addison rose steadily in political favor and office. He became in turn Undersecretary, member of Parliament, Secretary for Ireland, and finally Secretary of State. Probably no other literary man, aided by his pen alone, ever rose so rapidly and so high in office.

The rest of Addison's life was divided between political duties and literature. His essays for the Tatler and Spectator, which we still cherish, were written between 1709 and 1714; but he won more literary fame by his classic tragedy Cato, which we have almost forgotten. In 1716 he married a widow, the Countess of Warwick, and went to live at her home, the famous Holland House. His married life lasted only three years, and was probably not a happy one. Certainly he never wrote of women except with gentle satire, and he became more and more a clubman, spending most of his time in the clubs and coffeehouses of London. Up to this time his life had been singularly peaceful; but his last years were shadowed by quarrels, first with Pope, then with Swift, and finally with his lifelong friend Steele. The first quarrel was on literary grounds, and was largely the result of Pope's jealousy. The latter's venomous caricature of Addison as Atticus shows how he took his petty revenge on a great and good man who had been his friend. The other quarrels with Swift, and especially with his old friend Steele, were the unfortunate result of political differences, and show how impossible it is to mingle literary ideals with party politics. He died serenely in 1719.

A brief description from Thackeray's English Humorists is his best epitaph:

A life prosperous and beautiful, a calm death; an immense fame and affection afterwards for his happy and spotless name.

WORKS OF ADDISON. The most enduring of Addison's works are his famous Essays, collected from the Tatler and Spectator. We have spoken of him as a master of the art of gentle living, and these essays are a perpetual inducement to others to know and to practice the same fine art. To an age of fundamental coarseness and artificiality he came with a wholesome message of refinement and simplicity, much as Ruskin and Arnold spoke to a later age of materialism; only Addison's success was greater than theirs because of his greater knowledge of life and his greater faith in men. He attacks all the little vanities and all the big vices of his time, not in Swift's terrible way, which makes us feel hopeless of humanity, but with a kindly ridicule and gentle humor which takes speedy improvement for granted. To read Swift's brutal "Letters to a Young Lady," and then to read Addison's "Dissection of a Beau's Head" and his "Dissection of a Coquette's Heart," is to know at once the secret of the latter's more enduring influence.

Three other results of these delightful essays are worthy of attention: first, they are the best picture we possess of the new social life of England, with its many new interests; second, they advanced the art of literary criticism to a much higher stage than it had ever before reached, and however much we differ from their judgment and their interpretation of such a man as Milton, they certainly led Englishmen to a better knowledge and appreciation of their own literature; and finally, in Ned Softly the literary dabbler, Will Wimble the poor relation, Sir Andrew Freeport the merchant, Will Honeycomb the fop, and Sir Roger the country gentleman, they give us characters that live forever as part of that goodly company which extends from Chaucer's country parson to Kipling's Mulvaney. Addison and Steele not only introduced the modern essay, but in such characters as these they herald the dawn of the modern novel. Of all his essays the best known and loved are those which introduce us to Sir Roger de Coverley, the genial dictator of life and manners in the quiet English country.

In style these essays are remarkable as showing the growing perfection of the English language. Johnson says, "Whoever wishes to attain an

English style, familiar but not coarse, and elegant but not ostentatious, must give his days and nights to the volumes of Addison." And again he says, "Give nights and days, sir, to the study of Addison if you mean to be a good writer, or, what is more worth, an honest man." That was good criticism for its day, and even at the present time critics are agreed that Addison's Essays are well worth reading once for their own sake, and many times for their influence in shaping a clear and graceful style of writing.

Addison's poems, which were enormously popular in his day, are now seldom read. His Cato, with its classic unities and lack of dramatic power, must be regarded as a failure, if we study it as tragedy; but it offers an excellent example of the rhetoric and fine sentiment which were then considered the essentials of good writing. The best scene from this tragedy is in the fifth act, where Cato soliloquizes, with Plato's Immortality of the Soul open in his hand, and a drawn sword on the table before him:

It must be so--Plato, thou reason'st well!--
Else whence this pleasing hope, this fond desire,
This longing after immortality?
Or whence this secret dread, and inward horror,
Of falling into nought? why shrinks the soul
Back on herself, and startles at destruction?
'Tis the divinity that stirs within us;
'Tis heaven itself, that points out an hereafter,
And intimates eternity to man.

Many readers make frequent use of one portion of Addison's poetry without knowing to whom they are indebted. His devout nature found expression in many hymns, a few of which are still used and loved in our churches. Many a congregation thrills, as Thackeray did, to the splendid sweep of his "God in Nature," beginning, "The spacious firmament on high." Almost as well known and loved are his "Traveler's Hymn," and his "Continued Help," beginning, "When all thy mercies, O my God." The latter hymn--written in a storm at sea off the Italian coast, when the captain and crew were demoralized by terror--shows that poetry, especially a good hymn that one can sing in the same spirit as one would say his prayers, is sometimes the most practical and helpful thing in the world.

RICHARD STEELE (1672-1729). Steele was in almost every respect the antithesis of his friend and fellow-worker,--a rollicking, good-hearted, emotional, lovable Irishman. At the Charterhouse School and at Oxford he shared everything with Addison, asking nothing but love in return. Unlike Addison, he studied but little, and left the university to enter the Horse Guards. He was in turn soldier, captain, poet, playwright, essayist, member of Parliament, manager of a theater, publisher of a newspaper, and twenty other things,--all of which he began joyously and then abandoned, sometimes against his will, as when he was expelled from Parliament, and again because some other interest of the moment had more attraction. His poems and plays are now little known; but the reader who searches them out will find one or two suggestive things about Steele himself. For instance, he loves children; and he is one of the few writers of his time who show a sincere and unswerving respect for womanhood. Even more than Addison he ridicules vice and makes virtue lovely. He is the originator of the Tatler, and joins with Addison in creating the Spectator,--the two periodicals which, in the short space of less than four years, did more to influence subsequent literature than all other magazines of the century combined. Moreover, he is the original genius of Sir Roger, and of many other characters and essays for which Addison usually receives the whole credit. It is often impossible in the Tatler essays to separate the work of the two men; but the majority of critics hold that the more original parts, the characters, the thought, the overflowing kindliness, are largely Steele's creation; while to Addison fell the work of polishing and perfecting the essays, and of adding that touch of humor which made them the most welcome literary visitors that England had ever received.

THE TATLER AND THE SPECTATOR. On account of his talent in writing political pamphlets, Steele was awarded the position of official gazetteer. While in this position, and writing for several small newspapers, the idea occurred to Steele to publish a paper which should contain not only the political news, but also the gossip of the clubs and coffeehouses, with some light essays on the life and manners of the age. The immediate result--for Steele never let an idea remain idle--was the famous Tatler, the first number of which appeared April 12, 1709. It was a small folio sheet, appearing on post days, three times a week, and it sold for a penny a copy. That it had a serious purpose is evident from this dedication to the first volume of collected Tatler essays:

The general purpose of this paper is to expose the false arts of life, to pull off the disguises of cunning, vanity, and affectation, and to recommend a general simplicity in our dress, our discourse, and our behavior.

The success of this unheard-of combination of news, gossip, and essay was instantaneous. Not a club or a coffeehouse in London could afford to be without it, and over it's pages began the first general interest in contemporary English life as expressed in literature. Steele at first wrote the entire paper and signed his essays with the name of Isaac Bickerstaff, which had been made famous by Swift a few years before. Addison is said to have soon recognized one of his own remarks to Steele, and the secret of the Authorship was out. From that time Addison was a regular contributor, and occasionally other writers added essays on the new social life of England.

Steele lost his position as gazetteer, and the Tatler was discontinued after less than two years' life, but not till it won an astonishing popularity and made ready the way for its successor. Two months later, on March 1, 1711, appeared the first number of the Spectator. In the new magazine politics and news, as such, were ignored; it was a literary magazine, pure and simple, and its entire contents consisted of a single light essay. It was considered a crazy venture at the time, but its instant success proved that men were eager for some literary expression of the new social ideals. The following whimsical letter to the editor may serve to indicate the part played by the Spectator in the daily life of London:

Mr. Spectator,--Your paper is a part of my tea equipage; and my servant knows my humor so well, that in calling for my breakfast this morning (it being past my usual hour) she answered, the Spectator was not yet come in, but the teakettle boiled, and she expected it every moment.

It is in the incomparable Spectator papers that Addison shows himself most "worthy to be remembered." He contributed the majority of its essays, and in its first number appears this description of the Spectator, by which name Addison is now generally known:

There is no place of general resort wherein I do not often make my appearance; sometimes I am seen thrusting my head into a round of politicians at Will's [Coffeehouse] and listening with great attention to the narratives that are made in those little circular audiences. Sometimes I smoke a pipe at Child's, and, whilst I seem attentive to nothing but The Postman, overhear the conversation of every table in the room. I appear on Sunday nights at St. James's, and sometimes join the little committee of politics in the inner room, as one who comes to hear and improve. My face is likewise very well known at the Grecian, the Cocoa Tree, and in the theaters both of Drury Lane and the Haymarket. I have been taken for a merchant upon the Exchange for above these ten years; and sometimes pass for a Jew in the assembly of stock jobbers at Jonathan's.... Thus I live in the world rather as a spectator of mankind than as one of the species,... which is the character I intend to preserve in this paper.

The large place which these two little magazines hold in our literature seems most disproportionate to their short span of days. In the short space of four years in which Addison and Steele worked together the light essay was established as one of the most important forms of modern literature, and the literary magazine won its place as the expression of the social life of a nation.

SAMUEL JOHNSON (1709-1784)

The reader of Boswell's Johnson, after listening to endless grumblings and watching the clumsy actions of the hero, often finds himself wondering why he should end his reading with a profound respect for this "old bear" who is the object of Boswell's groveling attention. Here is a man who was certainly not the greatest writer of his age, perhaps not even a great writer at all, but who was nevertheless the dictator of English letters, and who still looms across the centuries of a magnificent literature as its most striking and original figure. Here, moreover, is a huge, fat, awkward man, of vulgar manners and appearance, who monopolizes conversation, argues violently, abuses everybody, clubs down opposition,--"Madam" (speaking to his cultivated hostess at table), "talk no more nonsense"; "Sir" (turning to a distinguished guest), "I perceive you are a vile Whig." While talking he makes curious animal sounds, "sometimes giving a half whistle, sometimes clucking like a hen"; and when he has concluded a violent dispute and laid his opponents low by dogmatism or ridicule, he leans back to "blow out his breath like a whale" and gulp down numberless cups of hot tea. Yet this curious dictator of an elegant age was a veritable lion, much sought after by society; and around him in his own poor house gathered the foremost artists, scholars, actors, and literary men of London,--all honoring the man, loving him, and listening to his dogmatism as the Greeks listened to the voice of their oracle.

What is the secret of this astounding spectacle? If the reader turns naturally to Johnson's works for an explanation, he will be disappointed. Reading his verses, we find nothing to delight or inspire us, but rather gloom and pessimism, with a few moral observations in rimed couplets:

But, scarce observed, the knowing and the bold

Fall in the general massacre of gold;

Wide-wasting pest! that rages unconfined,

And crowds with crimes the records of mankind;

For gold his sword the hireling ruffian draws,

For gold the hireling judge distorts the laws;

Wealth heaped on wealth nor truth nor safety buys;

The dangers gather as the treasures rise.

That is excellent common sense, but it is not poetry; and it is not necessary to hunt through Johnson's bulky volumes for the information, since any moralist can give us offhand the same doctrine. As for his Rambler essays, once so successful, though we marvel at the big words, the carefully balanced sentences, the classical allusions, one might as well try to get interested in an old-fashioned, three-hour sermon. We read a few pages listlessly, yawn, and go to bed.

Since the man's work fails to account for his leadership and influence, we examine his personality; and here everything is interesting. Because of a few oft-quoted passages from Boswell's biography, Johnson appears to us as an eccentric bear, who amuses us by his growlings and clumsy antics. But there is another Johnson, a brave, patient, kindly, religious soul, who, as Goldsmith said, had "nothing of the bear but his skin"; a man who battled like a hero against poverty and pain and melancholy and the awful fear of death, and who overcame them manfully.

"That trouble passed away; so will this," sang the sorrowing Deor in the first old Anglo-Saxon lyric; and that expresses the great and suffering spirit of Johnson, who in the face of enormous obstacles never lost faith in God or in himself. Though he was a reactionary in politics, upholding the arbitrary power of kings and opposing the growing liberty of the people, yet his political theories, like his manners, were no deeper than his skin; for in all London there was none more kind to the wretched, and none more ready to extend an open hand to every struggling man and woman who crossed his path. When he passed poor homeless Arabs sleeping in the streets he would slip a coin into their hands, in order that they might have a happy awakening; for he himself knew well what it meant to be hungry. Such was Johnson,--a "mass of genuine manhood," as Carlyle called him, and as such, men loved and honored him.

Life of Johnson. Johnson was born in Lichfield, Staffordshire, in 1709. He was the son of a small bookseller, a poor man, but intelligent and fond of literature, as booksellers invariably were in the good days when every town had its bookshop. From his childhood Johnson had to struggle against physical deformity and disease and the consequent disinclination to hard work.

He prepared for the university, partly in the schools, but largely by omnivorous reading in his father's shop, and when he entered Oxford he had read more classical authors than had most of the graduates. Before finishing his course he had to leave the university on account of his poverty, and at once he began his long struggle as a hack writer to earn his living.

At twenty-five years he married a woman old enough to be his mother,--a genuine love match, he called it,--and with her dowry of L800 they started a private school together, which was a dismal failure. Then, without money or influential friends, he left his home and wife in Lichfield and tramped to London, accompanied only by David Garrick, afterwards the famous actor, who had been one of his pupils. Here, led by old associations, Johnson made himself known to the booksellers, and now and then earned a penny by writing prefaces, reviews, and translations.

It was a dog's life, indeed, that he led there with his literary brethren. Many of the writers of the day, who are ridiculed in Pope's heartless

Dunciad, having no wealthy patrons to support them, lived largely in the streets and taverns, sleeping on an ash heap or under a wharf, like rats; glad of a crust, and happy over a single meal which enabled them to work for a while without the reminder of hunger. A few favored ones lived in wretched lodgings in Grub Street, which has since become a synonym for the fortunes of struggling writers. Often, Johnson tells us, he walked the streets all night long, in dreary weather, when it was too cold to sleep, without food or shelter. But he wrote steadily for the booksellers and for the Gentleman's Magazine, and presently he became known in London and received enough work to earn a bare living.

The works which occasioned this small success were his poem, "London," and his Life of the Poet Savage, a wretched life, at best, which were perhaps better left without a biographer. But his success was genuine, though small, and presently the booksellers of London are coming to him to ask him to write a dictionary of the English language. It was an enormous work, taking nearly eight years of his time, and long before he had finished it he had eaten up the money which he received for his labor. In the leisure intervals of this work he wrote "The Vanity of Human Wishes" and other poems, and finished his classic tragedy of Irene.

Led by the great success of the Spectator, Johnson started two magazines, The Rambler (1750--1752) and The Idler (1758--1760). Later the Rambler essays were published in book form and ran rapidly through ten editions; but the financial returns were small, and Johnson spent a large part of his earnings in charity. When his mother died, in 1759, Johnson, although one of the best known men in London, had no money, and hurriedly finished Rasselas, his only romance, in order, it is said, to pay for his mother's burial.

It was not till 1762, when Johnson was fifty-three years old, that his literary labors were rewarded in the usual way by royalty, and he received from George III a yearly pension of three hundred pounds. Then began a little sunshine in his life. With Joshua Reynolds, the artist, he founded the famous Literary Club, of which Burke, Pitt, Fox, Gibbon, Goldsmith, and indeed all the great literary men and politicians of the time, were members.

This is the period of Johnson's famous conversations, which were caught in minutest detail by Boswell and given to the world. His idea of conversation, as shown in a hundred places in Boswell, is to overcome your adversary at any cost; to knock him down by arguments, or, when these fail, by personal ridicule; to dogmatize on every possible question, pronounce a few oracles, and then desist with the air of victory.

Concerning the philosopher Hume's view of death he says: "Sir, if he really thinks so, his perceptions are disturbed, he is mad. If he does not think so, he lies." Exit opposition. There is nothing more to be said. Curiously enough, it is often the palpable blunders of these monologues that now attract us, as if we were enjoying a good joke at the dictator's expense. Once a lady asked him, "Dr. Johnson, why did you define pastern as the knee of a horse?" "Ignorance, madame, pure ignorance," thundered the great authority.

When seventy years of age, Johnson was visited by several booksellers of the city, who were about to bring out a new edition of the English poets, and who wanted Johnson, as the leading literary man of London, to write the prefaces to the several volumes. The result was his Lives of the Poets, as it is now known, and this is his last literary work. He died in his poor Fleet Street house, in 1784, and was buried among England's honored poets in Westminster Abbey.

JOHNSON'S WORKS. "A book," says Dr. Johnson, "should help us either to enjoy life or to endure it." Judged by this standard, one is puzzled what to recommend among Johnson's numerous books. The two things which belong among the things "worthy to be remembered" are his Dictionary and his Lives of the Poets, though both these are valuable, not as literature, but rather as a study of literature. The Dictionary, as the first ambitious attempt at an English lexicon, is extremely valuable, notwithstanding the fact that his derivations are often faulty, and that he frequently exercises his humor or prejudice in his curious definitions. In defining "oats," for example, as a grain given in England to horses and in Scotland to the people, he indulges his prejudice against the Scotch, whom he never understood, just as, in his definition of "pension," he takes occasion to rap the writers who had flattered their patrons since the days of Elizabeth; though he afterwards accepted a comfortable pension for himself.

With characteristic honesty he refused to alter his definition in subsequent editions of the Dictionary. The Lives of the Poets are the simplest and most readable of his literary works. For ten years before beginning these biographies he had given himself up to conversation, and the ponderous style of his Rambler essays here gives way to a lighter and more natural expression. As criticisms they are often misleading, giving praise to artificial poets, like Cowley and Pope, and doing scant justice or abundant injustice to nobler poets like Gray and Milton; and they are not to be compared with those found in Thomas Warton's History of English Poetry, which was published in the same generation. As biographies, however, they are excellent reading, and we owe to them some of our best known pictures of the early English poets.

Of Johnson's poems the reader will have enough if he glance over "The Vanity of Human Wishes." His only story, Rasselas, Prince of Abyssinia, is a matter of rhetoric rather than of romance, but is interesting still to the reader who wants to hear Johnson's personal views of society, philosophy, and religion. Any one of his Essays, like that on "Reading," or "The Pernicious Effects of Revery," will be enough to acquaint the reader with the Johnsonese style, which was once much admired and copied by orators, but which happily has been replaced by a more natural way of speaking. Most of his works, it must be confessed, are rather tiresome. It is not to his books, but rather to the picture of the man himself, as given by Boswell, that Johnson owes his great place in our literature.

BOSWELL'S "LIFE OF JOHNSON"

In James Boswell (1740-1795) we have another extraordinary figure,--a shallow little Scotch barrister, who trots about like a dog at the heels of his big master, frantic at a caress and groveling at a cuff, and abundantly contented if only he can be near him and record his oracles. All his life long Boswell's one ambition seems to have been to shine in the reflected glory of great men, and his chief task to record their sayings and doings. When he came to London, at twenty-two years of age, Johnson, then at the beginning of his great fame, was to this insatiable little glory-seeker like a Silver Doctor to a hungry trout.

He sought an introduction as a man seeks gold, haunted every place where Johnson declaimed, until in Davies's bookstore the supreme opportunity came. This is his record of the great event: I was much agitated [says Boswell] and recollecting his prejudice against the Scotch, of which I had heard much, I said to Davies, "Don't tell him where

I come from." "From Scotland," cried Davies roguishly. "Mr. Johnson," said I, "I do indeed come from Scotland, but I cannot help it."... "That, sir" [cried Johnson], "I find is what a very great many of your countrymen cannot help." This stroke stunned me a good deal; and when we had sat down I felt myself not a little embarrassed, and apprehensive of what might come next.

Then for several years, with a persistency that no rebuffs could abate, and with a thick skin that no amount of ridicule could render sensitive, he follows Johnson; forces his way into the Literary Club, where he is not welcome, in order to be near his idol; carries him off on a visit to the Hebrides; talks with him on every possible occasion; and, when he is not invited to a feast, waits outside the house or tavern in order to walk home with his master in the thick fog of the early morning.

And the moment the oracle is out of sight and in bed, Boswell patters home to record in detail all that he has seen and heard. It is to his minute record that we owe our only perfect picture of a great man; all his vanity as well as his greatness, his prejudices, superstitions, and even the details of his personal appearance:

There is the gigantic body, the huge face seamed with the scars of disease, the brown coat, the black worsted stockings, the gray wig with the scorched foretop, the dirty hands, the nails bitten and pared to the quick. We see the eyes and mouth moving with convulsive twitches; we see the heavy form rolling; we hear it puffing; and then comes the "Why, sir!" and the "What then, sir?" and the "No, sir!" and the "You don't see your way through the question, sir!"

To Boswell's record we are indebted also for our knowledge of those famous conversations, those wordy, knockdown battles, which made Johnson famous in his time and which still move us to wonder. Here is a specimen conversation, taken almost at random from a hundred such in Boswell's incomparable biography.

After listening to Johnson's prejudice against Scotland, and his dogmatic utterances on Voltaire, Robertson, and twenty others, an unfortunate theorist brings up a recent essay on the possible future life of brutes, quoting some possible authority from the sacred scriptures:

Johnson, who did not like to hear anything concerning a future state which was not authorized by the regular canons of orthodoxy, discouraged this talk; and being offended at its continuation, he watched an opportunity to give the gentleman a blow of reprehension. So when the poor speculatist, with a serious, metaphysical, pensive face, addressed him, "But really, sir, when we see a very sensible dog, we don't know what to think of him"; Johnson, rolling with joy at the thought which beamed in his eye, turned quickly round and replied, "True, sir; and when we see a very foolish fellow, we don't know what to think of him." He then rose up, strided to the fire, and stood for some time laughing and exulting.

Then the oracle proceeds to talk of scorpions and natural history, denying facts, and demanding proofs which nobody could possibly furnish:

He seemed pleased to talk of natural philosophy. "That woodcocks," said he, "fly over the northern countries is proved, because they have been observed at sea.

Swallows certainly sleep all the winter. A number of them conglobulate together by flying round and round, and then all in a heap throw themselves under water and lie in the bed of a river." He told us one of his first essays was a Latin poem upon the glowworm: I am sorry I did not ask where it was to be found.

Then follows an astonishing array of subjects and opinions. He catalogues libraries, settles affairs in China, pronounces judgment on men who marry women superior to themselves, flouts popular liberty, hammers Swift unmercifully, and adds a few miscellaneous oracles, most of which are about as reliable as his knowledge of the hibernation of swallows.

When I called upon Dr. Johnson next morning I found him highly satisfied with his colloquial prowess the preceding evening. "Well," said he, "we had good talk." "Yes, sir" [says I], "you tossed and gored several persons."

Far from resenting this curious mental dictatorship, his auditors never seem to weary. They hang upon his words, praise him, flatter him, repeat his judgments all over London the next day, and return in the evening hungry for more. Whenever the conversation begins to flag,

Boswell is like a woman with a parrot, or like a man with a dancing bear. He must excite the creature, make him talk or dance for the edification of the company. He sidles obsequiously towards his hero and, with utter irrelevancy, propounds a question of theology, a social theory, a fashion of dress or marriage, a philosophical conundrum: "Do you think, sir, that natural affections are born with us?" or, "Sir, if you were shut up in a castle and a newborn babe with you, what would you do?" Then follow more Johnsonian laws, judgments, oracles; the insatiable audience clusters around him and applauds; while Boswell listens, with shining face, and presently goes home to write the wonder down. It is an astonishing spectacle; one does not know whether to laugh or grieve over it. But we know the man, and the audience, almost as well as if we had been there; and that, unconsciously, is the superb art of this matchless biographer.

When Johnson died the opportunity came for which Boswell had been watching and waiting some twenty years. He would shine in the world now, not by reflection, but by his own luminosity. He gathered together his endless notes and records, and began to write his biography; but he did not hurry. Several biographies of Johnson appeared, in the four years after his death, without disturbing Boswell's perfect complacency. After seven years' labor he gave the world his Life of Johnson. It is an immortal work; praise is superfluous; it must be read to be appreciated. Like the Greek sculptors, the little slave produced a more enduring work than the great master. The man who reads it will know Johnson as he knows no other man who dwells across the border; and he will lack sensitiveness, indeed, if he lay down the work without a greater love and appreciation of all good literature.

LATER AUGUSTAN WRITERS. With Johnson, who succeeded Dryden and Pope in the chief place of English letters, the classic movement had largely spent its force; and the latter half of the eighteenth century gives us an imposing array of writers who differ so widely that it is almost impossible to classify them. In general, three schools of writers are noticeable: first, the classicists, who, under Johnson's lead, insisted upon elegance and regularity of style; second, the romantic poets, like Collins, Gray, Thomson, and Burns, who revolted from Pope's artificial couplets and wrote of nature and the human heart; third, the early novelists, like Defoe and Fielding, who introduced a new type of literature. The romantic poets and the novelists are reserved for special chapters; and of the other writers--Berkeley and Hume in philosophy; Robertson, Hume, and Gibbon in history; Chesterfield and Lady Montagu in letter writing; Adam Smith in economics; Pitt, Burke, Fox, and a score of lesser writers in politics--we select only two, Burke and Gibbon, whose works are most typical of the Augustan, i.e. the elegant, classic style of prose writing.

Bibliography

Amitav Ghosh's: *The Shadow Lines: Critical Essays*, New Delhi, Atlantic, 2002.

Arthur Miller: *As a Critic of Drama*, New Delhi, Anmol, 2004.

Bennett, J. A. W.: *Middle English Literature*, Oxford, Clarendon Press, 1986.

Bush, Douglas: *English Literature in the Earlier Seventeenth Century, 1600-1660*, Oxford, Clarendon Press, 1962.

Chambers, Kerchever: *English Literature at the Close of the Middle Ages*, New York: Oxford University Press, 1947.

Crystal, D.: *Prosodic Systems and Intonation in English*, Cambridge, Cambridge University Press, 1969.

Dobree, Bonamy: *Contemporary English Literature in the Early Eighteenth Century, 1700-1740*, Oxford, Clarendon Press, 1959.

Ferrence, G.: *Deadly Fashion: the Rise and Fall of Cigarette Smoking in North America*, New York, Garland, 1989.

Hogan, Robert Goode: *The Modern Irish Drama: a Documentary History*, NJ: Humanities Press, 1975.

James, Runcieman: *English Literature of the Late Seventeenth Century*, New York, Oxford University Press, 1969.

Nicoll, Allardyce: *A History of English Drama, 1660-1900*, Cambridge, University Press, 1952-65.

Rahilly, J.: *Phonetics: The Science of Speech*, London, Arnold, 1999.

Salzman, Paul: *English Prose Fiction, 1558-1700: a Critical History*, Oxford, Clarendon Press, 1985.

Vikram Seth: *Multiple Locations, Multiple Affiliation*, New Delhi, Rawat, 2001.

William, John: *A History of English Poetry*, London, MacMillan and Co., 1903.

Index